THE AZTEC GOD

AND

OTHER DRAMAS

BY

GEORGE LANSING RAYMOND

FOURTH EDITION REVISED

G. P. PUTNAM'S SONS

NEW YORK AND LONDON

The Knickerbocker Press

Made in the United States of America

CONTENTS.

iii

THE AZTEC GOD.

INTRODUCTION : PLACE AND TIME.

The scene of this drama is laid in Mexico near the opening of the Fifteenth Century, just when the Aztecs were beginning to overrun the country, and when, therefore, the peculiar forms of their religion may reasonably be supposed to have been comparatively unknown to the Tezcucans who, as will be shown presently, adhered, in the main, to the more mild religious observances of the ancient Toltecs.

The facts with reference to the Aztec human sacrifices, the selection for these of a captive without blemish, the allotment to him of certain maidens as wives, and the general luxury and adoration with which he was surrounded up to the time when, surrendering the flowers that crowned his head and the lyre that he carried, he ascended the pyramid to have his heart torn out of him while still alive,—all these facts are sufficiently well known to substantiate the delineations of the drama.

The exact religious conception which underlay these Aztec rites is not known. In the circumstances, it has been thought justifiable to surround them with a certain atmosphere of spiritual truth—though only in twilight—similar to that which is known to have formed the setting of the pagan worship of ancient Egypt and Greece. It has been recognized that doing this might not only enhance the poetic effectiveness of the presentation, but might also aid in imparting to it that contemporary import and application which, in every work of art, the intelligent reader ought to feel, even though he may not be able, in any wholly satisfactory way, to analyze or interpret.

A few historical quotations may be needed to explain the disposition which Haijo and the King are represented as proposing to make of Waloon. In a note referring to the inmates of the Aztec religious houses, in Prescott's "Conquest of Mexico," vol. I., p. 69, we read that "Tales of scandal . . . have been told of the Aztec virgins," etc., and in vol. I., pp. 110–112, of the same author's "Conquest of Peru," a country in which there prevailed a worship of the heavenly bodies very similar to that of the Aztecs, we are informed, with reference to the "Virgins of the Sun," as they were termed, that "they were young maidens, dedicated to the service of the deity, who . . . were taken from their homes and introduced into convents. . . . From the **moment they entered the establishment, they were cut off from all connection with the world, even with their own family and friends. Yet** . . . though Virgins of the Sun, they, **were** brides of the Inca (or king), and, at a marriageable age, the most beautiful among them were selected for the honors . . . of the royal seraglio . . . The full complement of this amounted in time not only to hundreds but to thousands. who found accommodations in his different palaces." An established custom like this among the Peruvians certainly seems sufficient to justify an illustration of the spirit underlying it among a people so much like them in other respects as were the Aztecs.

A few words may be needed too with reference to the range of thought and feeling attributed in the drama to Monaska and Kootha. Some may suppose the healthfully romantic chastity of the one and the philosophic cynicism of the other to be idealizations beyond the possibilities of the period.

With reference to the first of these suppositions it is only necessary to say that a very slight investigation of facts would enable the reader to recognize that Monaska represents a type of character by no means uncommon among the Indians of our own country to-day, or among other semi-civilized people. The elaborated systems of ethics, to which the enlightened nations are apt to attribute their virtue, are themselves merely developments of natural and normal instincts of which men, especially young men, are everywhere conscious, and by which they are often controlled. If this were not so, the ethics of civilized life would be a result without a cause.

With reference to the philosophic and religious attitudes of mind of Kootha, and of Monaska, too, so far as he is represented as indulging in these, something more, perhaps, should be said. And first of all, let the reader be reminded that, had this drama been written by one who had lived among the Aztecs, it would have been impossible for him, however desirous of being faithful to facts, looking backward, as he would be obliged to do, through the vista of time, not to have his whole representation tinged with the results of his experiences in life, thought and expression through the four hundred years intervening. But, besides this, were he a poet, it would be impossible for him not to have them tinged specifically with the results of his own imagination, inasmuch as the value of the contribution of poetry, in all cases, is exactly proportioned to the light with which it illumines facts in connection with the process of transferring them to the region of fancy. It is admitted, therefore, that the characters of this drama are presented as they appear through an intervening space of four hundred years; and that, as a consequence, the expressions used, and in some cases the substance of what is expressed, are more or less modern. But just as a magnifying glass modifies all the points of interest in an object to which it is applied, so it seems permissible at times for imaginative art to do—in case, like the glass, it does not change the relative proportions of the parts to one another and to the whole. A

poet, like a painter, has a right to increase the interest and
beauty of the life that furnishes his model by means of the
medium—the modern medium too—through whicn he is supposed to contemplate it.   Otherwise, the subject with which
he deals could not be treated from a present and poetic
view-point, and his works would not be worth the ink ex-
pended on them.   All the consideration for truth which it
seems reasonable to expect of the historic dramatist is
that, in a medium, the component parts of which are neces-
sarily made up of the language and methods of thought
natural to his own time, he should represent, in their relative
proportions, the particular motives and feelings as well as the
general atmosphere of thought natural to the conditions existing at the time of the events forming the basis of his plot.

There still remains another supposition to be met. It has
apparently been granted, thus far, that the range of thought
and feeling attributed to Monaska and Kootha may be beyond
the possibilities of the period.   But barring the modern
associations and suggestions, to which reference has already
been made, it is by no means certain that this need be con-
ceded.   The fathers of the Spanish church, at the time when
America was discovered, seeing in the distribution of bread
and wine, confession, penance, monasticism and sacrificial
ceremonies, as practiced by its aborigines, a resemblance to
their own religious observances, could attribute this to nothing
but contrivances of the devil to counterfeit the rites of Christianity.   But we all know now, or ought to know, that the
real explanation for resemblances of this kind is to be found
in the fact that humanity, wherever it exists, is the same ; and
that a similar stage of its development always tends to forms
of life, religious as well as civil, of the same general nature.
This fact, indeed, is the chief warrant for supposing that this
drama of the Aztecs can have any present interest, or suggest,
by analogy, any present lesson.   But this thought aside, the
fact being as stated, all that is needed to justify the character-

istics and sentiments of Monaska and Kootha is to show that the civilization of the Tezcucans at this period was sufficiently highly developed to produce them. To do this is not difficult. Of one of the kings of Tezcuco, Nezahualcoyotl, who died about 1470 A. D., the same author already quoted says in the "Conquest of Mexico," vol. I., pp. 192–196, that "He built a temple in the usual pyramidal form, and on the summit a tower nine stories high, to represent the nine heavens; a tenth was surmounted by a roof painted black and profusely gilded with stars on the outside and incrusted with metals and precious stones within. He dedicated this to the unknown God, the Cause of causes. . . . No image was allowed in the edifice, as unsuited to the invisible God; and the people were expressly prohibited from profaning the altars with blood, or any other sacrifices than that of the perfume of flowers and sweet-scented gums.'' He is also represented to have said: "Idols of wood and gold can neither see, hear nor feel; much less could they make the heavens and the earth and man the lord of it. These must be the work of the all-powerful, unknown God, Creator of the universe, on whom alone I must rely for consolation and support;" and in one of his poems—for many nobles and princes of this people were poets—he says: "The great, the wise, the valiant, the beautiful—alas! where are they now? They are all mingled with the clod; and that which has befallen them shall happen to us, and to those that come after us. Yet let us take courage, illustrious nobles and chieftains, true friends and loyal subjects,—let us aspire to that heaven where all is eternal, and corruption cannot come." Men educated where opinions like these prevailed and were expressed, could certainly be capable of sentiments of the kind attributed in this drama to Monaska and Kootha.

Each time you try to mold a spirit's life
With fingers grappling from the fist of force,
You clutch but at the air, at what is far
Too fine for force to handle.

THE AZTEC GOD, *IV, 1.*

Oh something surely must be wrong,
When that which rules without rules not within.

IDEM.

CHARACTERS.

MONASKA. A young Mexican or Acolhuan warrior of noble blood, captured by the Aztecs from the Tezcucans, a people who, before succumbing to the Aztec invasion, were distinguished by their comparatively mild religion and manners.

KOOTHA AND HIS COMPANION. Tezcucans of high rank and education, captured by the Aztecs years before the time when the drama is supposed to open, and now slaves of the priest, Haijo, and attendants at the temple.

HAIJO. A chief priest of the Aztecs.

WAPELLA. A Tezcucan warrior, captured by the Aztecs at the same time as Monaska.

THE KING. Sovereign of the Aztecs.

WALOON. A Tezcucan maiden of high rank, niece of Kootha, captured, when very young, by the Aztecs and adopted by Haijo the priest.

FIRST
SECOND } MAIDENS. { Admirers of Monaska, and assigned to him as wives, according to the customs of the Aztecs.
THIRD

WOMEN, MAIDENS, OFFICERS, WARRIORS, PRIESTS, PRIESTESSES, PAGES, ATTENDANTS, ETC.

PROPERTIES.

MONASKA. In Act First, Bow, Arrows, and Club. In Act Second, Club. In Acts Third and Fourth, Flower-wreathed Head-dress and Lyre.

KOOTHA AND HIS COMPANION. In Acts First and Fifth, a Spear.

HAIJO. In Act First, a Spear.

WAPELLA. In Acts First and Fifth, Bow, Arrows, and Club. In Act Second, a Club.

KING. In all the Acts, Belt and Hand Weapons appropriate for a king. In Acts Second and Fourth, some sort of a Crown.

WALOON AND HER MAID. In Act First, a Spear. In Act Second, a Wreath of Flowers.

MAIDENS. In Second Act, Wreaths of Flowers about their heads, shoulders, etc., and also carried in their hands.

WARRIORS with Bows, Arrows, Spears, etc. and all on the stage in the costumes of the place and period.

THE AZTEC GOD.

ACT FIRST.

Scene:—*A forest. Backing, a tree with a moss-
covered elevation or bench at its Right. Many
Entrances at the Right and Left through the
trees. The darkness of a storm by day, with
occasional thunder and lightning. Contending
bands of warriors in flight and pursuit cross
the stage from Left to Right.*

*Enter—Left—*Kootha *attended by his* Companion.

[1][Kootha (*to his* Companion).

Oh, what a whirlwind's wave-lashed sea is
    war!
Then hate breaks loose to over-flood the world,
Hurling all love-built order upside down
Till weal is drowned in darkness of the deep,
And wreckage rides the crest.—They might
    have known

[1] These brackets—[and]—are placed before and after
passages which, in reading or presentation, may be omit-
ted without interfering with the unfolding of the plot.

They would be tricked.   War's tactics all are
     acts
Of treachery—the one sole sphere where he
Who does the worst thing does the best, here
     faith
Falls crushed beneath the trampling foot of
     force;
And fair means trip, trailed mireward after
     foul.]

             *Enter—Right—*OFFICER.

OFFICER.   What, Kootha, you here?

KOOTHA.   Ay.

OFFICER.   What for?

KOOTHA.   To see
   The tragedy.

OFFICER.   Is over now.

KOOTHA.   The fight?—
   I mean not that; but you have captives.

OFFICER.   Crowds.

KOOTHA.   And them I came to see.

OFFICER.   Yes, you are he
   That waits on them till sacrificed.

KOOTHA.   I do.

OFFICER.   And you take pleasure in it?

KOOTHA.   So they say.—
   Why?—You would not?

OFFICER.   In part of it I might.—
   For you, too, like an angel, bring to each
   The maiden he is free to love and wed.

KOOTHA.   And I, too, ride the nightmare, sped
        him when
    His love o'erflows in dreams of Paradise.
    I come to tell him just the way to reach it,
    Describe the scene awaiting on the morrow—
    His own stripped, cringing form—and, over
        there,
    Each man, maid, child in town agog to see him;
    Then how the priests will throttle, throw him
        down,
    And, while yet living, writhing, yelling, sane,
    Gouge their blunt nails between his reeking
        ribs,
    And, by the roots, tear out his dripping heart.
[OFFICER.   Ugh!—I would rather be a soldier.
KOOTHA.   What?—
    And miss a spectacle so rare?—that play
    Of fright and agony, in white and shade
    Breaking in contrast o'er your victim's brow?
    Why, what is life without variety?
OFFICER.   You see too much of it.
KOOTHA.   Oh no!—no more
    Than all men do—perhaps concentered more
    Than hell vouchsafes to others!   That is all.]
OFFICER (*pointing toward the Left*).
    See there—the maids are coming now.
KOOTHA.   Of course,
    To snare the captive that your spears have
        spared.

They know the first with whom they fall in
    love
Will be the first one whom the priest will call
The chosen of the gods, and send to—heaven.
What cares a maid, be he her victim too?
OFFICER.   You mean her lover.
KOOTHA.   Victim.
[OFFICER.   Humph! I see:
A soldier's life seems lovelier, then?
KOOTHA.   Why not?—
A man-foe is a brute, a shark that whacks
The spirit's prow and whirls it from its course.
A maid may be a devil, seizing on
The spirit's helm to turn it where she will.
Her victim though—he thinks her will is his.
You never knew a man to dodge the touch
Of love-like fingers feeling for his heart.
That heart held once within a grip so gained,
Will take each wrench that wrings its life-
    blood out
To be its own pulsation.]
OFFICER.   I, at least,
Am not their victim yet, and so I leave.
            *Exit—Right—*OFFICER.
KOOTHA (*to his* COMPANION).
No, not their victim; but his captives are;
And they are our own kin, whom we, forsooth,
Must fool and lure to slaughter. How I
    longed

Why break their peace, before you get them
    home?
[FIRST WOMAN.   No fear for your peace! You
    may stay alone!
There are those, though, who want us.
KOOTHA.   There are men
    Who lose their senses. I have heard of those
    With ears too dull to hear a bat when squeal-
        ing.
    And flesh too tough to feel a flea when sting-
        ing.
SECOND WOMAN (*to* FIRST WOMAN).
    Why stand and talk? We have a right to see
    The captives. Kootha knows it too.
             (*To* KOOTHA). Stand back!
             (*To* FIRST WOMAN).
    Go forward!
KOOTHA.   Nay, leave forwardness to men.
    Have backwardness. It best becomes a
    woman.]
(*An arrow, coming from the right, falls upon the
    stage.* KOOTHA *picks it up.*)
    See there—an arrow! They are fighting still.
    You may get more of these through your own
        hearts
    Than even you could dream to send through
        others'.
WOMEN. Oh! oh!
    Exeunt—Left—the WOMEN *in fright.*

KOOTHA (*looking after them, and then toward the right*).   The fight and flight not over?—Humph!

*Exit—Left—*KOOTHA *and his* COMPANION.
(*After a little, amid thunder and lightning*),
        *Enter—Right Rear—*WAPELLA.
        *Enter—Right Front—*MONASKA.

WAPELLA. That you, Monaska?

MONASKA.   Yes, and you?

WAPELLA.   Wapella.

MONASKA.   What man can fight both earth and heaven?

WAPELLA.   Some fiend
Is raining down these fiery storm-bolts.

MONASKA.   Yes,
We meet the foe, and in their track, as if
Out-cowarding the just-caught cuttle-fish,
This gloom exudes upon the flooding light.

WAPELLA.   We might have scaled their hill, but not these heavens.

MONASKA.   We just had drawn our bows, each arrow aimed
To wedge eternal stillness in between
Unhinging joints of some affrighted heart,
When down upon us burst that thunder-flash.
The shock, so sudden, glanced the arrows up
As if to shoot them in the face of gods
Asail the clouds in yon black gulf.   It gave

Their men their chance. With one wild yell
    and bound
They closed like smoke about the lightning's
    fire;
And, all with darts whirled on like sparks
    before
A flame that followed, they came roaring on
To fill the gaps their shots had made. [Oh,
    hell!
Not one of us but saw, mount fiercely up
The dying body of some fallen friend,
What seemed wild fiends.
WAPELLA. How know you but they were?—
    Grim phantom-spirits of the earth and air—
    The same that now pursue us?—And from
      them
    You fled?
MONASKA. Fled?—Never! No, with them I
      fought,
    Till all I fought for but myself were not.
WAPELLA. Hush! They will find us.
MONASKA.   Ay, they will—too soon.
    Each fearful time this lid of heaven is lifted,
    The rays pour in and focus here on us.
    They axle here the foes' near wheeling lines,
    Ay, draw them like a whirlpool to its vortex.
WAPELLA. This tree will shield us.
(*The two move toward a tree at the Back Centre
    with a moss-covered bench at the Right of it.*)
   2

MONASKA. There is not a tree
Or leaf, or trunk, but what, to point us out,
These fiery fingers of the storm would dash
Aside to ashes—fume—thin air.]

WAPELLA (*leading* MONASKA *toward the moss-
covered bench, and sitting down, then
rising*). We here
Are hid as could be hoped for.

MONASKA. I hope not
For anything. Sweet hope is a bird of light,
The pulsing touch of whose aspiring wing
Thrills to new life the very air one breathes.
In gloom like ours the trembling heart but
leaps
To dodge the whir of some blind bat of fear.

WAPELLA (*looking toward the Left*).
Hark! There seems human rhythm in this
hell.
What hot pursuit is it comes burning through
These crackling branches?
(*Vivid lightning.*)

MONASKA (*pointing toward the Left*).
Did you see it?

WAPELLA. No.
But when I do——(*drawing his bow.*)

MONASKA (*placing his hand on the bow*).
Hold!—Could one ever see
An angel, hers would be a form like that.

WAPELLA. An angel?—fiend!

MONASKA. Right! Only fools have faith
In forms they have not wit to find unfrocked.
Not sages even see the spirit through them.
We flee.

WAPELLA (*placing his hand on his hip, and sinking down*). I cannot.

MONASKA. What?—Are wounded?

WAPELLA. Yes.

MONASKA (*sitting on the moss-covered seat beside
him*). Then I stay too.

WAPELLA. Nay, go.

MONASKA (*lying down on the moss-covered eleva-
tion*). Not I.—No man
Can wish us ill, the while our bodies bow
To do his wishes. Let us yield our wills
To save our lives, and feign that we are dead.
    *Enter—Left—*WALOON *and a* MAID.

WAPELLA. Sh—sh——

WALOON (*to the* MAID).
    The foe are fled. Our homes are safe;
(*Lightning. She sees* MONASKA *and* WAPELLA.)
Why, who are they?—How beautiful! What
    flowers
To bloom amid the desert of the storm!
What glow of vigor in their fair, round limbs,
Ay, how their colors warm this cold-hued air!—
Can they be wounded?—dead?—Oh, cruel
    man,
When spirits of the sunlight guise in flesh

And fringe the halo of the sunshine round
 them,
Have we so much to cheer us on the earth,
We can afford destruction to the frames
That form fit settings of a light so dear?—
Nay, I——
  (*She approaches, bends, and studies them.*)
  They both are breathing still!—But look——
    (*Lightning.*)
This garb?—Why, they will kill us yet un-
 less——
(*She lifts a spear that she holds in her hand, then
   drops it.*)
[Who made me heaven's avenging messenger?
Or bade me cull for those high gardeners there
What grow in nights of earth to greet their
 dawn?
I should not know them foes but for their
 guise.
And what is all their alien flesh but guise
A little nearer to their souls?   It gone,
What would they be but spirits, freed from
 space,—
From all the need of trampling others down
To find a place to stand in for themselves?—
The two here must be wounded.—Say, good
 friends—]
  (*They start up.   She draws back.*)
 Exit—Left—the MAID *as if frightened.*

Wait, wait!—A maid like me would do no
    harm.—
    (*As they sit still and look at her.*)
You—you are wounded?

MONASKA. Not to death.—And you?—
Why do you stand there, and not hurl the
    dart?
It would be sweet, if when one came to die,
His last sigh could breathe forth toward one
    like you.

WALOON. I kill you?—What?

MONASKA.   And why, pray, should you not?

WALOON. I am a woman!

(*The storm ceases; and from this time on the forest
        grows gradually brighter.*)

MONASKA.   And a woman's aim
Knows how to reach the heart. We should
    escape
The bungling work of men.
            (*opening his breast.*)
                    My heart—take aim—
Is open to you. Oh, how it will thrill
To feel it gets what you would give!

WALOON.   No, no;
You seem too strong and fair for earth to lose.
Some one, with you, would find it full of light.

MONASKA. But we are foes.

WALOON.   To me you seem like friends.

MONASKA. But to your brothers?

WALOON.   There are those they spare.
MONASKA.   At your wish?
WALOON.   I can plead.
MONASKA.   From such lips pleas,
   Like fragrance from the flowers upon a shrine,
   Might bring an answer.   I will trust in you.
      (MONASKA *and* WAPELLA *begin to rise.*)
*Enter—Left—*HAIJO *and* KOOTHA *with his* COM-
               PANION.
WALOON.   Nay, nay, lie still.   Wait, till I
   speak to them.
(*referring to* HAIJO *and* KOOTHA, *and moving*
    toward them and addressing them.)
   Here lie some wounded warriors.
KOOTHA.   Foes?
WALOON.   They are.
KOOTHA.   I hope then you have cured them of
   their wounds!
WALOON.   How so?
KOOTHA (*lifting his spear*).
      How so?—There is but one sure cure.—
   Ope wide the casket that the world has bruised
   And let the unbruised soul fly out of it.
(*makes as if he would move toward* MONASKA.)
WALOON (*lifting her hands, and moving forward*
      as if to shield MONASKA).
   No, no; not that; no!—They are beautiful.
KOOTHA.   Then send them upward while they
   are so.   Why

Outlive the happy moment for one's death!
A body maimed may mold a spirit maimed.
WALOON. Their wounds are not so bad as that.
KOOTHA.   Or good.
    (WALOON *looks at him in a puzzled way.*)
I mean it—good. I mean it. Let me see
    them.
(WALOON *gestures toward them and looks toward*
             HAIJO.)
[HAIJO (*to* WALOON, *as he looks toward the*
    prisoners).
You call them beautiful? When you have
    seen
As much of men as I, you will think more
Of greater spirits with their lives enshrined
In mountain, valley, forest, bush, and flower
Than of these little spirits framed in flesh.
WALOON. A great priest, you, and I a little
    maid.
HAIJO. And for our little maidens men like
    these
Are sent at times on little missions to us.]
KOOTHA (*waving his spear*).
Sire, pin them down where they shall kneel
    before us
And keep on kneeling till their life is through.
HAIJO. No, no!—but I wait here, and you go
    back
And tell them at the temple why I do so.

KOOTHA (*to his* COMPANION *as he moves toward the left*).

　　Oh, heaven, I thought to help them!—but
　　　　too late!

　　*Exit—Left—*KOOTHA *and his* COMPANION.

HAIJO (*to* WALOON).

　　You wish to save them, eh?—One way is——

WALOON (*eagerly*).　　　　　　　　　　What?

HAIJO. Why, make the king adopt them.
　　　　This, you know,

　Is often done.　Then they will be our own;
　As much so as if born here.　Can you think
　Of anything he would not do for you?—
　The trouble is, I hear, that there are things
　You would not do for him, ha, ha, ha, ha!
　Oh, no offense!　You know you are my
　　　　ward.

　For one, I ward you from his majesty.
　Suppose you go, and tell your tale to him—
　The beauty of the prisoners, and your wish.
　I think that he would grant it.

WALOON.　　　　　　　　　　Free them wholly?

HAIJO. Why, you can ask and learn.　Should
　　　　he refuse,

　They would be no more sure to die than now.
　　　　(HAIJO *waves his hand.*)

*Enter—from both Right and Left—*GUARDS *with
　　　　spears, and stand watching* MONASKA *and*
　　　　WAPELLA.

WALOON.   First I will tell them why I go away—
　And you will guard them here?
HAIJO.　　　　　　　　　　As if the king
　Himself had ordered it.
(*to a Chief of the Guards as* WALOON *walks to-*
　　　ward MONASKA *and* WAPELLA *who rise*
　　　to receive her)   The girl is right.
　She knows what beauty is—just what we need!
　And not another fair-formed captive left us!
　The king will save them, not a doubt of
　　that.
　We never found a pair of fairer gods.
WALOON (*to* MONASKA.)
　I go to ask our king here to adopt you.
　　　　　(*pointing to* HAIJO)
　This guardian of all our sacred things
　Will guard you sacredly till I return.
HAIJO (*to* MONASKA *and* WAPELLA).
　Unless you mean to fly.   Try that; no more
　Could you escape our warriors' darts, than
　　dodge
　The shadows of the trees through which you
　　flew.
　　　　*Exit—Left—*WALOON.
MONASKA (*to* HAIJO).
　You seem a prophet, sire?
HAIJO.　　　　　　　　　They hold me such.
MONASKA (*holding out his hand*).
　And you could read my fate?

HAIJO.   Not difficult.
  (*plucking a twig from a tree*)
  The tree's full growth is here, could one unfold
    it.
  Your future is the fruit of present dreams,
  The lure that leads the deepest wish within
    you,
  The goal that lights the farthest path of hope.
(*taking* MONASKA *by the hand, then dropping it*)
  A touch that feels the start can point the
    finish.
MONASKA.   You think so?
HAIJO.   There is nothing stops the flow
  Of thought betwixt my fingers and my brain,
  Betwixt your fingers and your brain; not
    so?—
        (*taking him by the hand again*)
  Now join these—what cuts off your brain
    from mine?
MONASKA.   Our wills.
HAIJO.   Yet if I yield my will to yours——
MONASKA.   But can you?
HAIJO.   And if not, what boots the priest
  His years of fasting and of discipline?—
  Besides, all lives are much alike.
MONASKA.   They are?—
  [How so?
HAIJO.   All thorns or roses, if you please,
  Grown on the self-same bush.

Monaska.   Do all lives grow
  Both thorns and roses?
Haijo.   Yes; we show the thorns
  To those who try to pluck us for them-
      selves;
  The roses to the ones that let us be.
Monaska.   And so you think all lives alike?
Haijo.   Allied.]
  All lives are summers, veiled at either end
  In shadows of the spring and autumn storms.
  We pass from tears of birth to burial;
  And in the brief, bright interval between
  There comes anon the fevered flush of life,
  Then paleness, then the fevered flush of
      death.
  Men leap and laugh, and then lie back and
      cough.
  Both but hysterical, betwixt the two,
  Warring for power that more of war must
      keep,
  Pushing for place that prisons those who seize
      it,
  Kneeling for love to tramp on when they
      get it,
  Their little rest is large-brought weariness,
  And what they wish for most is mainly
      death.
Monaska.   A cheerful view!
Haijo.   It was not volunteered.

[Monaska.   My fate seems dark then?

Haijo.   Brilliant.

Monaska.   Brilliant?

Haijo.   Yes,——

Monaska.   A fire is brilliant, yet it burns
   us up.

Haijo.   In time.

Monaska.   Yet all life is a thing of time.

Haijo.   You hunger for excitement, man.   You
   hail
 The trump of war, the tramp of onset, all
 That sweeps you on where drafts of life and
    love
 Fan up the flames that flicker in the breast
 And set the whole form's trembling veins
    aglow.

Monaska.   You read me well.

Haijo.   Suppose this heart a toy
 Wound up to run through just so many
    ticks——

Monaska.   I see, you mean a fast life is a short
   life.

Haijo.   The fleetest foot is first beside the goal.

Monaska.   But if the goal be high as well as
   far——

Haijo.   The bird of fleetest wing may fly the
   highest.

Monaska.   It may!—A chance that I could
   risk!—If not,

More blest the short-lived moths that fly to
    flame
Straight through a pathway lit by coming
    light
Than long-lived worms that crawl through
    endless mire.

HAIJO. Yours will be lit by coming light.

MONASKA.   And I,]
I shall not lose my life?

HAIJO.   In every life,
The first and final acts are tragedy.

MONASKA. But ere the final act?——

HAIJO.   The whole you wish
Will come.

MONASKA. All?

HAIJO.   All.

MONASKA.   But I am not unselfish.

HAIJO. You need not be—where all will rush
    to serve you.

MONASKA. And I am vain.

HAIJO. None will be clothed more richly.

MONASKA. And I have tastes.

HAIJO.   Each meal will be a feast.

MONASKA. I would not slave it to these lower
    aims.
  I have ambition.

HAIJO.   None will rank above you.

MONASKA. None?

HAIJO.   I have said it—none.

MONASKA. That cannot be.
  My birth——
HAIJO. Who knows the place that he was born
  To fill?
MONASKA. High aspirations thrill my soul.
HAIJO. Have higher still. You will be like a
    god.
      (*aside, to the Chief of the Guards.*)
  Now will I see if he divine my meaning.
MONASKA. It may be when I die.
HAIJO (*aside to the Chief again*).
        Is not divined;
  Or, if it be, in but a slight degree.
        (*to* MONASKA.)
  No; you mistook my thought. I spoke of
    earth.
MONASKA. Of earth?—You know, sire, I can
    tell it you—
  You know about the weaknesses of youth?
HAIJO. Yes, you can tell me all.
MONASKA. I am not one
  Has lived or worked with other men. My soul
  Has dwelt alone, and sails the waves of life
  Like some stray oil-drop lost upon the sea,
  Refusing still, however wildly tossing,
  To lose or fuse itself in things about it.
  I have so craved a mate! but, whoso came,
  The spirit that is in me would deny
  My clasping to a heart that might not beat

In time to pulses of another's purpose.
So what I would caress, I dared not touch,
For fear the rhythm throbbing in my veins
Would prove discordant and reveal us foes.

HAIJO. Ah! love you wish?

MONASKA. Ay, sire, I would be loved.

HAIJO. You think that strange at your age,
strange?

MONASKA. Not strange the wish—but could it
be fulfilled——

HAIJO. I said it should be. You shall be so
loved
That you will yearn for rivals more than see
them.

[MONASKA. Will yearn—but how can this be
true? You jest.

HAIJO. Is it my face or robe you deem a jester's?

MONASKA. You mean it?

HAIJO. It is in your hand, your face.
I told you I had had experience.
Why do you doubt?

MONASKA. Because life never brought
Aught like it.

HAIJO. Life brings day as well as night,
When day, the wise will use the sunshine.]

MONASKA (*looking at* WAPELLA, *who has been
watching them eagerly, and now rises*).

Come
And tell his fortune too.

WAPELLA.   Yes, mine.
   *Enter—Left—*WALOON *and the* KING.
HAIJO.   The King.
   (*All bow. The* KING *speaks aside to* HAIJO.)
   The King desires that you retire, you three.
(*motioning to* MONASKA, WAPELLA, *and* WALOON.)
*Exeunt—Right—*MONASKA, WAPELLA, *and* WA-
   LOON, *accompanied by some of the Guards.*
KING (*to* HAIJO.)   What think you?
HAIJO.   Just what she has told you, sire.
   No doubt, about the beauty of the men.
KING.   Nor of her love?
HAIJO.   It seems to augur well.
KING.   I feel not sure about your method.
HAIJO.   No?—
   In lands like ours, a land controlled by law,
   Illegal force will rouse the people's wrath.
   But let her love the one we make a god,
   And wed his ghost, and dwell within the
      temple;
   There he who is the head of our religion
   Can rightly represent the god,—not so?
KING.   I see—a portion of the heaven of which
   The priesthood holds the key, is on the earth.
HAIJO (*suddenly turning the subject*).
   Sire, we must have some foe to sacrifice.
   For this year——
KING.   You will furnish one insured
   To break this maiden's heart.

HAIJO.   A colt once broke
  Drives easily.
KING.   Let me not doubt again
  What power incarnates Providence on earth.
  Lead out this coming god.
HAIJO (*looking toward the Right*).
                              Waloon, the King
  Desires to see the prisoners.
[*Enter—Right*—WALOON, MONASKA, WAPELLA,
                and GUARDS.
KING (*to* HAIJO, *as he looks at* MONASKA).
                              Yes, yes,
  He is a fine one, no mistake!   Poor girl!—
  But what were life without its discipline?
  And what are kings and priests for but to give it?
  No fêtes are feasts with every course alike;
  And all fare better who begin with bitters.
        (*to* MONASKA *and* WAPELLA.)
  Young men, your warriors came a long, hard
      way
  To fight with us.   They should have stayed
      at home.
MONASKA.   Our king, sire, sent them forth.
KING.   Good!   We shall keep
  Their flesh to fertilize our fields, and see
  That he has less to send the next time.   Ha!
        (*The* GUARDS, *at a sign from the* KING, *draw
          their bows on* MONASKA *and* WAPELLA.)
  Waloon, stand back, there, from the prisoners.
  3

WALOON (*to the* KING).

Ah, but you will not kill them, will you, sire?

KING.   Why not?—They would kill us.   We
      only do

What they would do.

MONASKA (*aiming his bow*).

                    Perhaps, when this has gone

Through you, and through your pals too——

WALOON (*hurrying between the* KING *and* MON-
      ASKA, *and speaking to* MONASKA).   Wait.

MONASKA (*bowing to* WALOON).   For you.

WALOON (*to the* KING).

Ah, sire, was it for this I urged them not

To fly from here?—You surely will adopt
      them?

KING.   And you would save my life and save
      his too?   (*To* MONASKA.)

We both owe something to her love, you see.

MONASKA (*to the* KING).

I read my pardon in your own face now.

KING.   I feel no pity, and no love for you.

If you are saved here, she alone has done it.

Thank her.

MONASKA (*kneeling to her*).

            I will, as I would thank an angel.

KING (*to* HAIJO, *aside*).

You see—we made no promises.   Keep watch

And never let them be alone together.

                    CURTAIN.

ACT SECOND.

SCENE:—*A walled open space within an Aztec fort.
Backing at the Right is a closed gate guarded by
SPEARMEN, and at the Left a pyramid-shaped
structure such as formed an Aztec shrine. On
the lower steps of this structure, forming a sort
of throne for the KING, are rugs, etc. On the
Right Side of the Space are trees, on its Left
Side, near the rear are curtains before a building
evidently of the nature of a temple. Entrances:
several at the Right through the trees; at the Right
Center through the Gateway; at the Left Front
to one side of the Temple; at the Left farther
back, through curtains into the Temple; at the
Left Rear between the Temple and the Pyramid.
The Curtain rises on the gray light of dawn.
Guards are at the gates, prisoners grouped
about the space. MONASKA and WAPELLA
are near the Left Front.*

WAPELLA.   I do not understand this.

MONASKA.   No; but half
The interest of life is in its puzzles.

WAPELLA.   I thought they set us free.

MONASKA.   I often think
  Some one is just about to set me free.
  I never found him yet.
WAPELLA.   We fare no better
  Than these, our fellow-prisoners.
MONASKA.   That seems
  A lesson to our self-conceit.   The wise
  Are grateful to their teachers.
WAPELLA.   You are sanguine.
MONASKA. Some men are born with light,
      aspiring blood
  That, bounding brainward, keeps the whole
      frame glowing.
WAPELLA (*pointing to the other prisoners*).
  These men expect us to be put to death.
MONASKA. And some are born with heavy,
      sluggish blood,
  That will not leave the heart but keeps it
      weighted.
WAPELLA. They say they know the customs
      of the place.
MONASKA. We know its characters—the maid,
      priest, king——
WAPELLA. They say that captives here are
      sacrificed.
MONASKA. Not those the king himself has
      once adopted.
WAPELLA. Then say why we are prisoned in a
      temple.

MONASKA. Humph! your conundrum! Have
    not thought of it.

WAPELLA. No; nor of anything outside the
    maid

You have enshrined there in your heart.

MONASKA.   With reason!

WAPELLA. Would reason drop the curtain of
    the eye,

And dwell in darkness, and be proud of it?

Monaska, you are dreaming. You must wake

And join us in our effort to escape.

MONASKA. You make it for yourselves. Why
    wait for me?

WAPELLA. Why?—You outrank us.

MONASKA.   There are no ranks here.

WAPELLA. A leader, if he lead not, shames his
    birthright.

Besides, we two have weapons left with us.

You keep your club; I mine. The rest have
    none.

Perhaps they merely overlooked our arms,

And, when the morning comes, will take them
    from us.

Before that, when the other guards withdraw,

As they do always, when the signal sounds,
       (*pointing toward the gate*)

We can attack the two they leave behind,

Each kill his man, and, while the rest break
    down

The gate behind, can all of us rush out,
O'ertake our friends and fly with them for
    home.
MONASKA.   The home in which the spider traps
        the fly!
WAPELLA.   No soldiers watch that side the gate.
MONASKA.   And we,
    To show our gratitude for being saved,
    Will leave two prostrate, murdered forms
        behind
    To do obeisance for us!
[WAPELLA.   Rather than
    Harm them, we all here should be murdered,
        eh?
MONASKA.   If there were fear of that, the maid
        would never
    Have pleaded for us.]
WAPELLA.   They are all our foes.
    Can you a moment balance them against
    Your time-tried friends?
            Exeunt—Left—all the GUARDS *but two,
                who stand each side the gate.*
                Look!   Now the guards have left.
    Monaska, come—I said you would.—They
        wait (*pointing to other* PRISONERS).
MONASKA.   You seem suspicious.
WAPELLA (*excitedly*).   Dare you tackle them?
MONASKA (*angrily*).
    Talk not of daring!   I will tackle you.

WAPELLA (*excited, but trying to control himself*).

Forgive me—Why, you know I am your friend.

We all are friends. Monaska, will you join us?

MONASKA. Turn traitor to the ones that saved us?—No.

WAPELLA. But to your own land and your landsmen, yes.

MONASKA (*drawing his club, and springing toward* WAPELLA).

That you must prove, or——

(WAPELLA *draws his club and defends himself.*)

GUARD (*at the gate*). Hold!

  Enter—Left—other GUARDS *and* OFFICER.
   They separate, with spears, MONASKA *and* WAPELLA.

WAPELLA (*to* MONASKA).

     Now you have proved it.

OFFICER (*to* MONASKA *and* WAPELLA).

Your clubs.

MONASKA. We were adopted. We are free.

OFFICER (*as he motions to the* GUARDS *to take the clubs away from the two prisoners*).

You will not need these, then, to guard yourselves.

  (*The* GUARDS *take the clubs.*)

  Enter—through the curtains at the Left—
  HAIJO, KOOTHA *and his* COMPANION.

(HAIJO *ascends the steps of the pyramid near the rugs. In his hand is a
parchment.*)

OFFICER (*to* MONASKA, WAPELLA *and other
prisoners*).

Stand back, and hear the royal proclamation.

HAIJO (*reading*).

Know, all ye captives, who have proved your
worth
By warding off when in the brunt of war
The stroke aimed well to fell you, know to-day
This temple celebrates its yearly fête;
And hither wend the maidens of the realm.
Commend yourselves to them, and woman's
love,
Like that which gave our land its natural sons,
Will make you sons of its adoption, sons
And lovers, fit to claim their heart's devotion.
For why should brave springs flow to waste,
and not
Augment the channels of the nation's life?—
Go seek your cells, make ready, and come
forth,
And know the highest honors wait for him
Whose charms prove greatest for the greatest
number.

MONASKA (*to* WAPELLA).

There, there. I told you so.

WAPELLA.   Well, we shall see——

MONASKA. That I shall wed the woman of my
 choice.

Exeunt—Right—all the PRISONERS *except* WAP-
ELLA.

KOOTHA (*to his* COMPANION *and looking toward*
 MONASKA).

What fools we are when we would read
 ourselves.

He thinks he craves the honors promised him

Whose charms prove greatest for the greatest
 number.

Alas, the one thing that his nature craves,

Is not a number.

*Exeunt—Right—*WAPELLA, *followed by some of*
the GUARDS.

(KOOTHA *continues to talk to his* COMPANION.)
                    Ah! That proclamation

Was worthy of the priest that penned it.

COMPANION.   Why?

KOOTHA. Must be received with faith to seem
 a blessing;

And holds a promise that, whatever come,

Will stand.

COMPANION. And be fulfilled.

KOOTHA.   Oh, yes—in form!

But nothing like a priest's grip on a form

To squeeze the spirit out of it.

                *Enter—Left—*WALOON.

COMPANION.   In that

The promise pairs with life; for nothing
  earthly
Fulfills a promise just as it was given.
KOOTHA. Ay, while the eyes of hope are look-
  ing up,
The devil trips the feet. But why should gods
Make priests play devil?
[COMPANION (*noticing* HAIJO *advancing*).
      Hold; you may play die,
And go to him.
KOOTHA (*looking at* HAIJO).
       Oh, no, no! After death
I think I shall be freed from following him.]
   (*The day grows gradually brighter.*)
*Exit—Left—through the curtains—*KOOTHA *and*
    his COMPANION.
WALOON (*to* HAIJO).
 Can it be true?
HAIJO   What true?
WALOON.   Why, that the king
 Will put Monaska to the maidens' test?
HAIJO. Of course.
WALOON.   Of course?
HAIJO.   Why not?
WALOON.   Because the king
 Adopted him.
HAIJO.   But you would not deprive
 The captive of his rights?
WALOON.   His rights?

HAIJO.   What right
Can any man have grander than to be
A god?
[WALOON.   A few-weeks' god?
HAIJO.   Why, yes.   You know
The joy of life is in its quality,
Not quantity.   A heaven on earth—what is it
But having what one wishes?
WALOON.   This is cruel.
HAIJO.   There are a score or more of prisoners.
We need a man whose bearing can supply
Attractions that will draw the souls of all
Toward him and toward the god he represents.
The surest way of choosing such a man
Is this one which the royal will decrees.
WALOON.   You know his beauty.   They would
        all choose him.
HAIJO.   Oh, no no; only some!—and if they all
        did,
Would it be just in us to fail for this
To let him be the chosen of the gods?
WALOON.   No,—of the maidens.
HAIJO.   Of the maidens' love.
And what than woman's love is more like
        gods'?
WALOON.   Oh, this is fearful, fearful!   Think of
        me.
HAIJO.   Of you?]
WALOON.   I love him.

HAIJO.   Then, if he should be
   The chosen of the gods, this would confirm
   Your choice, and thus exalt both him and you.
[WALOON.   But then he would belong—oh, not
      to me!
   But to the world, and to the world of women.
HAIJO.   The thought of that is not inspiring?
WALOON.   No.
   And soon he would be gone——
HAIJO.   Among the gods.]
WALOON.   I would not have him there.   I wish
     him here.
HAIJO.   If earth held all our souls could wish,
     no soul
   Could ever wish for heaven.
WALOON.   My heaven holds love.
   And what thrives there thrives here, and has a
     right
   To all things men can rightly let it have.
[HAIJO.   Save when the gods——
WALOON.   The gods I cannot see:
   In front of me what I see is a man.
HAIJO.   Then pray the gods to give you light.
WALOON.   How can
   I pray the gods to give me light, if those
   That have been sent to lead me where it shines
   Forever stand betwixt my soul and it?]
    Enter—Left Rear—the KING *with* ATTENDANTS.
WALOON (*to the* KING).

Great sire, they plan to do a great wrong here.

KING. How so? It shall be righted.

HAIJO (*to the* KING). She would keep
Monaska from the test that makes him god.

KING. Oh—but—he has a right to it.

WALOON. Yet, sire,
A right that wrongs your kindly pardoning
him.

KING. Why no, no! all our captives have that
right.

WALOON. But, sire, he, he would be the choice
of all.

KING. So much more reason he should have his
chance.

WALOON. But I—I—love him.

HAIJO. If you loved him truly,
You scarce would dare to stand between him,
then,
And that which lifts him to the gods.

[WALOON. You know
I pleaded for his life.
(*turning toward the* KING.)
You gave it him.
Now all of you seem plotting for his death.

HAIJO. Monaska had his choice.

WALOON. His choice?

HAIJO. Why, yes.

WALOON. When was it?

HAIJO. In the woods. "More blest," he cried,

"More blest the short-lived moths that fly to
    flame
Straight through a pathway lit by coming
    light
Than long-lived worms that crawl through
    endless mire."]
(*The* KING *nods approvingly, and moves on with*
    ATTENDANTS *toward the pyramid.*)

WALOON (*to* HAIJO).
    You told him all?

HAIJO.   Oh, no, not all.   Why should I?

WALOON.   Then I will tell him.

HAIJO.   When the priests enjoin it.
    Till then, the only lips that can reveal
    One temple-secret speak from realms of
        death.
    And if as yet they have not entered these,
    It will become our duty to transfer them.

WALOON (*surprised*).
    I cannot speak to him?

HAIJO.   Speak all you wish.
    But if he learn too much, he cannot hide it.

WALOON.   Oh, cruel! I may speak—show all
        I wish—
    Except what fills the fount from which it
        springs.
    Alas, what pain—what pain alone—can keep
    The ever-swelling, surging, flood within?—
    Go bid the lake sleep on unheard, unseen,

Whose tribute-streams are dashed from cata-
    racts,
Or waves are whirled by winds up toward the
    clouds——

HAIJO.   Ah, has it gone so far?

WALOON.   Oh, sire, too oft,
A mood but half expressed is all distressed.
What now is left my soul!

HAIJO.   One course is left.
The surest way to keep from feeling things
Is not to touch them.

WALOON.   What were best for me,
Is not the question.   I would ward from him
The fatal blight that follows woman's love,
Accurséd love, that makes the brightest eye
A sunglass through which heaven would wilt
    the soul,
And by the very pleasure beauty gives
Mete out the measure of impending doom.

HAIJO.   What will you do then?

WALOON.   Save him if I can.
       (*Blast of trumpets, followed by music. The*
         KING *and* ATTENDANTS *arrange them-*
         selves on the rugs at the base of the pyra-
         mid. The gate backing at the Right
         Center is thrown open.)
      Exit—Right—very hastily, WALOON.

HAIJO (*to the* KING).
Poor fool!   She does not know the surest way

To guard her lover from the love of all
Is letting him alone.   About the lips
Found sweet by merely one, all swarm like
      bees.
But let that one forsake him all forsake him.

> *Enter—through the Gate backing at the
>   Right Center—Procession of* MAIDENS
>   *and others, bearing banners and wreaths
>   and decorated with flowers.   All sing
>   the following:*

Where dwell the gods?
Where dwell the gods?
Oh, dwell they in the sky?
Or come they near in gloom or gleam
Of earth or air or wood or stream?—
Oh, yes, the gods are all on high;
But, robed in all that teem or seem
Where eye can spy or fancy fly,
   The gods are always nigh.

How speak the gods?
How speak the gods?
In thunder from the sky?
In storms that o'er the cloud-banks pour,
Or dash in waves along the shore?—
Oh, yes, the gods are all on high;
But not alone in rush and roar,
   Wherever breeze or breath can sigh
   The gods are always nigh.

How touch the gods?
How touch the gods?
Oh, reach they from the sky

Wherever airy fingers brush
The leaves that throb, the cheeks that flush?—
  Oh, yes, the gods are all on high;
But in the thrills that fill the hush
  When naught without is passing by,
    The gods are always nigh.

    Where look the gods?
    Where look the gods?
  In glances from the sky
Down through the lightning's death-dealt blaze,
Or thrilling through the starry rays?—
  Oh, yes, the gods are all on high;
But in the looks that on us gaze
  From out the love-lit human eye
    The gods are always nigh.

    (*While singing, the* MAIDENS *arrange
      themselves in line from Front to Rear
      at the Left.*)

KING (*looking toward the Right*).

And now bring forth the prisoners.

OFFICER (*standing near the Right.*)   They come.

KING (*gesturing with his right hand*).

Arrange them there in line.

    *Enter—Right—*CAPTIVES, *and are marched
      and formed in a line at the Right
      between the gateway and the Front
      of the stage.* MONASKA *enters last,
      and stands nearest the Right Front.*

*Enter—at the Right Front—*WALOON, *and stands
    at the Right of* MONASKA.

King.   Now shall the eyes
  Of gods above look through the brightest eyes
  Whose glances light the earth; and whom
        those eyes
  Adore the most, him too shall all adore.

(*The* King, *looking at the* Captives, *converses
        with his* Attendants.)

(*The* Maidens *look at the* Captives, *especially
at those nearest the gateway, and converse together.*)

Waloon (*to* Monaska, *in a half whisper, and not
        observed by others except him*).

  Monaska.

Monaska.   What?

Waloon.   Look this way.

Monaska.   Could I else?—
  (*gesturing and looking toward the* Maidens.)
  Yet must I seek the favor of these maids.

Waloon.   Is not the favor of one maid enough?

Monaska.   Enough and more—yet here——

Waloon.   Confide in me.

Monaska.   Yes, wholly.

Waloon.   Then be wholly what I wish.

Monaska.   Be what?

Waloon.   One who will not attract attention.

Monaska.   Why, then——

Waloon.   You might seem wholly mine.

Monaska (*looking toward the other* Maidens).

                              I see—
  O brightest hour of all my life!—I see

You love—and love, if shorn of jealousy,
Drops half its charms, like maids whose locks
    are clipped,
And better might be boys, or bald-head-babes.

WALOON (*taking him by the sleeve*).

Monaska.

MONASKA (*continuing to look at the others*).

        Doubt me!—But I know, at times,
Deceit that spices daintily with doubt
The plain-served truth more seasons it to
    taste.

WALOON (*touching him again, and moving toward
    the Right Front Entrance*).

Here—something this way I would have you
    see!

MONASKA (*looking at her, then at the others*).

I must not lose my chances with the maids.
And yet—a moment—then I can return.

        (*turns toward* WALOON *and bows.*)

The highest honors wait for him alone
Whose charms prove greatest for the greatest
    number.

        *Exit—Right—*WALOON.
        *Exit—Right—*MONASKA.

KING (*to the* MAIDENS).

Now to select your mates.

        (*to the* CAPTIVES.)

        Come forward, men.

(*to* HAIJO, *looking toward the Right Front.*)

Saw you those two depart?—She plans to tell
　　him.

　　(MAIDENS *and* CAPTIVES *mingle and talk.*)

HAIJO (*to the* KING).

　　She will not; no.　She will not dare.

KING.　　　　　　　　　　　　　　What then?

HAIJO.　They will return.

KING.　　　　　　　　　　　　But if they love?

HAIJO.　　　　　　　　　　　　　　Then she
　　Will play the woman, try to fascinate
　　His eye, spell-bound till blind to charms of
　　　others.

KING.　And he?

HAIJO.　　　He is a man.　What man will barter
　　Self-love for woman's love?

KING.　　　　　　　　　　　　He may.

HAIJO.　　　　　　　　　　　　　　If so,
　　Some other will be chosen.

KING.　　　　　　　　　He must be it.

HAIJO.　Safe statement, sire!　Small danger any
　　　man
　　Will waive his chances for the highest
　　　honor
　　To please a heart whose love is won already.

KING.　You may be right.

HAIJO.　　　　　　　　　It might be well to send
　　A message to remind him of his chances.

(*to a* MESSENGER, *and pointing toward the Right
　　　　Front Entrance.*)

Saw you those two retiring to the right?—
Remind them of the royal proclamation.

Exit—Right Front—MESSENGER.

(*Music and dance in which* CAPTIVES *and*
MAIDENS *join.   As the dancing ends,*)

*Enter—Right Front—*MONASKA *and* WALOON.

MONASKA. You will not dance with me,
Waloon?

WALOON.   No, no;
[Not here.

MONASKA.   Then I shall have to dance alone

WALOON.   Why should you dance at all?

MONASKA.   Why?—Ask the leaves
The reason why they vibrate in the breeze,
Or ask the trees when swaying in the storm;
Ask of the spray-drop leaping from the rill,
Or up and down amid the waves at sea;
Ask of the circling smoke, tornado's cloud,
The sun and moon revolving round the
world,
But when the throb of music beats the air
And sets the currents of the breast in motion,
Sweeping the bounding rills to rhythmic waves
That dash like breakers through the heart and
pulse,
Ask not why every vein begins to glow,
Each nerve to tremble, all the frame to heave,
And to and fro to march, to leap, to dance,—
Enough—if natural!—When checking nature,

You lay your human hands upon the work
Heaven meant for what it is; you are profane.
  (*he makes motions of dancing.*)

FIRST MAIDEN (*pointing toward* MONASKA *and
  speaking to* SECOND MAIDEN).

There comes another.

SECOND M.   Where?

FIRST M.   There with Waloon.

THIRD M.   Oh, see!

FIRST M.   We go to him.

SECOND M.   No, no; not yet.
  Look there at that one.
(*pointing toward* WAPELLA, *who is near the Right
            Rear Entrance.*)

THIRD M.   Which one?

SECOND M.   That one there.
(*All three* MAIDS *move toward the Right Rear
            Entrance.*)]

WALOON (*trying to draw* MONASKA *toward the
  Right Front Entrance*).

Monaska, do come this way—do—I fear——

MONASKA.   You must not fear for me.

WALOON.   You do not know——

MONASKA (*taking her hand*).

  You tremble.

WALOON.   Oh, love, do have faith in
  me!

MONASKA.   And have I none? You tremble
  like a bird

That once I caught. Poor thing, I could not
    harm it,
So beautiful, so soft, with chirp so sweet!

WALOON. But if you look that way, you do not
    love me.

MONASKA. And am I everything to you that
    you
Should fancy you are everything to me?

WALOON. And am I not then?

MONASKA.   What a fire divine
  Must blaze within a woman's heart, who
    deems
That her one form all glowing where it kindles,
Must cinder all things else!

WALOON.   Do men love less?

MONASKA. Nay, but have eyes for things they
    do not love.
And I, you know, am young, have seen not
    much, (*looking toward the* MAIDENS
    again.)
And nothing of these rites you know so well.

WALOON. That whets my fear. I know them
    all too well.

MONASKA. My nerves are sensitive to form
    and hue.
A little flitting of the two but serves
To irritate and make me itch for more.
But let me once be free to bound and whirl
And scratch my gaze upon them in the dance,

What cures me will not scar below the surface.
Yes; I have better avenues through which
These outer visions reach the heart.   Besides,
That now is wholly filled.   No room is left
For more than one.   Believe me, I speak
      truth.

WALOON.   I know—I do not doubt you, but——
MONASKA (*laughing*).   You do.
   Come, come, confess now.   You are jealous of
      me.
WALOON.   Not so!   No, you mistake me.
      Would the gods
   Would tell you why, or let me tell you why!
MONASKA.   You dare not tell me?
WALOON.   Nay, I—Come.
MONASKA.   I will.
(*then, as* WALOON *moves toward the Right Front
               Entrance*)
   You mean some untold penalty awaits
   The one who fails to win the maidens' favor?
(*turns to follow* WALOON, *just as* HAIJO *reaches
         him, coming from the rear.*)
HAIJO (*to* MONASKA).
   What, man, you fear not you are losing time?
MONASKA (*to* HAIJO).
   When gaining something better?
HAIJO.   What is better?
MONASKA.   The worth of time is measured
      like a gem's

Not by its bulk but by its brilliancy.

HAIJO. Just what I told Waloon you thought.
(*to* WALOON *who is listening.*) Not so?
(*to* MONASKA.)

But you—you heard the royal proclamation?

MONASKA. I did.

HAIJO.   And you would waive the
highest honor?

MONASKA. For something else, could I not
have them both.

HAIJO. And wherefore not have both?—
(*to* WALOON.) You know, Waloon,
He can.

MONASKA (*to* WALOON).   I can, Waloon?

WALOON.   Have I not said?—
Will you believe?——

HAIJO   This maiden, or the king?—

MONASKA. This maiden.

HAIJO.   Treason!

MONASKA.   And the king.

HAIJO.   Prove that
By joining in the dance.—Come,—both together.

WALOON. Not I!

MONASKA (*aside to* WALOON).

                    Waloon, you need not fear for me,
For if I venture in the dance at all,
I dance to win.

WALOON (*anxiously*).   No, no; I meant——

(Maidens *gather around* Monaska *and* Waloon.)

First Maiden (*to* Monaska.)   Come, come.
  And dance with us if not with her.

Second M.   Come on.

Third M.   Yes, come.

First M.   You must.

Third M.   No backing out!

Second M. (*taking his hand*).   With me.
      (*They drag him with them into the dance.*)

Waloon (*to* Haijo, *as she watches* Monaska.)
  Why did he not believe me?   He is lost!
      (*All the* Maidens *and* Captives *dance.*)
          *Exit—Right—*Waloon.

King.   Now, silence!   Let the maids declare
    their choice,
  Their chief choice, gathering round his figure
      whom
  The god of love that looks through love-lit
      eyes,
  The spirit that inspires love-throbbing
      hearts,
  Finds dowered with dignity and manly grace
  And beauty, and all heart-inspiring charms
  That fitly can incarnate love's ideal.
          Music.
      (*The Captives stand in a line at the Right of
        the stage;* Monaska *not far from its
        front.   The* Maidens *march along
        the line of the* Captives, *and drop*

*flowers or wreaths in front of Mon-
aska. Some drop them in front of
others, but, seeing that Monaska will
surely be chosen, they take the flowers
from others and cast them before him,
and gather around him.*)

King (*descending from his seat on the pyramid
and taking Monaska by the hand, pointing
with his free hand toward the seat he has
just left, at the same time bowing to Monaska*).

Chosen of love, now bow we to your worth.

We yield to you, and lead you to your place.

(*All except the King prostrate themselves before
Monaska.*)

Monaska. You do me too much honor.

(*The King bows, and shakes his head,
while he begins to lead Monaska
toward the seat at the base of the
pyramid. Just as they reach it,
Enter—at the Right Front—throwing up her hands
in grief, Waloon.*)

Waloon. Chosen? Lost!

The People chant:

Where look the gods?
Where look the gods?
In glances from the sky
Down through the lightning's death-dealt blaze,
Or thrilling through the starry rays?—

Oh, yes, the gods are all on high;
But in the looks that on us gaze
From out the love-lit human eye,
The gods are always nigh.

CURTAIN.

ACT THIRD.

SCENE:—*Same as in Act Second. The Gate back-*
ing at the Right Center is open. Guards beside it.
*Enter—Left—*KOOTHA *and his* COMPANION.

KOOTHA (*to his* COMPANION).

[If what the priesthood teach us be the truth,
Ay, if the gods do everything, themselves,
Why should they smut our mortal souls to
  stoke
The fuel of their smoking fires on earth?
If they see everything, what need that we
Play spy here to Monaska and Waloon?—
Trail like a reptile's tail to prove them brutes,
Where'er the love goes, which but proves them
  human?
The power that makes a man who would stand
  straight
Prostrate and prostitute his nobler nature,
Sneak, dodge, crawl, shadow spirits bright as
  theirs
May come from gods, but, if so, they have lent
This part of their dominion to a devil.
Perhaps they have—who knows?—The priest-
  hood say,

When earth is dark, by contrast heaven is
    bright—
How could a mortal ever guess the greed
Of gods for being glorified, unless
What made mankind had damned the most of
    them
To show how good it could be saving others?—
How good!—Ah, strange how much would not
    be thought
Were it not taught! A plague on their
    presumption
Who first began to teach, and teach religion!
As if, forsooth, the heaven would be all dark
Without our great lights of the temple here
To thrust their smoking torches toward it!—
    bah!—
Well, well, who knows?—One thing, at least,
    I know:
They sin who shove a man and maid together;
And make it sin for them to touch each other.]
Enter—through the Gate at the Right Center—
    MAIDENS, *talking loudly.*

Hello! these belles of ours proclaim their
    presence
As ever by their tongues. Oh, for a pipe
To pitch them to my tune; ay, ay, a pipe
To blow them up with, make them flip, flap,
    flop
And whir for me, and stir the dust for me,

And make them all my puppets. I will
    try it.
Waloon might dodge away from them alive;
But from Monaska, be there none to check
The love she bears him, she will have no
    chance.

FIRST MAIDEN. Oh, he is lovely!

SECOND M.   An ideal god!

FIRST M. His form so graceful!

SECOND M.   Yes, and so well built!

THIRD M. His touch so gentle!

FIRST M.   Such a godlike flush
On all his flesh!

THIRD M.   And flowering in his cheeks!

[FIRST M. He seems a spirit lured to gates of
    dawn
Who, venturing near the clouds when all
    aflame,
Has been snatched up within their ardent arms
And borne to earth with all their glow about
    him.

SECOND M. And from his lips that have not
    lost the tint
Of daybreak yet, there breathe forth sweeter
    sighs
Than morning air brings when it drinks the
    dew.

FIRST M. Ay, ay, than morning air brings when
    it rings

With all the choruses of all the birds.

THIRD M.   That warmth of welcome in his eyes
        too!

FIRST   M.   Yes,
    And fire behind them, fire that when one
        feels
    The innermost recesses of the soul
    Begin to——

KOOTHA (*interrupting her*).
            Burn.—Confess they burn.

FIRST M. (*to* KOOTHA).
                        Who spoke
    To you, uncouth one?   Off!
            (*continuing to other* MAIDENS.)
                        They rout the gloom
    Within the heart sure as the morning sun
    That spreads new glory o'er the darkened
        world,
    The while its fire-sped lances tilt the shades
    That fly afar, and leave our lives with
        heaven.]

KOOTHA.   My, my! how mighty fine my fancies
        are!

SECOND M.   A woman's fancy may be near the
        truth.

KOOTHA.   As near as fire to water.   Yonder
        pool
    Is truth.   The sunbeam it reflects is fancy.
    One water is, one fire.   But, as you say,

The flaming of his eye has turned the sap
Once oozing from your useless lips to——
(*hesitating.*)

SECOND M. What?

KOOTHA. Why, flames turn sap to soft and
sticky sirup.

[Tell now which sweet lips were they that the
god's
Were stuck to last?

FIRST M. You heartless man! You know
We love the god.

KOOTHA. Oh, yes!—the god in man—
The god it takes a woman's eye to see.

SECOND M. And what, pray, is it that men
worship?

KOOTHA. Oh,
The thing that most men worship is them-
selves.
Or, look they upward, then it is the god
Most like themselves. You know religion's
aim
Is bringing gods and men together; so
To many men that creed seems best, which
best
Makes out how mean and small a god can be.

SECOND M. (*saucily*).

Does that mean anything?

KOOTHA. You think not?

SECOND M. No.

KOOTHA.   Not so? not so?—Come back then to
　　　　your range—]
　　Which one of you was it, the god kissed last?
FIRST M.   Is knowing that your business?
THIRD M.　　　　　　　　　　　　Just so!
KOOTHA.   Oh yes,—the business of all men.
FIRST M.　　　　　　　　　　　　　　Why?
KOOTHA.   Have you observed which maid it is
　　　　that proves
　　The most attractive to the most men?
SECOND M.　　　　　　　　　　　　　No.
THIRD M.   Tell which?
FIRST M.　　　　　　Yes, tell us.
KOOTHA.　　　　　　　Why, of course, the one
　　The most attractive to the most of them.
　　Ha, ha!
　　　　　(*continuing, as they turn away in anger.*)
　　　　　　　You see that most men are such apes
　　They never know which girl to go for next,
　　Until they see where some one else has gone.
SECOND M. (*sarcastically*).
　　Aha! you think that we wish you, then?
KOOTHA.　　　　　　　　　　　　　Yes,—
　　Away from here.   But, frankly now, my mind
　　Had stumbled on the impression that a maid
　　Looks on her lovers as a Toltec brave
　　On scalps: she likes to see them hanging on
　　Her neck—at least in presence of such mates
　　As make no conquests.

SECOND M. (*sarcastically*).

          Ah? and who are they?

KOOTHA. The town will find them out, some
      day, I guess.

THIRD M. Not our fault, then?

KOOTHA.   Humph, what are women for?
  And what are you about the temple for?

THIRD M. Go ask Waloon.

SECOND M.   Yes, yes, go ask Waloon.

KOOTHA. Ah, then there is a favored one I see.

SECOND M. Did I say that?

KOOTHA.   You had no need. You know
  A friend can heed the meaning of our thought
  Unhelp'd by word or gesture.

FIRST M.   You a friend?—
  Drive off Waloon then.

KOOTHA.   I?—a woman-driver?—
  But were she more the dove that he esteems
      her,
  And you still less old hens than you appear,
  I think you might find bills to settle with
      her,
  And raise a cackle that would make her fly.
        (*to his* COMPANION)
  Ugh! I have roughed their feathers now
      enough.
  Poor, poor Waloon!—and yet her only safety.
      *Enter—Left—*WALOON.
  Ah, there she is herself.

First M. (*noticing* Waloon).

                              Oh, here comes one
That loves the god.   How nice to love a god!
Second M.   But not so nice to pose as loving
        one,
And only love a man.
First M.   You wait awhile.
When they have spilt the spirit in that
        vessel,—
Ay, when the blood is drained, it may not then
Appear to her so rare and rose-like.
Second M. (*to* Waloon, *sarcastically*).   Ah,
You seem surprised?
Waloon.   I am.
Third M.   And grieved?
Waloon.   And more.
All the Maidens.   Ha, ha, ha, ha!
Waloon.   I am surprised and grieved,
And more than this—to think that you are
        women.
Kootha (*to his* Companion).
Aha!   Had not found out that fact before?—
She knows it now, for they know how to prove
        it (*to the* Maidens).
Come, come, be not so cruel.   Be more
        gentle.
First M.   Are cruel, are we?   If she like it
        not,
She need not strike at our likes.   Did she deem

It kind to push between us and the god
The wide-spread drapery of her greedy arms
As if, forsooth, our hope were killed, and she
A vulture feasting with foul wings aflap?

SECOND M.   Nay, more, too, make us laughed
    at, slighted, scorned?

WALOON.   I did not mean it so.   This friend
    of mine
Was mine before you chose him for the god.

FIRST M.   Was yours?—and now you mean to
    keep him yours?—
And so your eyes are always dodging his
To catch their glances?   Did you turn your
    back,
You fear he might forget you?

ALL THE MAIDENS.   Ha, ha, ha!

        *Enter—Left—*HAIJO.

*Exeunt—Right—*KOOTHA *and his* COMPANION
    as soon as they catch sight of HAIJO.

HAIJO (*to the* MAIDENS).
    Why, what can be the matter here?

FIRST M.   Waloon.

SECOND M.   Waloon.

THIRD M.   Waloon.

FIRST M.   She says the god is hers.

HAIJO.   Of course, but not hers only!

FIRST M.   Yes, hers only.

HAIJO.   Oh, you mistook her!

THIRD M.   No.

SECOND M.   Is what she meant.
FIRST M.   She called him "mine."
HAIJO.   Meant hers?
FIRST M.   Yes, hers.
SECOND M.   Hers.
THIRD M.   Hers.
HAIJO (*to* WALOON).
   Can this be true?
WALOON.   I said my friend was mine
Before they chose him.
HAIJO.   Ah, but they did choose him;
   And now, according to the temple's law——
WALOON (*half weeping*).
   You mean he is not mine, I know.
HAIJO.   My child,
   I hoped your training——
WALOON.   Do not think that men
Can ever change our nature by their training.
Nay, clip, abuse, deform it as you may,
The weakest bush will bear its own flower still,
And every heart the love life made it for.
[HAIJO. Ah, so! You think!—Who taught
      you, pray, to think?
WALOON.   My mind, sire, and the gods from
      whom it came.
HAIJO.   Be careful, child; nor force us to use
      force.
WALOON.   Ah, sire, sire, when you come to deal
      with thought,

The only influence force can have upon it
Is to suppress, but leave it still possessed.
If error be in mind, it seems far better
To let it out, and so be rid of it.

HAIJO. No need that we discuss that now!
You know
The temple's law, that when one will would
stand
Against the general good, that will must yield.

WALOON. I was not speaking of my will, but
heart.

HAIJO. Well, call it heart then. You have
thrust your love
Between these maidens and the god. They
claim
The joy and profit of his intercourse.

WALOON. They might have shared these with
me. Never yet,
Have I been left alone with him.

HAIJO.   And who
Could claim exclusive rights when with the
gods,
Whose eyes view all, whose arms embrace the
world.
And if incarnate for a time in man,
How base in us to tempt their high, pure life
Toward our low, selfish, human love for *one!*

WALOON. Is that why we were watched?

HAIJO.   Did you not need

A hint that others too had claims upon him?
What profit is it though a god may dwell
In human form, if souls, whom else the god
Would lure to love and draw to sympathy
With heavenly thought and deed and light and
  life,
Be kept away from him by one like you?
FIRST M. Just what we ask.
HAIJO.   What all the wise would ask.]
SECOND M. She keeps us from him.
HAIJO.   If she do this more
The law will interfere, and part them wholly.

   *Enter—through the gate backing at the
   Right Center—a line of* PRIESTS,
   PRIESTESSES, *etc., singing before a
   chariot in which* MONASKA *is drawn
   upon the stage. His head is crowned
   with flowers, and he thumbs a lyre-
   like musical instrument. All sing
   the following:*

All hail the god! All hail and laud
 The god we now enthrone,
Whose realms extend, all bright and broad
Beyond the seas and stars and aught
That ears have heard, or eyes have sought,
 Or hands could ever own.
All hail the god! All hail the god!
 Upon the man we call;
But bright behind the gaze we greet,
There gleams the glory yet to meet

Our souls beholding past the gloom
Of toil and trouble, tear and tomb,
   The god beyond it all.

All hail the god!   All hail and laud
   The god we bow before,
Whose altar fires, while all are awed,
Are lit in souls that flash through eyes
That light for heaven itself supplies,
   Nor could one wish for more.
All hail the god!   All hail the god!
   Upon the man we call;
But bright behind the gaze we greet,
There gleams the glory yet to meet
Our souls beholding past the gloom
Of toil and trouble, tear and tomb,
   The god beyond it all.

FIRST M.   (*to* MONASKA, *as he descends from
      the chariot, while all bow to him*).
   All hail the god!
SECOND M.   All hail!
THIRD M.   All hail!
FIRST M. (*noticing that he pays no attention to
      the salutation of the* MAIDENS, *although
      they are making every effort to attract his
      attention*).   All   hail!
MONASKA (*to the Maidens*).
   I like not hail-storms but the gentler sunshine.
      [(*pushing through them toward* WALOON.)
   Yet sometimes through the arch-bow of the
      storm

Life enters on its heritage of hope.]

(*takes* WALOON *by the hand, then, as she does not speak.*)

You do not speak to me.—Why this?—Why this?

WALOON (*gesturing toward the other* MAIDENS).
They chose you.   They have claims upon you too.

MONASKA.   Claims to my gratitude—I yield them these.

Claims to my love?—Ah, no.

HAIJO.   And you will not Accede then to their claims?

MONASKA.   Their sex's claims
Are well acknowledged, as I think, by him
Who plights his whole soul's faith to one of them.

[HAIJO (*gesturing toward the other* MAIDENS).
Nay; plight your faith to all of them.

MONASKA.   To all?—]
Why, I would not insult these women so
As to suggest that love for one alone
Did not fill my whole heart to overflowing.

You seek here room for more?—Then you mistake.

(*addressing the* MAIDENS, *who seem offended at his language.*)

And can it be that I had not revealed
The truth?   Forgive me.   I had meant to do it.

The time has come to end your doubt?—I will.
Here stands the holy father.   Here stand we.
(*looking toward* Haijo *and taking* Waloon's
    hand, then leading her toward the Right.)
Yes, it is time our vows were made in public.
What? what?—you hesitate?—you do?—you
    do?——

    *Exeunt—Right—*Monaska *and* Waloon.

First M. (*to* Haijo).
    And would we better follow?

Haijo.   Wherefore not?
The mood is on her now to thrust him off,
And if she do but push him far enough,
What should he do but tumble then toward
    you.

Enter—through the gate at the Right Center—the
    King *and* Attendants.
        *Exeunt—Right—*Maidens.

King (*to* Haijo).
    How fares it with the god?

Haijo.   His heavenly mood
Is yet upon him.

King.   He does not suspect?

Haijo.   Not he!—Why, he was just now order-
    ing me
To seal his vows, and wed him to Waloon.

King.   He does not deem it strange we honor
    him?

Haijo.   Each to his own conception is a god.

Proclaim him this, you but concede a claim
Long felt within.   He knew it all before.
[KING.   The egotist!
HAIJO.   Yes, but we all are that.
The spirit, we are told, is made of air.
Like air it is in this,—will force its way
And feel full right to enter and possess
Whatever space a crack or crevice opens.]
KING.   How to himself, does he explain the
      way
That all the maidens wait upon his wishes?
HAIJO.   He thinks they deem him lord of all
      creation.
And so they do, forsooth.   Their bearing
      proves it.
KING.   He deems Waloon?——
HAIJO.   His only, through and through.
KING.   She never can be more completely his?
HAIJO.   Impossible.
KING.   The time to pluck a flower
Is just when in its bloom.
HAIJO.   I think so, sire.
The hour has come to tell him of his fate.
A member of our nearer tribes would know it.
He knows it not.   Waloon now shuns him.
      Look (*pointing to the Right.*)
And he must find excuse for this, or else
May turn away from her, and seek another.
If so, he may not always keep her love.

Besides, Monaska ought to know the truth;—
Is wasting time with her.

KING.   Has naught to do
With others?

HAIJO.   No; and therefore should be told
Our laws must part him from her.

KING (*looking and pointing to the Right*).

                                        You are right.
I see him coming this way now.

HAIJO.   With some
Request, I warrant.

KING.   Wise men do not greet
A suppliant with too open hand and heart.
Did gentleness not midwife his desires,
His cries would sooner die for lack of nursing.
And so I think they best refuse requests
Who best refuse to hear them.   Let us go.
            *Exeunt—Left—*KING *and* HAIJO.
*Enter—Right—*MONASKA *followed stealthily by*
      WALOON.   (*He notices the* KING *and* HAIJO).

MONASKA (*to* WALOON).   A generous mind is
            never loath to face
The object of its benefaction.   No;
Had all that they have done been kindly done,
They would not thus have turned their backs
            upon us.
That Haijo is no man to harbor trust.
[He never holds a steady eye to greet
The look that rests on him.   It seems as if

He feared that one might spy within his brain
Some secret that a dodging glance could
    shield.
I fear the secret may concern yourself.
For ever when I lead you where I hope
No mortal will be present to profane
Vows fit for only gods to hear, some form,
With eyes omniscient as a very devil's
Incarnate in an earthly messenger,
Outspawns its fouling shadows on the light
Like night-shades to the lost who pray for
    day.
Just now, when here I came, he too was here.
We left him then, and you were deaf to me.
What drug to hearing poured he in your ear
To deaden nerves hereto so sensitive
To slightest whispers of my thrilling love
That hands, voice, lips and eyelids, all your
    frame
Went trembling like a willow in a wind?
It cannot be the cause is in yourself?—
Or is it?—May you merely pity me,
Whose life you saved, as thousands might be
    saved;
And, moved by pity still to note my state,
Thus hinder me from fully asking what,
If rightly answered, would but seal my
    doom?—
No, I have asked you fully—ay, and you—

Those eyes—ah, naught but light divine as
   love's
Could so illumine, so transfigure them!——
*Exit—Right—*WALOON, *as if in fear of* HAIJO
whom she has apparently seen approaching.

Enter—Left—Haijo.

HAIJO. Alone, Monaska?
MONASKA.   Yes.
HAIJO.   Alone?   Alone?—
   With all those maidens praying for your
      presence?
MONASKA. I dodged behind a tree, then, when
      they left,
   Came here.
HAIJO.   A valiant warrior!
MONASKA.   Yes—with men.
HAIJO. With women?
MONASKA.   He with her I think is valiant
   Who waives what would be force.
HAIJO.   And runs away?
MONASKA. Why, yes, if elsewise he might be
      ungentle.
HAIJO. Your waste of time does not yet weigh
      upon you?
[MONASKA. My what?
HAIJO.   You chose a life not long, but
      brilliant.
MONASKA. If so——
HAIJO.   Is brilliant now, but will be brief.

MONASKA. Be brief?——

HAIJO.   Enough, I hope, to make you ply
   Your opportunities.

MONASKA.   And what are they?]

HAIJO.   You craved for love.

MONASKA.   Ay, and you promised it.

HAIJO.   You have it.

MONASKA.   Have it?—No, I have it not.

HAIJO.   Your heart must be a very glutton then.
   With all these maids——

MONASKA.   And what are they—to love?—

HAIJO.   They chose you, yet you turn your
              back upon them.

MONASKA.   But you know why: I turn my
              back on lust
   That I may turn my face to love.

HAIJO.   Poor fool,
   But one life can you live, and yet you lose it!

MONASKA.   But one love can I keep, and I shall
              keep it.

HAIJO.   Too bad you had not thought of that
              before.

MONASKA.   Before?

HAIJO.   Ay, ay, before the maidens chose you.

MONASKA.   Chose me, and not I them.

HAIJO.   You courted them.

MONASKA.   Oh, no.

HAIJO.   You sighed, you smiled, you sued, you
              wooed.

MONASKA. You overstate——
HAIJO. What made you leave Waloon?
MONASKA. I leave her?
HAIJO. You.—When, just before the dance,
  She talked with you aside, and begged you not.
  Were you so wholly satisfied with her,
  That was the time to show it.
MONASKA. But—the king—
  His proclamation, and the highest honor——
HAIJO. You have it now. You gained it leav-
      ing her.
MONASKA. I left her for a moment only.
HAIJO. So!
  Great fires are kindled in a moment only.
  Where hearts are tinder, and a glance a spark,
  [Why, there——
MONASKA. Aha, those dusky robes of priests
  Astride the broken beam of every ray
  That bridged my prison's gloom have not
      been ghosts
  To haunt my love alone? They have been
      fiends
  To turn it to a curse.
HAIJO. Blame your own choice.]
MONASKA. But how could I have known the
      choice meant this?
HAIJO. Who knows the fruitage of the seed he
      plants?—
  Like seed, like fruit.
  6

MONASKA.   The seed was very small.

HAIJO.   The fruitage large?—Yet both were
      one in kind.

MONASKA.   Nay, tho' my transient look went
        wrong, my feet
   Have followed righteousness.   Ah, sire, you
        know
   Some think the only harvests heaven can find
   Unfold from germs dropped near enough to hell
   To fear its heat and grow away from it.—
   Why was it wrong to seek the highest honor?
   How could one know it could not come with
        her?

HAIJO.   You think that one small man's experi-
        ence
   Embraces in its clasp the whole broad earth?—
   Nay, it is finite.   Every path has limits.
   Climb up to mountain-tops, you turn away
   From flower and verdure, spring and warmth,
        to dwell
   With rock and weariness and thirst and chill.

MONASKA.   Oh, this is preaching!   And you
        promised me
   A brilliant life——

HAIJO.   Life brilliant far beyond
   Your highest hope.

MONASKA.   Nay, nay, you promised love.

HAIJO.   The choicest maidens of the realm are
        yours.

MONASKA.   But not Waloon!

HAIJO.   Is his experience then
So strangely brilliant who is loved, forsooth,
By one maid only?

MONASKA.   It may not be brilliant,
But like a star in heaven it fills with light
One point—that where the gods have placed it.

HAIJO.   You—
May be a sun round which mere stars revolve.
Your dignity has larger, broader range
Than gains fit homage from the love of one;—
Which, if you have not learned, you should be
          taught.

MONASKA.   And yield Waloon?

HAIJO.   Waloon—till you can yield
Your love to others.

MONASKA.   What?   When I have let
Their lustful kisses drain the dew of youth,
Give her the parched and lifeless remnant?—
          No.
Go take that wolf-skin from the snarling
          hounds
When all the blood has been sucked out of it,
And flesh gnawed off, and fling it, cold and
          limp,
Out to another wolf panting for a mate;
But ask me not to fling love's foul cold carcass
Out to her arms to whom I owe my life.—
Oh, cursèd fate!

*Exit—Left—*HAIJO *shrugging his shoulders.*
*Enter—Right—*WAPELLA *with a* WOMAN.

                         Wapella, you here? Oh
  Wapella, you were right!—And who is this?
     (*gazing at the* WOMAN.)

WAPELLA. My wife.

MONASKA. Your wife?—Beware—you cannot
    keep her.

WAPELLA. Oh, no one cares what I do here!
    Not I,
  Not I, but you have won the highest honor.

MONASKA. Yes—won the highest honor. I,
    forsooth,
  I have, Wapella. Ah, why are the scales
  That measure what our world is worth so poised
  Betwixt the outward and the inward life
  That what lifts up the one must lower the
    other?
  Why, when we reach the highest earthly place
  Must this be balanced by the spirit's fall?

Enter—Right—other MAIDENS *and* WALOON,
who is back of them.

(MONASKA *continues—pointing to* WALOON.)
  Wapella, there is heaven; and all the world,
  A world that will the more pollute my soul,
  The more I try to cross it, lies between
  Myself and it, and keeps me here in hell.

CURTAIN.

ACT FOURTH.

Scene First:—*Interior of a hut or tent hung with curtains, evidently used as a prison for* Monaska. *Entrance at the Left. The Curtain rising discloses* Monaska *dressed in gorgeous apparel. He has on a garlanded head-dress and in his hand a large lyre-like musical instrument.* Kootha, *who apparently has just finished robing him, stands regarding him.*

[Kootha.   You seem a rising sun.   Each time the crowd
  Renew their gaze on you, your splendor grows.

Monaska.   And when, at last, they tone me to a pitch
  That no new height of splendor can transcend,
  To get more halo, will they burn me up?

Kootha.   Oh, no, not that!

Monaska.   How long now will it be
  Before this play will climax?]

Kootha (*looking toward the Left*).

                    Some one comes.

          *Enter—Left—*Haijo.

Haijo (*to* Monaska).
  Good day.

(Haijo *motions to* Kootha *to retire.*)
*Exit—Left—*Kootha.

Monaska.   I have my doubts if it be good.
  Each time you come to me and call it so,
  Your coming makes me more your prisoner.

Haijo. Of course, if you will yield not to our
      ways——

Monaska. If I gulp not the feast you gorge me
    on,
  And bury all my soul beneath the spoils
  Of foul and glutton appetite—why then
  I will not prove the bloated beast you wish.

Haijo. We hope that you will prove a god.

Monaska.   What forms
  Your test of godhood?

Haijo.   What is it shall bring
  The spirit of the fair-god back to earth,
  When once again his white-winged vessels
      leave
  Their land of ease, and brave the sea for us?

Monaska. I know not—What?

Haijo.   Self-sacrifice.

Monaska.   Yes, yes,
  I see—perhaps I wronged you. You may
      light
  These fires of fierce temptation round me but
  To test my metal.—Have I triumphed then?

Haijo. Triumphed? O'er what?—I spoke of
      sacrifice.

MONASKA.   And I have sacrificed low love for
　　　higher.

HAIJO.   You call that sacrifice?

MONASKA.　　　　　　　　What?   Is it not?—
　To give up what is earthly for the heavenly?—
　Turn from the serpent coiled within the loins
　To follow in the flight of that fair dove
　Whose wings are fluttering within the heart?

HAIJO.   To turn from those you loathe to those
　　　you like?—
　I did not speak of that.

MONASKA.　　　　　　　Ah, not of that?
　Of what?

HAIJO.　　　Self-sacrifice.

MONASKA.　　　　　　That sacrifice
　Is due to self.

HAIJO.　　　　　　　And if it be?

MONASKA.　　　　　　　　Why, sire,
　You think to force my fate; and if you do,
　There may be sacrifice, but not by self.

HAIJO.   That does not matter.

MONASKA.　　　　　　Does not?—in a spirit—
　You would make godlike?

HAIJO.　　　　　Should it?   Why?

MONASKA.　　　　　　　　Because,
　Each time you try to mould a spirit's life
　With fingers grappling from the fist of force,
　You clutch but at the air, at what is far
　Too fine for force to handle.

[Haijo.   May be, too,
  That what you speak of, is too fine for some
  To care to handle.
Monaska.   Care not for the spirit?—
  What are your gods?
Haijo.   The sovereigns of our temple.
Monaska. The outward temple only, not the
        inward?
Haijo. You deem the sovereigns of the two
        may differ?
Monaska. I do. I know of priests who judge
        of gods
  Like altars by their gilding, to whose greed
  One god in hand is worth a score in heaven.
  For every time they kneel to touch their
        puppet,
  It shakes to sprinkle gold-dust on them.
Haijo.   Hold!
  Where were you reared to such impiety?
Monaska. Where sun, moon, stars rained
        from the blue above
  And flowers were fountained through the
        green below,
  Where lights we knew not what, but they were
        heaven's,
  Looked down on eyes that looked up from the
        earth,
  And men, whatever might impel their souls,
  Were guided onward by a goal to mate it.

HAIJO. Ay, and by priests and prophets.—
    Tell the truth.
MONASKA. Yes, there were those who dreamed,
    and those who deemed
  In darkness they saw forms that had been
    earth's,
  And heard their words, and they believed it
    true
  That there was life behind the sights we see.
  But those who stood the highest of the high,
  And knew our poet-king, were taught to look
  Upon a God beyond the reach of men.
HAIJO. Beyond their reach, what were he
    worth! Young man,
  You have your priests, your temples, ay, we
    know it,
  And have but one religion.
MONASKA.   And we speak
  One language too, but differ in the accent.
  The language gives the passwords of the race,
  The accent keys the culture of the home,
  And some were welcome at the royal home.
HAIJO. And there were taught religion?
MONASKA.   There we heard
  The poems of our prince; and prized them not
  Because his tongue controlled us, but his truth.
HAIJO (*contemptuously*).
  Religion of a poet!—upside down
  And inside out, to fit each freak of fancy!

MONASKA. Religion of a man, sire. You would
   say
   One cannot see the spirit save through
   forms.
   Yet who can see through forms, except as
   these
   Obscure the spirit? Be it so, why, then
   Our king was right to bid us use our eyes,
   Yet not believe that what we saw was all.
   And what we cannot see, yet feel exists,
   We cannot think of, save as we imagine.
   And so the phase that best reports the spirit
   Is that of poetry,—so said our king.

HAIJO (*sarcastically*).
   His was a vague religion!

MONASKA.   Not so vague
   As that religion is whose forms befriend
   A life to which all laws within the soul
   Are foes. Our king with his one queen would
      never
   Have sanctioned, much less led himself, a life
   Like that. Oh, something surely must be
      wrong
   When that which rules without rules not
      within.]

HAIJO. And you will not be ruled——

MONASKA.   By what you urge?—
   I cannot.

HAIJO.   Yet they chose you as their god.

Monaska. Then it befits me like a god to live.
  Oh, sire! those are most worth our help on earth
  Whose eyes look up, and he who stands above
    them,
  Would he fulfill their soul's ideal, must show
  A life worth while their looking up to see.
Haijo. Well, then, prepare to die.
Monaska.   To die?
Haijo.   To-day.
Monaska. Ye gods! I had not thought of
    that—so soon?
  So soon?—why, you had promised I should
    have
  My fill of love!
        (Haijo *stands sneering at him.*)
                  What fool is more a fool—
  What foe is falser—than one false to self?—
  And false, forsooth, because of flattery—
  Nor of the soul— but of this outward frame,
  Frame destined for a shattered wreck to-day.
  No, no!—not that—it cannot be! No, no;
  It is against all nature I should die.
  What have I lived for, if I am to die?
*Exit—Left—*Haijo, *beckoning, as he goes out
    to some one beyond the entrance.*
        *Enter—Left—*Kootha.
(Monaska *continues to* Kootha.)
  You come to deck me for my death? Faint
    heart!

(putting his hand upon his heart.)

And it had so much life!   I thought its thrills
The rilling of a fount whose brook should flow
Out to a sea of life, as wide as earth,
And upward to a golden clouded heaven.
Why, all my moods—they banner spring-
    time yet,
The buds but just unfolding, scarce a flutter
To balm the breeze with their sweet promises!
Must all be now cut off?—uprooted?—what?
The prickliest cactus clutches, at the last,
The flower toward which it grows; and shall
    these nerves,
All tender to the touch of life, so live
Themselves, so hungry to be fed, yet void
Of all with which hope pledged them to be
    filled—
Shall they be cheated out of this they craved?
Are all the visions of the fancy frauds
That fool our faith, anticipating joy
That never comes?   Is that mysterious power
That prompts our lives to be, and pushes on
Toward what it promised them, so vilely weak
That, like a knave who fears to be outwitted,
It needs must lash and lure us with a lie?—
Yet now—O heaven!   I will not so believe it.
I cannot; no, I cannot!——

KOOTHA.   What is this
  You will not do, and cannot?

MONASKA.   You saw that priest
  That just now left me?
KOOTHA.   Haijo?—Yes, I saw him.
MONASKA.   He says I am to die.
KOOTHA.   Most people die.
MONASKA.   He says, to-day.
KOOTHA.   Bad jobs are near their best
  When nearest ended.
MONASKA (*in surprise*).   You?—indifferent?
KOOTHA.   Same thing—am old.
MONASKA.   And so are hard?
[KOOTHA.   No, soft;
  Have learned to yield to what could not be
      blocked
  By my opposing it.   I know no rose
  That blooms but fades.
MONASKA.   Yet men——
KOOTHA.   Oh, yes, yes, men
  Are different, I know.   I know, for men
  Not only fade but worse—
MONASKA (*distressed*).   Why picture it?
KOOTHA (*intentionally harsh*).
  I own no pigment dull enough.—You know
  What human life is?—all a fight of soul
  To keep the body sweet,—a fight a bird
  Or beast knows nothing of.   A babe when
      born
  Is dipped in water; every following day
  Is dipped again.   If not, ere long will come

Disease and death, and, when a mortal dies,
His fellows all thank heaven that they have
    hands
To keep the fight up for him; for, if not,
Be he not burned or buried in a jiffy,
The air of heaven may find the spirit sweet,
But not the air of earth—pugh!—well he left
    it!

MONASKA.   You judge of men by their outsides.

KOOTHA.   Oh, no!
Some of our people here so love a man
They feast upon him. Who, pray, could
    know more
Of his insides? They say—their sense is
    trained—
That nothing has a taste as much like man
As has—what would you guess?—a hog.]

MONASKA.   You think
By drugging me with bitters, you can whet
An appetite for death?   Man, I am young.

KOOTHA.   Be thankful, then, that you have not
    grown old,
Worn out, diseased and full of pain.

MONASKA.   To think
That all this glowing blood within these
    veins
Should be spilled out, before my soul has
    drunk
The pleasure that is in them.

KOOTHA. When thus drunk,
The veins will be exhausted, have no stock
To treat the sense with longer; and the soul,
Intoxicated with the joys of earth,
Will be too heavy weighed to rise above them.
[MONASKA. But I——
KOOTHA. The worst of prisoners is a soul
Severed from its own realm by appetite
That lets naught pass that pays no toll to
greed.
Mere soulless brutes are better than are men
With souls that love but that which they can
lust for.]
MONASKA. Nay; not of low desires I spoke. I
meant
That I had never tasted love.
KOOTHA. Then you
Have never found it bitter.
MONASKA. Cynic!
KOOTHA. One
Must be what earth has made him.
MONASKA. Let me die
Before I learn a lesson sad as that!
KOOTHA. Wise prayer! Ay, it is mercy lets us
die
Before our souls decay—makes life more sweet
To those who have to live it with us here.
MONASKA. No, no! You do not understand—
Waloon——

KOOTHA. I understand the world. It frames
    her soul,
  And yours, and souls in this world fit their
    frames.
MONASKA. You deem my disposition too
    despotic
  To be appeased by service of her love?
  Yet not myself I think of, but of her.
KOOTHA. Think of her as she is then.
MONASKA.   How is that?
KOOTHA. A woman.
MONASKA.   What, pray, is a woman?
KOOTHA.   What
  Is made to woo a man.
MONASKA.   What man?
KOOTHA.   What man?——
  Why, any man.
MONASKA.   You villain, to say that!
KOOTHA. Humph! I have seen the world, and
    tell you truth.
  You deem the truth is villainy?—it is—
  The truth about this world.
MONASKA.   You think Waloon——
KOOTHA. Will mourn you?—Yes, a while; but
    woes like hers
  Are troubles which a kindly Providence
  Will always raise up some man who can cure.
MONASKA. Waloon—I must believe she knows
    this now—

Has made a solemn vow, if aught should come
To me, to serve as priestess in the temple.

KOOTHA. Oh yes; oh yes; with you to be her
  god.

MONASKA. Sad, lonely servitude!

KOOTHA.   Oh, no.

MONASKA.   With none
 To love?

KOOTHA. But there are others there.

MONASKA.   What for?

KOOTHA. To represent the god.

MONASKA.   You mean——

KOOTHA.   Oh, no!——
No, not this week, nor month, not that, not
  that.
But when the time comes—when this lonely
  soul
Desires content, and cannot leave the place
Without dishonoring herself and us——

MONASKA. Your evil mood is master of your
  thought——

KOOTHA. Say, makes my conscience conscious
  that no law
Can legislate the devil out of life.
You block a maiden of one lover——

MONASKA.   Knave!

KOOTHA. Nay, some would call him both a
  knave and brute—
Who failed to make her seem less lonely.

7

MONASKA (*angrily*). The king
would not permit this.

KOOTHA. No?

MONASKA. He would?

KOOTHA. You see——
The king—he chiefly represents the god.

MONASKA. What?—I have heard he loves
her.—Can this be
A plot of his to get her, will or nill?
You mean to say——

KOOTHA. I do not need to say it;
I think a man might, if he had some sense,
Put two and two together.—Times will come
When they two will be two together. Humph!
One ought to guess the rest.

MONASKA. And ought to swear
To level every wall that can shut out
The sun that brings to light man's every act—
The only weapon that can ward off ill
From souls allured to wrong through
secrecy.—
And you—what cause had you to hint this
to me?

KOOTHA. You thought Waloon would suffer——

MONASKA. So she will.
A thousand deaths were better for her.

KOOTHA. Whose?—
(*insinuatingly.*)
You mean the king's?

MONASKA (*suddenly changing his manner*).

Are you a native here?

KOOTHA. Not I.

MONASKA. Of what tribe then?

KOOTHA. Sh—sh—of yours.

MONASKA. Mine? mine?

KOOTHA. I said it—captured years ago.

[MONASKA. And here?

KOOTHA. Dishonored.

MONASKA. Why, you seem a priest?

KOOTHA. I am what priests would be, did they
believe

In being what they seem.

MONASKA. How so?

KOOTHA. A man

Yet not a man.]

MONASKA. You wish me?——

KOOTHA. Yes, of all

The captives taken by us, you alone,

When tempted, have not let them drain your
veins

Of healthful soul-strength, to inject therein,

In place of it, their foul sense-fevering virus.

MONASKA. And you would save me?

KOOTHA. Do you think a man

Can save a god?—It is the god saves men.

You see this point here?

(*pointing to a sharp protuberance on one
end of the musical instrument carried*

by Monaska. Monaska *examines
it.*) I have known a man
Who had no weapon——

Monaska.   Yes, I see the point!

Kootha. A time will come when you stand
        near the king.
If then you choose to give a benediction,
The people's eyes will all be looking downward;
And if there be confusion, and some gate
About the pyramid be open, then
Quick feet might pass it, and quick eyes might
        see
A friend of mine who might be sent to guide
        them.

Monaska. When is it that I stand so near the
        king?

Kootha. Just when he bids you give this lyre
        to him.

Monaska. And I will give it!—What comes
        just before?

Kootha. Our adoration.

Monaska.   What just after?

Kootha.   You
Begin to mount the pyramid;—meanwhile,
Keep dropping off you, one by one, your
        robes.
The king takes first this lyre, and Haijo next
Your head-dress; then, the other priests the
        rest.

MONASKA. Till everything be taken from me?

KOOTHA.   Yes.

MONASKA. Before the people?—an indignity!

KOOTHA (*sarcastically*).

    They will have done your spirit so much
        honor,

    It will be too much honored for this body.

MONASKA. You mean the body will be too
        dishonored

    For any spirit to remain in it.

KOOTHA. Oh, not dishonored ere the godship
        leaves.—

    Then what does flesh devoid of god deserve?

MONASKA. Damnation, if devoid of godship
        mean

    Devoid of spirit to defend the flesh.—

    And so they kill me?

KOOTHA.   In the end they do.

MONASKA. They mutilate me first?

KOOTHA.   That lasts not long.—

    You are to see Waloon now.

MONASKA.   See Waloon?

    How cruel both to her and me!

KOOTHA.   Oh, then,

    If you wish not——

MONASKA.   Nay, but I do—and you—

    You are to watch us, as has been your
        wont?

KOOTHA. Why—

MONASKA.   It will be my final word with her.—
　　Were you to be a god, what would you give
　　To speak that word and not be overheard?
KOOTHA.   Eternal benediction.
MONASKA.　　　　　　　　　　So will I.
　　Or god or spirit, here I pledge you it.
KOOTHA.   I shall not overhear.
MONASKA.　　　　　　　　One hope is left.
　　I have the lyre—
　　　　(*making motion of using lyre as a weapon.*)
　　　　　　　　　　　　can give it to the king.
　　[Though I may die, I need not leave Waloon
　　To her worst enemy,—that spider-soul
　　Bating his web of lust with my pure love,
　　And, for his foul embrace, entrapping thus
　　The vainly fluttering wings of her fair spirit
　　　　　　(*looking toward the Left.*)
　　But ah,—she comes.   I must not think of self,
　　But of this better self.   If any soul
　　Had ever need yet to believe in God
　　Through a belief in man, that soul is hers.]
　　　　　　*Exit—Left—*KOOTHA.
　　　　　　*Enter—Left—*WALOON.
WALOON.   Monaska.
MONASKA.　　　　　Here I am, Waloon.
WALOON.　　　　　　　　　　You know
　　The truth?
MONASKA.   I do.   Oh, love, but it is hard.
　　[You knew it all these days?

WALOON.   I feared—

MONASKA.   It was
   For this I deemed you jealous of me?

WALOON.   Yes.

MONASKA. A fool that I have been! But who
     could think
   Humanity could be so base?

WALOON.   Be what?

MONASKA. They are to kill me; and you had
     not heard?]
   Or do you think it right that I should die?——

WALOON (*in surprise and reproach*).
   Monaska!

MONASKA. Have I no friends left? not one?—
   Not even you?—you wish to kill me too?

WALOON. No, no, not that——

MONASKA.   I, all my life, Waloon,
   Have served a spirit larger than myself.
   These limbs but fit it on a single side,
   Their utmost only half what it would have.
   And now, athrill with spirit-arms that stretch
   Up toward the heaven and onward toward
     heaven's love,
   My balanced being had embraced in you
   That other side. We are not two, but one.
   And—think—to part two factors of one life
   Is murder—not of body but of spirit.

WALOON. Monaska—what?—Monaska,   are
     you mad?

MONASKA.   Not yet, not quite.

WALOON.   But think—you are the god.

[MONASKA.   Do you believe this?

WALOON.   I?—why should I not?

MONASKA.   Have always heard it, eh?—and
     most of us

   Commune with reason through our mem-
        ory;

   And not the work of our own minds we
        heed,

   But rôte-repeated phrases framed by others.—]

   Do you believe me then to be a god?

WALOON.   You must be.

MONASKA.   Your   god,   yours,   Waloon?

WALOON.   My god.

MONASKA.   To hear you say so, I could think it
     too.

   Thank heaven, thank heaven! But if I leave
        you here,——

WALOON.   I still will love you—-serve you in the
        temple.

MONASKA.   Nay—say not that!

WALOON.   I must though—if I love you.

MONASKA.   You must?—and why?

WALOON.   Because their souls are cursed

   Who loved the god, and serve not in the
        temple.

MONASKA.   Is that what they have taught you?

WALOON.   Yes.

MONASKA. A part
Of that instruction which they call divine?
(WALOON *drops eyes and head in assent.*)
I thought so!—and they say they make me god.
No, no; they make me devil!—Would they
could!
What happy hours in hell would heat the hate
My heart could hurl at what they call divine!
WALOON. What said you?
MONASKA. Said I? said I?—It was naught
[But practicing to be a god. You know
A coming glory casts a glow before it.
Those who shall be the lords of fowldom
gobble
A gobble at times before their gills are grown.]
WALOON. You seemed in anger.
MONASKA. So are gods at times.—
They think of men.
WALOON. Of women too?
MONASKA (*changing his tone*). Oh yes;
Of women:—they are said to be in bliss.
Waloon, you love me?
WALOON. Yes.
MONASKA. Will always love me?
WALOON. I will.
MONASKA. Then if a devil come to you,
In human shape, and say he represents me,
Swear you will not believe him—though the
king!

WALOON (*startled*).

    What can you mean?

MONASKA.   You do it, I will damn you—

    Not only I—but all the gods there with me.

(WALOON *draws back in fear.* MONASKA'S *tone
changes.*)

    Waloon, are you afraid of me, Waloon?

WALOON (*hesitatingly*).

    Why—no—

MONASKA.   I have a last request to make.

    I have to die in public,—is that so?

        (WALOON *bows in affirmation.*)

    They strip and mutilate me first?

WALOON.   You mean

    When—when they tear your heart out?

MONASKA (*in horror*).   Tear?—what, what?—

    While I am living, feeling, tear my heart out?

WALOON.   Oh, do not speak of it!   It—let me

    rest.

    (*almost swooning, and seating herself.*)

MONASKA.   You faint!—Oh, horror!—and for

    me, Waloon?

(*bending over her, and talking huskily and rapidly.*)

    We have but one brief moment more together.

    (*trying to rouse her, and succeeding.*)

    Wake!—there is one thing you must promise

    me.

    When I am gone—their ghastly deed been

    done—

I wish you to recall me as I am,—
One fit for all things almost, save to die,
Each factor, organ, limb of me complete,
And, at this moment, hot against the fire
Blazed through me by your love-enkindled
    eyes,
No sinew but is trembling with the draft
Of that delicious flame; and yet none too
Not strengthened by a power divine like that
Propelling all creation,—I am god,
Not man. Nay, nay! Remember me as god.
You must not see that unveiled, writhing
    frame,
Weak, color-void, save where the death-blood
    dyes it.
Waloon, you must not be there. I shall
    writhe
More like a god to know you are not there.—
But go you where we met first—in the woods—
You know the place—to me the holiest place
My life has ever known! Waloon, go there.
Oh, swear to me you will.—My soul will
    swear
To meet you.
WALOON.   What?
MONASKA.   By all that makes me god,
In form, perchance, in spirit certainly.—
[Will you, Waloon?
WALOON.   I——

MONASKA.   Swear it. So your soul,
  As I depart this life, may draw mine own
  Off in the current of that sympathy
  Forever sweeping from my life to yours;
  Away from ways where human wills out-
    wit
  The wisdom that has made earth what it
    is,
  To where, in that true temple of the spirit,
  The winds are whispering what men know not
    of,
  And flower and leaf are trembling like the
    heart
  That feels the presence of the power divine.—]
  There go I, darling—you?

WALOON.   I too.

MONASKA.   Thank heaven!
  *Enter—Left—*KOOTHA, *and his* COMPANION.

KOOTHA.   Your time is up.

MONASKA.   Farewell, Waloon.

WALOON.   Farewell.
  Oh, bitter, bitter, bitter word farewell,
  So bitter when the lips belie the heart
  That knows too well that life will not fare
    well.

  *Enter—Left—*HAIJO *with two* ATTENDANTS.

MONASKA (*to* WALOON).
  Things may turn brighter than you fear,
    Waloon.

WALOON.   Could they be darker?   Oh, my god,
     my god!

(*She bows before* MONASKA, *clinging to his hand.*)

KOOTHA (*to* HAIJO *as he gestures toward* WALOON).
     Note how complete is her devotion, sire.

HAIJO (*to* KOOTHA, *but at the same time motioning
     to* WALOON).
     Remove her.

(*pointing to* MONASKA *and speaking to the*
     ATTENDANTS.)
          Lead him forth.

MONASKA (*to* WALOON).   Farewell.

WALOON (*to* MONASKA).   Farewell.

MONASKA.   Do not forget—we meet where only
     gods are.

WALOON.   Yes—there.

MONASKA.   Have faith and hasten.

WALOON.   Yes, farewell.
          *Exit—Left—*WALOON.

HAIJO (*to* MONASKA).
     Now comes the hour in which you triumph.
     The people at the temple wait for you
     To do you adoration.

MONASKA (*lifting up his hands*).   With their
     hands?

HAIJO (*also lifting up his hands*).
     To lift your spirit to the skies.

MONASKA.   You think
     I crave that?

HAIJO.   Most men would.

MONASKA.   A wingless hand
Lifts only to a wingless height.   A rôle
Not past the common reach of common men
Cannot incite uncommon aspiration.
Lead me on.

*Exit—Left—*MONASKA, *led by the two* ATTEND-
ANTS.

[HAIJO (*to* KOOTHA).

                        How does he seem to take it?

KOOTHA.   Just like a god when made by man;
   or if
You like not that, a man when made by a god.—
Is there much difference between the two?

HAIJO.   And how Waloon?

KOOTHA.   She thinks as all the world do;
So lives enough in hell to please a priest.

HAIJO.   You villain!

KOOTHA.   Yet! I always do your bidding.

HAIJO.   Ungrateful cur!

KOOTHA.   Nay, do not say ungrateful.—
Nay; I am thankful for what you have
   taught me.

HAIJO.   My curses on you!—To the sacrifice!
   (HAIJO *moves towards the Left Entrance.*)

KOOTHA (*to his* COMPANION.)
The two things go together.   And how kind,
When one has curses loaded on him so,
To let him load them on another!

HAIJO (*turning toward* KOOTHA). What?—
  Away.

         *Exit—Left—*KOOTHA.

(*to the* COMPANION). His insolence must end,
  or I
  Must find a way to put an end to him.]
*Exit—Left—*HAIJO *and* KOOTHA'S COMPANION.

CURTAIN.

SCENE SECOND:—*Same as the Scene in Act Second.
Enter—through the gateway,—in a procession
marching to the music of the orchestra,* AT-
TENDANTS, PRIESTS, PRIESTESSES, MAIDENS,
PAGES, HAIJO, *the* KING, MONASKA *sitting
in his chariot, and apparently playing his lyre,
and, near the chariot,* KOOTHA *and his* COMPAN-
ION. GUARDS *end the procession, and station
themselves near the gate. This is not closed.
The* ATTENDANTS *and* PRIESTS *station themselves at the Right facing the Left; the* PRIEST-
ESSES *and* MAIDENS *at the Left facing the
Right. The* PAGES *are in Front of the Pyramid.*
MONASKA *descends from the chariot and stands
beside* HAIJO, *facing the pyramid.* KOOTHA
stands nearer the gate. His COMPANION
stealthily gets behind one of the GUARDS, *and
then Exits, at the gate. The* KING *ascends the
pyramid a few steps, and, standing in front of*

the rugs forming a seat near the base of the pyramid, faces the audience. The following is then chanted:

Oh, not what life appears to be,
  Is what in life is true.
Inveiled behind the forms we see
  Are things we cannot view.
What but the spirit working through
The guise men wear to what they do
Reveals the force that, foul or fair,
Awakes and makes the nature there.

The sunshine shows the worth of suns,
  The moisture, of the shower;
The stream, of rills from which it runs,
  The fragrance, of the flower;
And, oh, the spirit when it springs
Above the reach of earthly things,
As fall the limbs that feed the shrine,
Reveals the life to be divine.

(HAIJO *ascends the pyramid a few steps
    and stands beside the* KING *facing*
    MONASKA, *who mounts a lower step
    and whom* HAIJO'S *hands can touch.*)

THE KING. Now once again, unveiled for
    mortal gaze,
Immortal mystery and man have met.
The heavens bend low to touch the earth, and
    earth
Is lifting up its longing hands to heaven.

HAIJO (*lifting both hands*).
   Oh, ye that dwell less in the earth and sky
   Than in the meditations of the mind,
   We thank thee that the power of old imposed
   On ministers of earth can downward call
(HAIJO *here places both palms on* MONASKA'S *head.*)
   Upon a form in fashion like their own
   The presence of the gods' own power above,
   Till in a human form it sits enthroned.
         (*As he utters the last words, the* KING *takes*
         MONASKA *by the hand.* MONASKA
         mounts the pyramid between the KING,
         who is at his right as he turns to face
         the PEOPLE, *and* HAIJO *who is at his*
         left. The moment MONASKA *stands*
         on the step between the KING *and*
         HAIJO *both the latter and all the*
         PEOPLE *kneel, while all chant the*
         following:)
HAIJO.   All hail the heavenly sun,
PEOPLE.   The heavenly sun!
HAIJO.   All hail the glory won,
PEOPLE.   The glory won!
HAIJO *and* PEOPLE.

   All hail the sun that brings the light,
      All hail the rays that shower,
   And wake the barren wastes of night
      To germ and leaf and flower.
8

HAIJO.   All hail the heavenly sun,
PEOPLE.   The heavenly sun!
HAIJO.   All hail the glory won,
PEOPLE   The glory won!
HAIJO *and* PEOPLE.

> All hail the life behind the sun,
>   All hail the gods that dwell
> Where men whose earthly race is run
>   Are borne, and all is well.

HAIJO.   All hail the heavenly sun,
PEOPLE.   The heavenly sun!
HAIJO.   All hail the glory won,
PEOPLE.   The glory won!
HAIJO *and* PEOPLE.

> All hail the form of him who dies,
>   All hail the soul that wends
> Up through the skies, and onward hies.
>   All hail the gods, our friends.

(*The stage grows darker, indicating an approaching storm.*)

KING (*rising, as do all the* PEOPLE).
  Now comes the deed that all the gods await,
  The final act of solemn joy that gives
  The life we prize to those that reign on high.
  But ere his lyre be given to the king,
  Let those appointed for the sacred task

Be led here to conduct their holy charge
On his most holy way.
   (HAIJO *moves, as if to descend the pyramid,*
    but stops, and turns back upon hearing
    the voice of MONASKA.)
MONASKA (*to the* KING.)   Your majesty?—
 Sire, may I ask?——
KING.   What would you?
MONASKA.   A request,
 If I may speak.
HAIJO (*to the* KING).   Sire, he needs nothing.
MONASKA (*to the* KING).   Slight
 The last request of him who is your god?
KING (*to* MONASKA).
 Say on.
MONASKA. I merely thought, sire, that my spirit,
 To be inspired the better toward the light,
 Should gaze upon yon rising sun; but here
 It cannot,
  (*pointing toward the gateway at the Rear.*)
KING.   Not?
MONASKA (*motioning toward the guards between*
   the pyramid and the gateway).
       Could these but step aside!——
KING (*to an* OFFICER *at his Left*).
 Yes, let the guards there stand aside, nor hide
 The sunlight from the sacrifice.
HAIJO (*to the* KING, *making a gesture of dissent*).
        But, sire——

King (*hesitating, and looking from* Monaska *to* Haijo, *then addressing the* Officer *again*).
You need not give the order.
   (*to* Haijo.) Now proceed.
Let those appointed for the sacred task
Be led here to conduct their holy charge
On his most holy way.
   (Haijo *descends the steps of the pyramid.*
    Those about separate to let him pass
    them. Exeunt—through the Curtains
    *at the Left—*Haijo, *followed by a pro-*
    cession of Priests. *A sudden peal*
    of thunder with lightning.)
Monaska (*to the* King, *availing himself of the*
   general commotion at the suddenness of the
   peal).   You dare deny me?
The gods have joined me in my last request.
Beware, lest by the charm yourselves invoke
These gods, that you but half believe in, check,
In ways that pride like yours deserves, the course
And curse of most foul infidelity.
King. Well, well, it matters little.
(*to the* Officer, *and motioning toward the gate-*
   way.) Officer,
Give orders that the guard there stand aside.
   (Officer *moves toward the gateway and*

> *gestures. The* GUARD *move toward
> the Right.* KOOTHA *takes a station
> between the pyramid and the gateway.
> The* KING *continues to* MONASKA.)

Now are you ready?

MONASKA.   If the man be naught,
Let not the spirit that you deem divine
Depart, ere it invoke the powers above
To rest in endless benediction here.

KING. This proves how wisely you were
        chosen god.—(*to the* PEOPLE.)
He whom we worship calls upon us now
To kneel and all receive his benediction.

> (The PEOPLE *kneel, and bend their heads.*
> MONASKA, *lifting one hand, motions
> to the* GUARD *near the gate that
> they too kneel.* KOOTHA, *by motions,
> seconds his wish, bidding them all
> kneel down, which they do, bending
> their heads forward, and casting
> down their eyes. They are in front
> of the gateway, with their backs
> toward it.*)

MONASKA (*noticing that the* KING *is still stand-
                ing*).

I would include you too, sire.

KING.   Me?

MONASKA.   You too—

(*The* KING *kneels. While he is doing so,* Mo-

NASKA *looks toward* KOOTHA *and bows, then
        speaks to the* PEOPLE *in a slow, loud
        manner.*)

This is—my—benediction—for the people.

> (*Bright flash of lightning, followed by a loud
> peal of thunder.* MONASKA *hurls the
> lyre down upon the head of the* KING,
> *then flies past* KOOTHA *behind the*
> SOLDIERS, *and through the gateway
> backing at the Right.*)

KING. Help, help!

KOOTHA (*running toward the* KING *and motioning
        the* GUARDS *to do the same*).

> What is it?

KING (*to an* OFFICER, *who is bending over him*).

> He has murdered me,

KOOTHA. Oh, murder, murder!

> (*to the* GUARDS.)

> Shut the gates. Let none

Escape.

(GUARDS *hasten and close the gates backing at
        the Right.*)

OFFICER. Where is he?—Stop him.

KOOTHA (*standing on a step of the pyramid at the
        Back and looking toward the Right*).

> Ah! too late!

CURTAIN.

ACT FIFTH.

SCENE:—*Same as in Act First. The darkness
of an approaching storm.*
*Enter—Right—*WALOON *attended by her* MAID.
WALOON (*to the* MAID).

[Yes, yes, it is the place; no doubt of that;
Yet, in the dark, is all so vague and wild.
How the whole air is weighted with the gloom!
Even to draw it in, my lungs, o'ertaxed,
Would rather choose not breathe than bear
    the burden.
These clouds are curtained like a funeral pall,
Fit funeral pall, round my dear dying hope.—
My dying hope?—Oh, selfish, cruel soul,
To think of it when, even now, perchance,
That dear, dear heart, so eager-sped by love,
Whose each pulsation, like a paddle's beat
Seemed furthering some canoe's o'erladen
    prow
Where it should rest and empty at my feet;
That dear, dear heart, so pliant to my wish
That, at my lightest breath, the brightening
    smiles

Would open round his lips in hues as fair
As rosebuds parted by the breeze of May;
That dear, dear heart, the germ of all he was—
The sweetest outgrowth of the sweetest life
This earth has ever molded into form;—
To think that even now a heart like that,
Its nerve-roots quivering in their agony,
Is being torn out from the bleeding breast
As if some foulest weed that could pollute
A soil that, just to hold it—that alone—
Is more than sacred.   Oh, how can the
  heavens
Be so unjust?   Far better not to think
Than think but of that fearful, bleeding
  vision.
Would, would that I could veil it out—but no!]
              (*Thunder.*)
The voice of thunder?—Can it be that he
Would speak to me through that?—No, not
  through that,
Not he!—He loves me.—Yet he may have
  changed.
[Some tell us that the fairest forms on earth,
Most full of mirth and softness and caress,
Whose mildness tames life's wild, coquettish
  blood,
Leave in the tomb their loveliness and charm,
And go thence, fiends.—And he?—no, no, not
  so!—]

I almost had forgot he is a god.
Though what would gods be for, if man were
    good?
And if he be not good, what are they for,
Except to punish him?—and am I doom'd?—
Why not?—Is not my spirit in rebellion?
Perhaps it was the man in him, not god,
The man they rightly killed, that tempted
    me
To leave the temple and to wander here.
And now the god, then prisoned in the man,
May wreak his vengeance on me.
                (*Thunder.*)   Hark—again!—
And rain too! I must find a shelter.   What?—
        (*looking toward the Left.*)
Can they be warriors?—Can we be pursued?
    *Exit—Right—*WALOON *and the* MAID.
      *Enter—Left—*TWO WARRIORS.
        (*Thunder and lightning.*)

FIRST WARRIOR (*looking toward the Right*).
A woman, I am sure.

SECOND WARRIOR.   If so, not he.
No noise!—Were he to think himself pursued
He might escape us.

FIRST WARRIOR.   That could never be.
The woods are wholly circled by us now;
And him we know to be inside.
    (*moving toward the Right Rear.*)
      (*Thunder and lightning.*)

SECOND WARRIOR (*looking earnestly toward the Right, but moving toward the Left*).

This way!
I saw a form there coming; and the price
Of capturing by surprise is keeping silence.

FIRST WARRIOR. Ay, you are right. No wise
men spring a trap
Till sure their prey is in it. We withdraw.
Exeunt—Left—the TWO WARRIORS.
(*Thunder and lightning.*)
*Enter—Right rear—*MONASKA *attended by Kootha's*
COMPANION.

MONASKA. At last, the place! I feared we
should be lost,
So many in pursuit, and those who know
The ground so well, and we alas, so ill!
Strength speeds the feet, but knowledge aims
the bow,
And where the one but just begins the race,
The arrows of the other cleave the goal.
Who could have thought so many cross-roads
here
And short-cuts to a pathway well-nigh straight?
At last, we seem now to have dodged the foe;
And if I find Waloon—what then?—I fear
We might attempt escape in vain.—Perchance
It may be best that she should not be here,
To die disgraced if found with me—no, no;
Did she but dream of life I plan for her,

Disgrace from its foes would to her seem
    honor!—
[What sanguine brain is mine! How know I
    this?
To most men no disgrace can loom like theirs
Who dare do aught save by the grace of custom.
Where earth's esteem is what all strive for first,
Her customs make them cowards to the call
Of conscience; and the foulest crime
Seems not a curse, if it be only common.
Waloon too—could I ever dare reveal
To what departure from all common ways,
To all that she deems holy, I had led her?
What right have I, more than those priests
    have there
To slay me for the safety of their souls,—
What right have I to shade her future life,
Or slay her, as it may be, for my love?
And were she now to come and find in me
A murderer, where she hopes to find a god,
A coward, driven in fright from ordeals
Which she had prayed would prove him fit for
    heaven,—
Oh, how might she abhor these treacherous
    arms,
Thrown open to receive her! how detest
Lips that to keep her love must keep their lies!
What has my rashness wrought? Is it so well
For one man to resist what all men wish?—

The customs that the centuries have crowned?
How many have dared all to thwart the world
And only thwarted good the world could do
    them!
I might have passed from earth upon a throne,
Revered by all men, and beloved by her,—
Her god!—and shall I now become her fiend?—
Live on condemned by her, because I dared
To fight against a world that all should serve?
Ah, if my dying could have given one heart
That comfort of the spirit which all crave,
How could my soul have wrought a godlier
    deed?
We live our lives for use; if men misuse us,
Far better so than that we lose all use.
And yet,—what is our use?—Oh, would some
    power
Could tell us how to balance, in our lives,
The rule of others and the rule of self!
How can we, when the two conflict, serve both?
And which one should we serve?—which
    first?—Which chiefly?—
Till spirit seem no more than matter is,
Let me serve that which rules me through the
    spirit.]
        (*Thunder and lightning.*)
    (MONASKA *looks toward the Right Front.*)
Who come?—more warriors?—No, my soul—
    she?—yes—

Ye gods, if I have not deserved the doom
Of deepest hell, for her sake, god me now.

Exit — Right — KOOTHA'S COMPANION *as if to
guard* MONASKA.

*Enter—Right Front—*WALOON.

WALOON. Monaska!—Oh, ye angeis, can it
be?—(*kneeling.*)

Nay, blast me not that these unworthy
eyes

Should have presumed to gaze where earth is
blest

With this transcendent vision.

MONASKA. Yes, Waloon,
You see me.

WALOON. You?—Oh, love, chastise me not.

MONASKA (*taking her by the hand.*)

Rise up, Waloon, rise up. I merely love
you.

WALOON. You love me?—what?—this poor
weak fainting flesh? (*She rises.*)

MONASKA. Yes, it is this I love.—I thank you,
friend,

You had such faith, and came here.

WALOON. Thank the gods
That I have lived to do what pleased a god.

MONASKA. Waloon, do I fulfill your soul's
ideal

Of what a god should be?
(*The sky begins to grow brighter.*)

WALOON. Ah, more, far more.

MONASKA. If I came back to live on earth with
you——

WALOON. Nay, hint not that. Earth would
be too much heaven.

MONASKA. And if I were to tell you this,
Waloon,
That, far away from here, there lies a realm
Where gods like me can live with maids like
you,
But that, to go there, you must rend yourself
Forever from the land that is your home,
Where dwell your friends and kindred, would
you go?

WALOON. Though you be god, you know not
woman's heart,
If you believe I would not.

MONASKA. Swear it then.

WALOON. I swear——

MONASKA. To leave this land and all
you love here,
And fly to live alone with me forever?

WALOON. And fly to live alone with you.

MONASKA. Forever?

WALOON. I do.—What moved?

> (*She points toward the Left. The sky
> grows darker again, with a sound of
> distant thunder and slight flash of
> lightning.*)

MONASKA (*looking toward the left*).

　　　　　It seemed a flash from weapons.

WALOON.　The woods are full of warriors, as I
　　think.

MONASKA (*anxiously looking around*).

　I see—are all about—each side of us.

　O heavens, our time has come!—Yet all draw
　　back!—

　We have a moment more.

(*pointing to the moss-covered bench, apparently
　　hidden behind a tree near the Right Rear.*)

　　　　　　　Waloon, in here!

WALOON (*gazing around, and apparently seeing
　　the* WARRIORS, *then seating herself on the
　　bench, where* MONASKA *sits beside her*).

　I know not what it means.

MONASKA.　　　　　　　You never heard

　Of hosts that come with gods to visit earth?

　Waloon, were I to tell you that the realm

　In which the gods dwell could be reached by
　　you

　In one way only,—in the self-same way

　That severs in the temple soul from form

　In him your priests and people choose as
　　god?——

WALOON.　Then I would thank the force that
　　severed me

　From all that could weigh down a soul so light

　That but for them I too might soar to heaven.

MONASKA. Swear you mean truly what you
    say, Waloon.
WALOON (*lifting her hand*).   I swear it.
MONASKA (*motioning her to drop her hand*).
                Wait—could you return again
  And be a priestess in the temple there,
  As you have told me that you would become,
  With all the honor that a priestess has,
  And all the consciousness of deeds divine,
  And could you, as the years wore on, forget
  The love you once had borne this god——
WALOON.   No, no.
  I never could forget that.
  (*The sky from here on keeps growing brighter.*)
MONASKA.   Hear me through.
  Your king is absolute.   He could do all
  Your heart desires.   What say you, should
      there come
  A time when he—he loves you now, Waloon—
  Should choose you for his queen. If this,
      Waloon,
  This exaltation over all the earth,
  Were your bright destiny, say, would you
      choose
  To die, die here alone with faith in one
  Whose only welcome for you is a blow?—
            (*doubling and lifting his fist.*)
  Would you choose this?
WALOON.   I would.

MONASKA. In truth?

WALOON. I would.—

(*half rising and looking toward the Left.*)
Who is that coming?

MONASKA (*looking the same way, then at her*).

Do not be afraid.
Why should a soul with faith sublime as yours
Fear aught?—Your love alone, if nothing else,
Could here create of me the god you think me.
(*hurriedly and nervously, as he induces her to lie
on the moss-covered bench.*)
These come to summon both of us to heaven.
Here darling, rest your head upon this mound.
Cast one look more at me, then let me veil
These loving, earthly eyes from all of earth.
A look like this must never see the stroke
That drives the soul-light out of them.—
There, there,
You are content, my darling, you are sure?—
Content to live with me in spirit only?

WALOON. I am. I am.

MONASKA. Farewell.—I mean farewell
To earthly presence.

(*placing a branch or wreath over her eyes.*)

Now to angel hands
I leave my angel—nor a whit too soon.

(*gazing anxiously toward the Left.*)

WAPELLA (*from behind the Left Entrance*).
Monaska.

9

WALOON.   Who is that?

WAPELLA.   Monaska.

MONASKA (*rising*).   What?
   I know that voice.
          (*to* WALOON.)   Lie still, dear.   I return.
               *Enter—Left Front—*WAPELLA.

WAPELLA.   Monaska.

MONASKA (*moving to meet* WAPELLA.)
                    What?—Wapella?

WAPELLA.   Yes,—with friends.—
   To save you.

MONASKA.   How can this be?   How came you
   To seek me here?
               *Enter—Left—*KOOTHA.

(*Enter—Right—*KOOTHA'S COMPANION.   *Enter
   —from Right and Left—*WARRIORS.)

WAPELLA.   We tracked you.   Weeks ago,
   When learning what would be your fate, I
      fled.
   I found our comrades, many still not slain.
   We all returned, and watched here in the
      woods.
   Then Kootha met us—vowed to do his best
   To save you, and this morning, when you flew,
   We watched, we dodged, we circled round
      your path,
   And now have trapped you.   We shall all
      escape.
      (*in surprise, as they approach* WALOON.)

Waloon is with you?

MONASKA (*taking* WALOON *by the hand*).

Yes.—Rise up, Waloon.

WALOON (*rising and gazing about in a dazed way*).
And who are these?

MONASKA.   Kind friends to welcome us,
And lead us to the realm of which I spoke.

WALOON.   The realm?—What realm?

MONASKA.   What realm, Waloon?—My heaven.

CURTAIN.

END OF THE DRAMA.

COLUMBUS.

COLUMBUS.

INTRODUCTION: PLACE AND TIME.

This drama is intended to be a study, psychologic rather than historic, though not unhistoric, of the character of Columbus, as manifested and developed in connection with his experiences before, during, and after his discovery of America. The general outline of the plot is as follows:

ACT FIRST: *In Portugal.* SCENE FIRST: A public square. Talk about the plans of Columbus and about himself. His entrance, his introduction to Felipa, and invitation to her house. SCENE SECOND: Room in the house of Felipa. Reasons why Columbus hopes for success, the failure of his hopes, and his betrothal. SCENE THIRD: Same room ten years later, rearranged as study of Columbus. Hounded by his creditors and wronged by the King, he loses Felipa by death and decides to leave Portugal.

ACT SECOND: *In Spain.* SCENE FIRST: A Spanish camp at midnight. Columbus has enlisted as a soldier, is ridiculed for his schemes, has a talk with Beatrix, is present at an attempted assassination of the Queen, and thus comes to meet the King. SCENE SECOND: The Council of Salamanca, called to confer with Columbus and discuss his projects. A summary of the popular objections urged against them. SCENE THIRD: The exterior of the convent of La Rabida. To prevent Columbus from leaving her country, and to insure the success of his plans, the Queen pledges to him the Crown jewels of Castile.

ACT THIRD: *In Transit.* SCENE FIRST: A street in Palos near its harbor. The difficulties and opposition encountered by Columbus when preparing to sail, coming from his friends, as Beatrix, and from his enemies, who try even to destroy his boats. SCENE SECOND: The deck of his ship at sea. The mutineers, their talk when alone and when with Columbus, and his dealing with it. The midnight discovery of land, and the morning approach to it.

ACT FOURTH: *In Triumph.* SCENE FIRST: Room in a house in Spain. Columbus welcomed by Beatrix, and urged to secure benefits from the Crown ; and his description to her and to Diego of his voyage and the new land. SCENE SECOND: Reception at the palace of Barcelona by the King, Queen, and populace. SCENE THIRD: Dining hall in the house of Cardinal Mendoza. The egg story.

ACT FIFTH: *In Chains.* SCENE FIRST: Camp in Hispaniola. Opposition to Columbus on the part of noblemen and imported criminals. Placed in chains by his enemies. SCENE SECOND: House in Seville. Death of Columbus. SCENE THIRD: A final tableau with hymn, representing a vision of the dying Columbus, portraying the progress and present condition of America.

THE FOLLOWING CHARACTERS APPEAR ONLY
IN THE FOLLOWING ACTS.

———

In the First Act Only.

James of Mallorca,
Correo,
Tailor,
Grocer,

Waiter,
Felipa,
Dona Correo,
Woman.

In the Second Act Only.

Fernandez,
Talavera,
St. Angel,

Zalora,
Perez,
Other Monk,

Attendant.

Only after the First, in the Second and later Acts.

King Ferdinand,
Gutierrez,
Sanchez,

Arana,
Beatrix,
Queen Isabella,

Mendoza.

Only after the Second and in later Acts.

Escobar,
Pintor,

Roldan,
Citizen.

Only in the Fifth Act.

Velasquez,
Gamez,

Young Diego,
Fernando,

Indian.

137

What moves me seems beyond all conscious thought ;
Seems like the lure that leads the summer bird
Southward when comes the fall.   It is enough,
It is my destiny.   I weigh it well,
And find it rational ; yet why I first
Conceived it as I do, I cannot tell.

                                                COLUMBUS, *III, 1.*

            Think not I lived my life
To beg men for a badge to brag about !—
Enough, if I have been an influence.

                                                IDEM, *V, 2.*

CHARACTERS.

(CHRISTOPHER) COLUMBUS.	The Discoverer of America.
DIEGO (COLUMBUS).	} Brothers of Christopher Columbus.
BARTHOLOMEW (COLUMBUS).	
FONSECA.	Archdeacon of Seville, Traveler in Portugal, afterwards Bishop of Badajos, Palentia, and Burgos ; then Patriarch of the Indies.
BREVIESCA.	A Portuguese friend of Fonseca, then later his Secretary, Treasurer, and Agent in Spain.
KING FERDINAND.	Of Aragon, and, after Marriage, of Spain.
GUTIERREZ.	Gentleman of the Spanish King's Bedchamber, and Officer.
SANCHEZ.	Officer, Inspector-General of Columbus' Expedition.
JAMES OF MALLORCA.	President of the Portuguese Naval School.
CORREO.	Husband of Sister of Felipa, Columbus' Wife.
FERNANDEZ.	Physician and Scientist of Spain.
MENDOZA.	Archbishop of Toledo, Grand Cardinal of Spain.
TALAVERA.	Bishop of Avila, Confessor to the Queen.
ST. ANGEL.	Receiver of Ecclesiastical Revenues of Aragon.
ZALORA.	} Bishops of Spain.
ARANA.	
PEREZ.	A Monk, subsequently Prior of the Convent of La Rabida near Palos.

Escobar.
Pintor.
Roldan.
Gamez.

} Sailors with Columbus, Settlers in the New World.

Velasquez. Subtreasurer in Hispaniola.
Young Diego. Eldest Son of Columbus.
Fernando. Youngest Son of Columbus.

Tailor.
Grocer.
Waiter.

} In the First Act.

Moor.
Other Monk.
Attendant.

} In the Second Act.

Indian. In the Fifth Act.
Felipa (Perestrello). Wife of Columbus, Mother of young Diego.

Beatrix (Enriquez). Companion of Columbus after Felipa's death, Mother of Fernando Columbus.

Queen Isabella. Of Castile and, after Marriage, of Spain.

Dona Correo. Sister of Felipa, wife of Correo.
Woman. In the First Act.
Maid. In First and other Acts.

Citizens, Officers, Soldiers, Courtiers, Sailors, Settlers, Women, etc.

COLUMBUS.

ACT FIRST.

SCENE FIRST.—*A street or square in Lisbon, Portugal. Backing at the Right, a wineshop, in front of which are two tables each with four chairs about it. Backing at the Left, a convent wall ending against a chapel, the door of which faces the audience. Entrances at the Right Center through the door of the wineshop; at the Left Center through a curtain hanging in the doorway of the chapel ; and at the Right and Left Sides through streets. The rising curtain reveals* FONSECA *and* JAMES OF MALLORCA *seated at the Right. The following is chanted in the chapel.*

> O Life divine, from thee there springs
>   All good that germs and grows,
> Thy Light behind the sunlight brings
>   The harvests to their close.
>
> O Life divine, thou art the source
>   Of truth within the soul;
> Thou art the guide through all the course
>   That leads it to its goal.

O Life divine, what soul succeeds
  In aught on earth but he
Who moves as all desires and deeds
  Are lured and led by thee!

Enter—from the Wineshop—BREVIESCA, *and a*
  CITIZEN.

FONSECA (*to* JAMES).   You came to see?—

JAMES.   That man Columbus.

FONSECA.   Him?
  A crank,—and worse, a creaking crank!

JAMES.   Without
  Some crank to creak of it, men might forget
  The wheels of thought were made to move
    them on.

FONSECA.   You place thought on the right track
    once, you find
  What moves it on is not what moves it off.
  They differ.

BREVIESCA (*to the* CITIZEN).   I must wait till
    church is out;
  Then meet by accident—go home with her,
  And fish an invitation to her house—
  A lovely girl, Felipa!—As I live!
            *Enter—Left—*DIEGO.
  That man I met when traveling in Spain!
  Is always looming up.   I wonder what
  Should bring——

DIEGO (*to* BREVIESCA).   Good-day to Senior
    Breviesca.

BREVIESCA (*to* DIEGO).   Good-day to you.
      Exit—Left—the CITIZEN.
DIEGO (*looking toward the chapel*).   Your servant,
    Senior.—So!—
  At your devotions that you told me of—
  Front door ones, too!—No wonder you deemed
    strange
  My studying for the priesthood!
BREVIESCA.   But you said
  That you had turned from it.
DIEGO.   Oh yes! Truth is
  That I too am in love—but love myself.
[BREVIESCA.   Are candid.
DIEGO.   Wish to be.   For that I changed.
  God started man; man's deviltry the priest.
  For one, I like the thing God started best.
BREVIESCA.   Like others, eh?—yet like yourself.
DIEGO.   I do;
  That is, we two do—God and I.
BREVIESCA.   And now
  They style you, "Your Irreverence"?
DIEGO.   I am reverent.
BREVIESCA.   A different way of looking!
DIEGO.   Looking downward,
  One seems irreverent; looking upward, not
    so.]
FONSECA (*to* BREVIESCA, *rising and going toward*
    him with JAMES).   Is this not Senior——?
BREVIESCA (*to* FONSECA).   Senior Breviesca?

FONSECA. And I, Fonseca—Spaniard—met you
　　once
　In Seville. You recall?—
BREVIESCA. 　　　　　　Archdeacon—yes.
　You honor me.
FONSECA. You pleased me when we met.
　　　　　　(*introducing* JAMES.)
　Professor James—Mallorca—naval school.
BREVIESCA (*introducing* DIEGO).
　And Senior Diego of——(*hesitating*).
DIEGO. 　　　　　　The world.
BREVIESCA. 　　　　　　　　Quite true!
DIEGO. A traveler, knowing little—would know
　　more.
JAMES. A wish to my own heart! I came to
　　meet
　The mariner Columbus here.
Enter—from the Chapel—FELIPA, CORREO,
　　　　and DONA CORREO.
BREVIESCA. So? (*then seeing* FELIPA). Ah!
DIEGO (*to* JAMES *as he looks at* FELIPA).
　A pretty point, too, for his exclamation.
JAMES (*to* DIEGO). Would you see more of
　　it?
(*To* FELIPA.) Good-day.
FELIPA *and* DONA CORREO. Good-day.
CORREO (*to all*). Good-day.
JAMES (*introducing* DIEGO).
　　Allow me, Captain—Senior Diego,

A traveler like yourself.—

 (*introducing to the ladies*) Seniora C'rreo,
And Seniorita F'lipa Perestrello.
Will sit?—and, Waiter?

  *Enter—from the Wineshop—*WAITER.
    Wine here.

[WAITER.   Red or white?

JAMES (*to all*).   What say you?

DONA CORREO.   None for me, thanks.

JAMES (*to* FELIPA).   You?

FELIPA.   Nor me.——

JAMES (*to the others*).   The gentlemen, at
  least?

CORREO.   I will perhaps.

JAMES. I thought it. (*to the other gentlemen.*)
  You too?—White, not so? Its hue
Will fit this sunny air, and make us think
Of drinking in the sunshine!]

  (*He pays the waiter for the wine.*)

   *Exit—into the Wineshop—*WAITER.

  (*All seat themselves at the tables, from left
   to right, in this order : first empty
   chair, then* DIEGO, D. CORREO, COR-
   REO, FELIPA, JAMES, BREVIESCA *and*
   FONSECA. JAMES *continues to* COR-
   REO.)

       Was that man
Columbus in the church?

CORREO.   Not met him.

 10

JAMES   No?—
  A sailor, drawing maps now for our school—
FONSECA, Who should be kept to that and
        facts—not draw
  So much upon his fancy.
[JAMES.   You should hear
  His arguments.
FONSECA.   Say feel them—all their points
  Well dipped in pagan poison.
JAMES.   Oh, not all!
FONSECA. Enough to make all deadly.
JAMES.   Beg your pardon;
  But I lack scent to follow up your trail.
FONSECA. You know a priest should save the
        world from lies?
JAMES.   Have no scent yet!—am senseless?]
  *Enter—from the Wineshop—*WAITER *with five
        glasses of wine, and sets them before
        the gentlemen.*
FONSECA.   Put it thus:
  If what he says be right, the church is
        wrong.
JAMES.   Oh, not so bad as that!—has not found
        out.
FONSECA. If what he says be wrong, his dupes
        will drown.   (*to* CORREO.)
  Not so?
CORREO.   It is the first time yet that I
  Have heard of him.

Fonseca. You will hear soon enough.
　The surest proof we men are not all fools,
　Is in the way we bruit them when we find them.
Diego. Ay, and the surest we are not all brutes,
　　　Exit—into the Wineshop—Waiter.
　Is in the way our thinkers make us mind them.
James. A friend of his, eh?
Diego. Yes.
Correo. Have known him long?—
　Can tell us of him?
Diego. Is from Genoa;
　A mathematician, studied at Pavìa.
　Since then, till now, for more than twenty
　　　years,
　A sailor and a soldier—in the scrubs
　At Naples, Tunis, famous for his fights
　Against the infidel—last year, the man
　Who clampt his frailer bark against a huge
　Venetian galley, and when both took fire,
　Driven to the water, holding but an oar,
　Swam in to Lisbon; and that oar of his,
　All that he brought here, may yet prove to be
　The scepter-symbol of a mightier sway
　Than your King ever dreamed of.
Correo. Ah!—How so?
Felipa. Yes, yes!
Diego. His plan is now to sail around
　The world; and in the trail he leaves behind
　Loop all to Portugal.

FELIPA.   Around the world?

JAMES.   Oh, you should hear him talk!

FONSECA.   No, no, should not—
  A mad dog to be muzzled!

DIEGO (*to* FELIPA).   You should not—
  Unless you wish to think and feel, and thrill
  To feel, there is a larger world than ours.

BREVIESCA.   In one's imagination.

DIEGO.   Be it so.
  Imagination is the soul of thought.

[BREVISCA.   Well, take the soul, but we will
    keep to sense.

       (FONSECA *nods at him approvingly*.)

DIEGO.   Humph! many a joke would better not
    be cracked.
    The kernel's——

BREVIESCA.   Not entirely to your taste?

FONSECA.   Well, well!—Quite frank for stran-
    gers!

JAMES.   Come, come, come.
  Enthusiasm needs a margin.

FONSECA.   But
  We may not need enthusiasm.

JAMES   So?—
  And you say this?—a priest?

BREVIESCA.   And pray, why not?

JAMES.   Why not?—Why, friend, enthusiasm
    is
    The essence of religion——

DIEGO. Valueless
Without its uplift and its oversight.
If these it lack, it is a lifeless corpse
Not measured by its worth but want of it.
(*to* JAMES.)
Not true?
JAMES. I think your training has been good.
DIEGO. It came from him we speak of.
FELIPA (*to* CORREO). How I wish
That I had known him!
CORREO. You?
FELIPA. Why, any man (*pointing to* DIEGO)
To kindle fire like that——
CORREO. Must have enough
To keep a maiden warm and cosy, eh?—
Think you that follows? I have known of
men
Whose thought would flash like lightning,
lighting up
Half heaven besides the whole of earth; and
yet
A whirlwind, did you trust to its caress,
Would never lead you in a madder dance.
DIEGO. Not true of him we speak of.—One less
mad
Does not exist.
FONSECA. Oh, you seem bit by him!
JAMES. Come, come, the church is wise, per-
haps, to put

Her brake on wheels that else might whirl us
 down,
But how about those wheels when mounting
 up?]
 *Enter—from the Chapel—*COLUMBUS.
DIEGO. Ah, here he comes to argue for himself.
 (*rising and extending his hand to* COLUMBUS.)
 Good-day.
COLUMBUS (*aside*). What! you here?
DIEGO (*aside to* COLUMBUS). Yes, but no one
 knows
We two are brothers. Better so, perhaps.
COLUMBUS. I see—can help me more.
JAMES (*rising and greeting* COLUMBUS).
     The Captain! Welcome.
   (*introducing* COLUMBUS.)
 Permit—Seniora Correo—Seniorita
 Felipa Perestrello—the Archdeacon
 Fonseca, Senior Breviesca—Captain
 Correo—sailor of experience.
   (*All rise and bow to* COLUMBUS.)
COLUMBUS (*to ladies and* CORREO). It gives me
 joy to meet you.
CORREO.   Shall we sit?
 (*All sit from left to right in this order :* COLUM-
  BUS, DIEGO, DONA CORREO, CORREO,
  FELIPA, JAMES, BREVIESCA, *and* FON-
  SECA.)
JAMES. You come here every day, I take it?

COLUMBUS. Almost.

JAMES. Are making up for time you lost at
    sea?

COLUMBUS. Yes, making up and mounting up.
    I like
The uplift of the services.

JAMES (*to* FONSECA). There, there,
    Archdeacon, one point scored against your-
    self!
Dull not the blade that carves at your own
    feast. (*to* COLUMBUS *in explanation*.)
Oh, nothing serious!—an argument
About good churchmen and enthusiasts.

COLUMBUS. I see—and me. Yet men were
    told to preach
The truth to all the world.
        (*to* FONSECA.) You think it done?
No, no; I am no mere enthusiast.

BREVIESCA. And yet would sail across the un-
    known sea.

COLUMBUS. I would.

BREVIESCA. But that——

COLUMBUS. I have good reasons for.

FONSECA. And where, pray, do you find them?

COLUMBUS. Everywhere—
Without a single fact against them.

BREVIESCA. Ha,
Without a single fact!

COLUMBUS. Well, name one, then.

BREVIESCA.   Enough for me, if one could cross
        the sea.
    We should have found it out.
[COLUMBUS.   So?—How?
DIEGO (*to* BREVIESCA).   No, no;
    The world has had too many men like you.
FONSECA.   And well for its own good!   If lands
        were there,
    The Lord would let us know it.]
COLUMBUS.   There are lands
    Men have not known.
FONSECA.   And that would make you brave
    The blazing waves, and have your ship burned
        up?
COLUMBUS.   Ten years ago, the waters just
        beyond
    Cape Bojador were said to burn thus; now
    Men sail them, far as Cape de Vere.
FELIPA.   Is true.
COLUMBUS.   And they return with branches,
        leaves and flowers
    That float from further west; and you have
        read
    The ancients?
BREVIESCA.   Yes, about Atlantis, yes;
    But that was lost.—Yet easily found, you
        think.
    I grant it—found by sinking.
FONSECA.   Ha, well said!

COLUMBUS. Oh, there are other tales! Late
      travelers too,
  Like Marco Polo and John Mandeville——
FONSECA. Now pardon me; but stick, man, to
      your text.
  It was of facts that you began to speak——
COLUMBUS. And that which gives them value.
BREVIESCA.   Fancies, eh?
COLUMBUS. Not fact-full only, but a mind that
      you
  Deem fanciful is needed, would a man
  Put this and that together, and build up
  The only structure that can make his facts
  Worth knowing.
JAMES (*rising, as do the others*). True as gospel
      that! But now
  I must be going. (*to* COLUMBUS.)
              You will come with me?—
  Another map—I would explain. Besides,
  Prince Henry will be there to-day.
BREVIESCA (*to* COLUMBUS).   And he
  Would let you sail your ship up to the moon,
  Were he not in it.
FONSECA (*to* BREVIESCA). Good! I like you,
      man.
  [You have some sense.
CORREO (*aside, to* JAMES). The Prince believes
      in him?
JAMES. If not in him, at least in enterprise.

COLUMBUS (*to* JAMES).   Is just the meeting I
    had prayed to have.
  Too good in you to further it!—will come.]
CORREO (*to* COLUMBUS).   And we shall see you
    soon at our home too?
BREVIESCA (*to* FONSECA).   At their home—
    what? that madman, and not us?
COLUMBUS (*to* CORREO).   I keep quite busy and
    have little time——
FELIPA (*to* COLUMBUS).   But we have maps my
    father made; and these
  You might find helpful.
COLUMBUS (*to* FELIPA).   Thank you. I will come.
  Good-day.
[FELIPA *and* DONA CORREO.   Good-day.
  (COLUMBUS *and* JAMES *exchange bows with all.*)
      *Exeunt—Left—*COLUMBUS *and* JAMES.
CORREO (*to* FELIPA *and* DONA CORREO).   But we
    too must be going.
      They bow to those that are left behind them.
        *Exeunt—Right—*CORREO, FELIPA *and*
        DONA CORREO, *followed by* FONSECA.
DIEGO (*to* BREVIESCA).   Ah, Senior Breviesca,
    even here
  Enthusiasm has been king to-day;—
  Within a single hour thrown wide apart
  The palace bars, and parlor doors that
    guard
  The prettiest girl in Portugal.

BREVIESCA.   Oh, yes!
    But wait you till the end come.
DIEGO.   In the end,
    As the beginning, nothing thrives but spirit.
    If trusted, it survives too, every time.
    A prince——
BREVIESCA.   Is mortal——
DIEGO.   Is a lord of earth;
    And on the earth he sometimes has the power
    To make a man immortal.
BREVIESCA.   Humph! How strange
    You like that egotist—insufferable!
DIEGO. Why, no. The insufferable is you—
    I mean to him. He dreams of destiny,
    His whole soul in his work. That soul speaks
        out
    And like a sovereign. Souls are sovereign
        always.
BREVIESCA. One's destiny you think, is made
        by talk?
DIEGO. One's destiny was never yet fulfilled
    By one whose coward conscience dared not give
    Expression to the spirit that inspired it.
        *Exeunt—Right—*BREVIESCA *and* DIEGO.]

SCENE SECOND.—*A Parlor in the house of* DONA
    CORREO *and* FELIPA *at Lisbon.* FELIPA *and
    an elderly Chaperon sit working in the rear.
    Entrances at Right and Left.*

*Enter—Right—*DONA CORREO *in an outdoor dress as in the First Act.*

FELIPA. I feared that you would not be back.
 Our Captain
Columbus will be here to-day. They say
No doubt that he will get the ships.
D. CORREO.   I doubt it.
FELIPA. Prince Henry promised him——
D. CORREO.   The Prince is ill.
Yet, could I, I should like to stay with you.
Give my excuses, please—ay, ay, and yours.—
Breviesca too is coming.
FELIPA.   That man, humph!
D. CORREO. We all accept the suit.
FELIPA.   Except the one
That should be suited.
[D. CORREO.   Whom we all so trust,
We trust her wisdom also. (*kissing* FELIPA.)
       With the Captain
Be not too cordial.
FELIPA.   Not too cordial?
D. CORREO.   No.
Cordialities that make the backward friends
But tempt the forward to presumption. Force,
Alive to clear its own approaches, flouts
A welcome meant for weakness.
FELIPA.   He is forward?
D. CORREO. A civil man enough!—But then
 they say——

Felipa.   The one that everybody's bid can bind
Is everybody's bondsman.

D. Correo.   But I know
The neighbors——

Felipa.   And I know myself.   The wise
Make self the mistress of their choice, I think.

D. Correo.   Now, now, fair play!   Fair play
   in argument,
Will catch our thoughts before it throws them
   back.
They call him flighty.

Felipa.   So are birds—and so
Are—angels——

D. Correo.   What?

Felipa.   And every kind of life
Above the common.]

D. Correo.   Why, my girl!
One might suppose——
        (*looking toward the window at the right.*)
                But see!   He comes.   I go.
Be on your guard—and think.   Good-bye.
                (*kissing her.*)
        *Exit—Left—*Dona Correo.

Felipa (*to her* Chaperon).   And think?—
I need that caution?—when this beaker all
        (*placing her hand on her heart.*)
Is brimming to its overflow?—And think?—
When all my thoughts are radiant with his
   form

Like surging sea-waves glancing back the
  sun?—
*Enter—Right—*COLUMBUS *carrying a roll of maps.*
    (FELIPA *signals her* CHAPERON *to retire.*)
        Exit—Left—the CHAPERON.
  (*to* COLUMBUS) Good-day to you.
COLUMBUS.   Good-day: was good enough
  For me before you called it so.
FELIPA.   With all
  Your disappointments?—It is true! Prince
    Henry——
COLUMBUS. Has promised all I wish. I shall
  succeed.
(*They sit together on the sofa, while* COLUMBUS
      hands her the maps.)
FELIPA. Thank God!
COLUMBUS. Ay, ay! Oh, I have sailed in
  nights,
  Dark nights, and prayed to heaven for one
    small star
  To guide me. Now it sends the Prince and
    you.
FELIPA (*unrolling the maps and looking at one*).
  You do me too much honor.
COLUMBUS.   Could I? Nay;
  A soul that summons all that does one's best
  To do still better, sits upon a throne
  Than which none higher is conceivable.
FELIPA. I was not conscious——

COLUMBUS. Nay, nor is a child
Of aught in her of movement or of form,
That, fitting sweet ideals of loveliness,
Makes fancied grace and beauty visible.

FELIPA (*looking down at the map*). And yet, I
had not thought my father's maps——

COLUMBUS. Ay, they confirm twice over all my
plan—
Not they alone, but your directions with
them.

FELIPA. Mine? (*sitting with one hand resting
on the map.*)

COLUMBUS. Yes, your fingers pointing out the
course.
It all is there, just there beneath your hand.
A sailor steers the way his compass points.

FELIPA (*looking down at her hand on the map*).
Is that your compass?

COLUMBUS. It might compass me—
I mean my soul.

FELIPA. That little hand? Oh, what
A little soul!

COLUMBUS. Do souls have size? One might
Be universed in this; yet not contained
(*pointing to her hand.*)
In all the universe outside of it.

FELIPA. To put your soul thus in another's
hand,—
Would that be wise?

COLUMBUS.   Why not?—the hand that serves
The soul one loves may serve but selfishly,
And yet serve best the one who trusts to it.
FELIPA.   But should it fetter him?—
COLUMBUS.   Then would he thrill
In every atom of his frame to feel
Its fingers' throb and pressure.
FELIPA.   Would not bound
Away?
COLUMBUS.   Away and up, but always back
      again,
Like grains of sand in earthquakes.
FELIPA.   Foolish man!
COLUMBUS.   Why, only God is wholly wise; and I
Am but a man—so never quite so manly
As when—why, say—made foolish.
FELIPA (*rising, as does also* COLUMBUS).

                        Some one comes.
Enter—Right—a SERVANT, *bringing a note.*
FELIPA.   A note for me—from whom?—
         (*opening and reading the note.*)
            *Exit—Right—*SERVANT.

                        Can this be true?
Bad news for us!   Oh very, very bad!—
The Prince is dead.
COLUMBUS.   Prince Henry?   What?—No, no!
FELIPA.   It must be so.   You see who sent it—
      look.
   (*handing the note to* COLUMBUS, *who reads it.*)

COLUMBUS. Impossible! Heaven cannot be
    malicious!
  What? build so high a structure for my hope,
  Then knock the prop from under? All, all
    gone?
FELIPA. There may be others.
COLUMBUS.   May be?—There are none.
FELIPA. But you have me still.
[COLUMBUS.   That is it. We must
  Forget all this—at least for years and years.—
  Oh, I know what it means!—have seen years
    like them.
FELIPA. Forget all this?
COLUMBUS.   You do not understand.]
  Prince Henry was my patron. Backed by
    him,
  Success was possible; I felt I trod
  An equal plane with others of your suitors.
  [I now am worse off than a beggar.
FELIPA.   No!
  You have your pencil—still can draw——
COLUMBUS.   Yet not
  The outlines I had hoped—of that new land,
  And you, its princess. No; there looms a
    face
  With more care-lines upon its wrinkled brow
  Than e'er I blacked a map with.
FELIPA.   There are ships
  That still need captains.

    11

COLUMBUS.   Could one see their sails
   Like arms, white-surpliced, praying heaven
      for wind,
   Yet keep his prow still turned away from
      that
   Which he had vowed to heaven that he would
      seek?]
FELIPA. But you can wait—you are so strong!
    —can wait——

[COLUMBUS. I can—but you—when lit by hope,
    rebuffs
   Are merely clouds aglow where dawn brings
      light.
   But when no ray of hope is visible,
   The dark seems full damnation.
FELIPA.   You say this?—]
   I thought——
COLUMBUS.   Oh, I!—yes, I can wait forever.
   The light is in me.   But could you see through
   These forms that cloak it, worse than worst of
      rags,
   Discourtesy, suspicion and contempt
   Of those who know Columbus as the fool?
FELIPA. Why——
COLUMBUS. No, deny it not.   I know it, feel
    it.
   Your mother, sister, brother—yes, I grant
   They tolerate me; but when patronless
   And penniless, it were a different tale.

FELIPA. Nay, nay; that cannot be! But they
with me
Will feel how noble is a man like you——
COLUMBUS. A pauper and fanatic——
FELIPA.   No, a man
Who all alone, can stand with but one friend,
His own brave soul, and trample underfoot
A hissing world that, coiling like a snake,
Would clutch him to its clod and hold him
there.
COLUMBUS. Too much! To-day you think it,
but to-morrow—
Next year—in ten years——No, I have no
right
To put you to the test. No, let me go—
Farewell.
FELIPA. Will you fare quite as well without me?
COLUMBUS. Felipa, nay, it cannot be.
FELIPA.   You think
A woman's heart, if tested through long years
With burdening love, would break? You
think it kinder
To break it at the start?
*Enter—Right—*BREVIESCA *shown in by a*
SERVANT.
COLUMBUS (*not observing* BREVIESCA). Felipa,
no—
A faith like yours—my God, what shall I do?
I would not harm you, yet have done the harm.

BREVIESCA (*sarcastically to the two*).　Ah, so!—
　　I see I come too late—
FELIPA (*aside, anxiously to* COLUMBUS).　Except
　For one thing!
COLUMBUS (*to* BREVIESCA).　Yes—we are be-
　trothed.
　　*Exit, with sarcastic bow—Right—*BREVIESCA.
　　　　　　　CURTAIN.

SCENE THIRD.—*The same as in* SCENE SECOND,
　now the home of COLUMBUS.　*Maps and
　charts are hanging on the walls, and lying on a
　large table at the Back Center; also books, in-
　struments for navigation, and implements for
　measuring and drawing.　A window at the Right.
Entrances at the Right and Left.
Enter—Right—a* MAID *and a* WOMAN, *followed
　　　　　　by other Women.*

WOMAN.　Is he at home?
MAID.　　　　　　Not now.
WOMAN.　　　　　　　What seems he doing?
[MAID.　Oh, just the same as ever!
WOMAN.　　　　　　　　　　Nothing eh?
(*to the other Women who have remained near the
　　　　　　　door.*)
　Come in.　(*to* MAID)
　　We thought that we should like to see——]
　(*handling charts and implements on the table.*)
MAID.　You really should not touch them.

WOMAN. No? Why not?

MAID. He would not like it.

WOMAN. Oh, of course not! but
He need not know it; need he?—
       (*pointing to a chart.*)
               What a blotch!

MAID. A chart, you know.

WOMAN. A chart?—A chart of what?
I never saw a chart like that—looks like
A crazy quilt. And so he wastes his time
On things like these?—Felipa dying too!
[No wonder!—Think of it!—Ten mortal years
Of this, and no one knows what more. At
    night,
I would not dare to stay alone with him,
Would you?—say, would you?

MAID. Why! I—no—he never——

WOMAN. Of course not. You would be afraid,
    of course.
I had a cousin once who went insane.
And all his family had to play insane
To keep him company. The sport was royal
Till, sure that he was royal and they slaves,
He ordered off their heads.

MAID. And then?

WOMAN. And then
They left off playing, and made war on him;
And so dethroned him. They should do so
    here;

The sooner, too, the better!   Look at this:]
     (*taking up a sharp instrument.*)
Not safe in hands like his!
     (*knocking at the door at the Right.*)
             Hark!   What is that?
Can it be he?   Say, you can let us out
     (*starting for the Left.*)
The other door, not so?
MAID.   No need of that!
Is no one but the tailor.
WOMAN.   Sure of it?
(*crossing the room and looking out the window at
     the Right.*)
[MAID.   Comes every day.
WOMAN.   What for?
MAID.   To bid us think
Of Adam's fall that made men civilized,
Wear clothes, and bear the curse of paying
   for them.]
     (*opening the door at the Right.*)
*Enter—Right—*TAILOR, *to whom she speaks.*
Is out.
TAILOR.   Oh, yes, I know—is always out—
Out of his head at least.   Were he but out
My clothes, it would be better.—Left no word?
MAID. He bade me say that he expects the
   king——
[TAILOR. If all the kings that are expected
   came,

Few would be left for subjects. I will strip
And cage his bareness for a jail-show. Ugh!

MAID. But, really, he is honest. He expects——]
Enter—Right—suddenly, the GROCER.

GROCER. Tell him his expectations are too old.
Fresh expectations, like fresh eggs, may hatch.
Not so with stale ones, though, however
white.

WOMAN (*turning from the window at the Right,
where she has been looking out, and gazing at
the* GROCER).
The grocer, eh? (*speaking to the other women.*)
    And all the family
Are coming—and the Captain too. I saw
them.—
Will be a scene here. I prefer the background.
*Exit—Left—*WOMAN, *followed by the other Women.*

[TAILOR (*to* GROCER). Suppose we club together
 —ay, let fly
Our blows at him together—down him sooner!]

GROCER (*to* MAID, *and holding a paper toward
her*). I cannot fill this order.

MAID.   But you must.
His wife is needing it.

GROCER.   But I myself
Cannot afford a wife——

TAILOR.   When keeping his.

*Enter—Right—*DONA CORREO *and* CORREO *pushing* FELIPA *in a chair upon wheels.*

Maid (*to* Grocer).

   His wife is ill.   You would not let her die?

Grocer.   Not I, but he; and there are other
         shops——

Maid.   But we have tried them all.

Grocer.   Then try the jail.

   They feed men there,—or let him sell——

Dona Correo (*bowing to* Grocer).   You
         say?

Grocer (*pointing toward the charts and imple-*
         ments on the table).   He ought to sell
         these things and pay us off.

Dona Correo.   Not paid you yet?   Oh, well,
         you may be right!

Felipa (*to* D. Correo).   They may be right?
         Why, this would ruin him.

Dona Correo (*to* Felipa).   Not outside things
         that men can take away

Bring ruin, but the things that stay within,

Which would they could take!

             (*to* Grocer *and* Tailor.)

                         He himself is coming.

         *Enter—Right—*Columbus.

Columbus (*to* Grocer *and* Tailor).   You
         seek for me?

Tailor (*holding his bill toward* Columbus).   I
         brought your bill.

Grocer.   And I.

Tailor.   We say an honest man——

COLUMBUS (*motioning toward* FELIPA). But not,
please, now.

My wife is ill.

TAILOR (*pointing toward the table*). We say—
your sister too—

[An honest man would sell these traps; not
let

His creditors go begging.

GROCER.   Ay, or come so.
           (*appealing to* FELIPA.)

You think it too.   (*to* COLUMBUS.)
                    You see it in her face.

TAILOR (*to* GROCER). Oh, he sees nothing!
Give one's brain a whack.

It flies from earth to stars—but all in here.
               (*pointing to his head.*)

COLUMBUS (*referring to the implements on the
table*). These are the tools I work with—
all of them.

GROCER. Humph, they work poorly, better give
them up!

COLUMBUS. The king——

TAILOR. For ten years we have heard of him.

COLUMBUS. Your bill is only three months
old.

TAILOR.   Yes; this one.

COLUMBUS. The present king has not been on
the throne.

But——

GROCER.   All kings are the same to us—as you
  Will find.

COLUMBUS.   You need but wait——

TAILOR.   Have learned that lesson.]

COLUMBUS.   My brothers will be here to-day.

TAILOR.   And they?

COLUMBUS.   Will bring me proofs of favor at
     the court.

TAILOR.   If so?

COLUMBUS.   Why, they will bring me what will
     pay
  A score of times and more your paltry bills.
  What say you?

GROCER (*to* TAILOR).   Shall we wait?   Fact is,
     one finds
  It hard to break old habits.   Shall we, eh?

(TAILOR *bows in acquiescence*.   GROCER *continues*
       to COLUMBUS.)

  But see we get what balances our claim,
  Or we shall weigh these things against them
    yet, (*pointing to the table.*)
  And sell them too by weight.

    *Exeunt—Right—*GROCER *and* TAILOR.

COLUMBUS.   No doubt they will.
  Too often in the judgments of this world
  Worth yields to weight.

DONA CORREO.   A scandal and disgrace—
  A scene like this in my own sister's house!

FELIPA.   Why, sister, when the king——

DONA CORREO. Oh, dear, you know
That talk is fiction, like the most things
here.
FELIPA. But yet the king took interest in his
charts,
And sent for them.
CORREO. Ay, ay, and found out so—
Quite likely—that he cannot draw at all—
Except from his own fancy. Who wants
that?
A visionary man produces visions;
And in the world that is, men want what is.
[COLUMBUS. Why, brother, I am accurate.
DONA CORREO. Perhaps.
Who knows it though? Yourself? If one
besides,
He too has made your own discoveries.
And if no mortal knows it, all will judge
By what they hear. What do they hear of
you?
CORREO. Humph, I can tell. (*to* COLUMBUS.)
Forgive me; it is time
You knew the truth. I thought, perhaps, to
lease
A ship that you could sail,—make money by,
But——
DONNA CARREO. Been too long from practice?
CORREO. No, no; worse!
DONA CORREO. Is but an idler, as they think?

CORREO.   Worse yet—
  One who should not be trusted, sure to do
  The wrong thing for the right.
COLUMBUS.   And you say that?
CORREO. Not I, but those that give you repu-
        tation.
COLUMBUS. Am I to blame?
CORREO.   Who else is, pray? They say
  That you would sail but heaven alone knows
        where.
  And I confess, I half believe you would.]
FELIPA. Oh, brother!
COLUMBUS (*aside to* CORREO). Cruel, talking
        thus to her! (*to* FELIPA.)
  The other room will be far better, dear,
  Than this. And they?—they but exaggerate.
  They hurt my feelings? Oh, why, why, why,
        why,
  You never saw a fisher catch a fish
  Whose hook would not get tangled in the line.
  Just wait, and see me get the better of them.
  You trust in me.   There.
      (*gesturing to the* MAID *to wheel* FELIPA.)
                          I am coming soon.
*Exeunt—Left—*MAID *wheeling* FELIPA *in her
                chair.*
DONA CORREO (*to* CORREO). Quite right!—
  The time has come to tell him truth.
  (*to* COLUMBUS *and gesturing toward* CORREO.)

You think him cruel. What are you, your-
    self? (*pointing toward the Left.*)
See what ten years of this have made of her?
I come, and find her wanting everything—
Food, physic—nearly dying at your hands.
DONA CORREO. Do not say that.
DONA CORREO.   Humph! It is time I did.
COLUMBUS. She still believes in me.
DONA CORREO.   As infidels
In their Mohammed, and are cursed for it.
[COLUMBUS. I think that you forget. How
    many men
Of humble, foreign birth demand and get
A summons to an audience with the king?
Say that of such importance that the king,
To weigh it, calls his wisest counselors?
Who argue it for days, with some, at least,
That side with him whom you think stands
    alone?
DONA CORREO. How many side with him?
COLUMBUS.   Enough to make
The king request his charts—the work of years
That you think wasted.
DONA CORREO.   That was months ago;
And nothing followed.
COLUMBUS.   There is too much life
In truth of any sort, when sown, to doubt
Its growing. I have made a good beginning.
DONA CORREO. A very small one.

COLUMBUS.   So a seed is too,
Whose growth is great.   When one awaits the
     dawn,
A flush is better than a flash, which oft
But bodes a rush-light.]
Enter—Left—the MAID, *crosses the room, and
     opens the door at the Right.*
*Enter—Right—*DIEGO *and* BARTHOLOMEW, *to
     whom* COLUMBUS *now turns.*
                    Ah, they come at last!—
My brothers, welcome!
DIEGO (*to* COLUMBUS).   So to you.
        (*to* DONA CORREO *and* CORREO.) And you.
BARTHOLOMEW.   And all.
             (*All greet each other.*)
             Exit—Left—the MAID.
COLUMBUS (*to* DIEGO).   You bring me news?
DIEGO.   Ay, by and by.
      (*glancing at* DONA C. *and* CORREO.)
COLUMBUS (*to* DONA C. *and* CORREO).   You will
     excuse us?
DONA CORREO.   We will leave.
      *Exeunt—Left—*DONA C. *and* CORREO.)
COLUMBUS (*to* DIEGO).   This news?
DIEGO (*sadly*).   My brother, can you bear
     it?
COLUMBUS.   I have borne
With much.
DIEGO.   Yes, you have been misunderstood,

Misjudged, maligned; but all were less than
    this.

COLUMBUS. How so?

BARTHOLOMEW. The king——

COLUMBUS. He has not sent the money?

BARTHOLOMEW. The money?

COLUMBUS. Yes, his agent promised it.

BARTHOLOMEW. We had not thought you cared
    so much for that.

COLUMBUS. Not I, but these—my wife, my
    family.

  The king sent here requesting all details.

  It took me weeks to draft them, had to turn

  My methods upside down and inside out,

  And mass and multiply and magnify,

  Till truth was large enough for all to see it.

  Meantime, what gaze had I to fix upon

  My earnings? They all fled, and now——

DIEGO. I see.

  No watch-dog keeps a creditor at bay

  Like well-housed earnings.—But we heard no
    talk

  Of pay.

COLUMBUS. When it was clearly promised?—
    what?

  [Then I, who trusted in the royal word

  And gave it currency, am made for this

  A charlatan who trades upon a cheat?]

DIEGO. And worse. He holds your charts.

COLUMBUS.   He keeps them?—Why—
   With truth, the longer kept, the longer
      thought of;
   And thinking feeds conviction.   On my soul,
   The king will let me sail yet.   You shall see.
BARTHOLOMEW.   Oh no, not you!
COLUMBUS.   Not me, not me?—and why?
DIEGO.   My brother, all your draughts, your
      work for years
   Rest like a charter in another's hands.
   That other is the pilot of a ship
   Now sailing west; and his head is decreed
   To wear the wreath for what your own con-
      ceived.
COLUMBUS.   Impossible!
DIEGO.   I tell the truth.
COLUMBUS.   His name?
DIEGO.   A secret—but no cowardly soul like
      his
   Will ever cross the sea.
COLUMBUS.   I could prefer
   He should, than by a failure earn my scheme
   Discredit.
DIEGO.   Which he surely will.
COLUMBUS.   Too true!
[DIEGO.   Oh, curse the king!
COLUMBUS.   But could you have conceived
   Such baseness?
DIEGO.   Why ask me?   Am I the devil?]

COLUMBUS. What reasons could he have?

DIEGO. Enough of them
  In such a world!—You, you have genius,
    brains;
  And those without them must get even with
    you,
  If not by higher then by lower means.
  You are original and they derived;
  And thought full-centered in itself, owns not
  A parentage that puts another first.
  And you are foreign, they are Portuguese.

COLUMBUS. But such dishonor in a king!

DIEGO. Why not?
  A king is human; place is relative;
  Down honor, and you boost dishonor up.
  Make men in common kneel, and common men
  Stand up like giants. Banish out of sight
  The bright minds, and the dull ones beam
    like beacons.

  (*A knocking is heard at the Right Entrance.*)
      Enter—Left—the MAID.

MAID. My master?

COLUMBUS (*to the* MAID). Well?

MAID. Your wife desires to see
  you.

COLUMBUS. I come; but there is knocking at
  the door.

      Exit—Right—the MAID.

  (COLUMBUS *continues to his brothers.*)

12

If she were not so ill now, I should leave
This Portugal forever.

BARTHOLOMEW.   Yes; you should.

COLUMBUS.   There certainly is elsewhere enter-
    prise
With honesty.   I think that I should try
The court of England.   You have seen their
    men:—
White skinned, the spirit just behind the face,
Their very faults the proof they are not false;
Too impudent for truthlessness, too bold
To stab behind one's back, too proud of push
To trip with little tricks, too fond of sport
To keep one down, when down.

BARTHOLOMEW.   Why, I might go there.

COLUMBUS.   You might and would, Bartholo-
    mew?

BARTHOLOMEW.   I will.

      Enter—Right—the MAID.

COLUMBUS (*to* MAID).   A visitor?

MAID.   A message from the king.

DIEGO.   We thought it coming.   Now you are
    prepared.

COLUMBUS.   My soul demands in one whom I
    obey
A moral equal, at the least.   It comes
In vain.   (*to the* MAID.)
      And messengers?

MAID.   Yes.

Columbus.   Show them in.
> *Exit—Right—*Maid. *The eyes of* Colum-
> bus *follow her, and look through the*
> *door, which she leaves ajar.*

Breviesca?   He alone makes both of them
Birds of most evil omen.

*Enter—Right—*Breviesca, *a* Companion, *and*
the Maid, *who exits at the Left.   All bow.*
                    Gentlemen?—

And will you sit?
> (*He motions towards seats.   Their manner*
> *indicates refusal, and they remain*
> *standing.*)

Breviesca.   I thank you, no.   The king
Sends here requesting you to visit him.

Columbus.   Requesting me to visit him?   For
what?

Breviesca.   Your charts.—He would examine
them with you.

Columbus.   With what intent?

Breviesca.   To satisfy you——

Columbus.   Me?
[Why, I am satisfied remaining here.

Breviesca.   But he demands your presence.

Columbus.   He demands?
Ah, not for my sake,—but for his, you come.]
He sends me then the means with which to go?

Breviesca.   How so?

Columbus.   The money? or conveyance?

BREVIESCA.   What?

COLUMBUS.   I need the one or other.

DIEGO.   Certainly.

BREVIESCA.   But when the king demands——

COLUMBUS (*in a hesitating way*). He promised me
  A sum of money for my charts. I thought——

BREVIESCA.   You dare dispute the royal will?

COLUMBUS.   I dare
  Do nothing to impugn the royal honor.

  Enter—Left—the MAID, *evidently in distress.*

MAID.   My master?

COLUMBUS.   Why, what is it?

MAID.   She—seems—dying.

COLUMBUS.   What, what? my wife?

  (*He starts for the door at the Left—*BREVIESCA
        makes a gesture of disapproval.)

BREVIESCA.   Give us your answer first.

COLUMBUS.   You press this now?

BREVIESCA.   We represent the king.
  Do you forget that he must be supreme?

COLUMBUS.   I do in presence of a Higher King.
  Oh, what has happened?

  *Exeunt—Left—*COLUMBUS *and the* MAID.

BREVIESCA (*bowing sarcastically to* DIEGO *and*
        BARTHOLOMEW).   What we shall report.

  *Exeunt—Right—*BREVIESCA *and his* COM-
        PANION.

[BARTHOLOMEW (*starting to call* BREVIESCA *back*).
  Ah, Diego, if the king excuse this yet——

DIEGO.   His creditors who hear of it will not.
       (*pointing toward the Left.*)
  If she be flown, I fear we all must fly.
BARTHOLOMEW.   But why should he so suffer!—
    I half think
  In truth to spirit there is that which makes
  All earth its enemy.
DIEGO.   Yet conquers it.
  *Exeunt—Right—*BARTHOLOMEW *and* DIEGO.]

CURTAIN.   END OF ACT I.

ACT SECOND.

SCENE FIRST:—*A Spanish camp by night, lighted up by distant camp-fires. Backing at the Left a gateway into a plaza reserved for royalty. At the Right, the tent of* COLUMBUS, *its curtains drawn aside revealing a cot or lounge on which two or more can sit, also a chair or two. Just outside the same tent on the side toward the center of the stage is a log on which two or more can sit. To the Left of the stage are trees. Entrances at the Left Center through the royal gateway; at the Right, behind the tent of* COLUMBUS; *also through his tent and between his tent and the audience; and at the Left, Rear and Front, through trees.*

Enter—Right, from behind the tent of Columbus —a MOOR *with a* COMPANION.

[MOOR (*to his* COMPANION). Darkness for deeds
      of darkness!   Thank the stars,
We well nigh touch the queen's pavilion; yet
In all this Christian camp, blood-red as life,
Not one suspects the Moor—this heathen
      worm

Who wriggles toward its core. Her tent!—
    steal in!
  (*addressing his steel dirk as he looks at it, then
        lifts it upward.*)
Be that our motto: Steel in, till we start.
The spirit of the queen, steel it away!
Hark!—some one comes here. Let us hide.—
    Aha!
    (*looks around, then apparently the two hide
       in the folds of the canvas at the Back
       of the tent of* COLUMBUS.)
Convenient folds these!—Thank you, Chris-
    tian friends.]
Enter—Left-Rear—a SENTRY, *and guards the
    gateway.*
Exeunt—Right—behind the tent of COLUMBUS—
    the MOOR *and his* COMPANION.
Enter—Right—through this tent, DIEGO *and*
    COLUMBUS, *dressed as a soldier.*
    (*The two are at first inside the tent ; but, as
       they talk, they gradually come out onto
       the stage in front of it.*)
COLUMBUS. Have heard from England and
    Bartholomew?
DIEGO. I have.
COLUMBUS.   He had success?
DIEGO.   They thought us
    fools.
  And how fared you in Genoa and Venice?

COLUMBUS.   They knew we were.   I half be-
    lieve that flight
Was all that saved me from a mad-house.   [Oh,
The world plays tyrant to the soul would
    serve it.
It treats him like a female relative
Whose drudgery is deemed supremely paid
By her own love.   But when the wage one
    wants
Is not within one, love is never paid.]
DIEGO.   Yes, yes; I fear that we must give it up.
COLUMBUS.   My voyage?
DIEGO.   Yes.
COLUMBUS.   Not till I die; and that
I will do soon as hope dies out of me.
DIEGO.   You have enlisted?
COLUMBUS.   It will help me on.
Men judge of us by standards in themselves;
And so like us when they see us like them.
Kings take to tales, too, writ with points like
    this—
    (*pointing, with a gesture, to his sword.*)
To underscore "your humble servant" when
He signs requests.
            Enter—Left—two young OFFICERS.   *They
            stand looking at* COLUMBUS *and*
            DIEGO, *making signs to indicate that
            they consider* COLUMBUS *out of his
            mind.*   COLUMBUS *notices them.*

DIEGO. And have you met the king?

COLUMBUS. Am waiting for a chance——

DIEGO. It promises?
What seem your prospects?

COLUMBUS (*pointing to the officers*).
Watch those men and see.
We ape sign-language here. Theirs means
"Columbus."
The women, children, all have learned it, too.
And point it now and then with exclamations.

DIEGO (*glancing angrily at the men*). Outrageous! I will stop them.

COLUMBUS (*staying him with his hand*). Why,
what use?
Far better have men point at us and laugh,
Than never have them point to us at all.

DIEGO. Do you say this, who were so sensitive,
High-spirited?

*Exeunt—Left—*OFFICERS.

COLUMBUS. One may have so much sense
It holds the spirit down. Besides, our spheres
Are stagnant and need movement. Make
men take
You gravely if you can; if not, what though
They laugh? You move them that way.
There are times
The tiniest tinklings that can tap the air
Ring up life's curtain for its grandest acts.

DIEGO. You talk as if all friends were lost.

COLUMBUS. Nay, light,
It trails the shadow. It is those with friends
Are sure of foes; and only those with neither
Are sure of neither.

DIEGO. Then you have friends?

COLUMBUS. Yes.

DIEGO. What class of people?

COLUMBUS. Oh, both Dukes and Dons;
And, to make life complete, at least one woman.

DIEGO. Aha!

COLUMBUS. The image of my lost Felipa.

DIEGO. You mean to marry her?

[COLUMBUS. Had I the wish
I could not have the will. Her family
Are not agreeable——

DIEGO. To you?

COLUMBUS. To her,
When seen with me; and—well!—enough
For one man to have sacrificed one woman
To appease what he esteems as God.

DIEGO. How so?

COLUMBUS. A woman craves attention and a
home.
Her lover's mission, let it oft withdraw
His ear or sphere from her, seems then her rival.

DIEGO. It would not, did she love the man's
true self.

COLUMBUS. Perhaps,—and yet the kinds of
love men feel

For mistress and for mission are so like!——
What, if behind the mission's love should be
Some sentient spirit too in realms unseen?
These women may be right.   They may have
        rivals.
But what Felipa felt I could not help.
Yet may avoid its repetition.
Diego (*doubtfully*).   Humph!]
Columbus.   This one is but a sister, name more
        sacred
Than wife, I think, as wives go now.
Diego.   She thinks
    This too?
Columbus.   She should, and you?
Diego.   I think, perhaps,
You ought to marry.
Columbus.   Oh no! I have vowed
Religiously—
Diego.   And might not be the first
Religion led astray.
[Columbus.   Astray! how so?
Diego.   A brotherly or sisterly regard
Grows up from family relationship.
Train boys and girls together, side by side,
As in one loyal household, holding all
Humanity, and then, perchance, may love's
        dishonor
Seem foul as incest, and imperilers of it,
No longer vehicles of life humane.

Unsouled of self-control, all flag themselves
The death-trucks that they are, and make
    health scud
From their contagion as from carrion.
COLUMBUS.   You mean——
DIEGO.   The young are not so trained in Spain——
Not schooled to know each other, soul by soul;
And nothing but the soul can outweigh sense.
COLUMBUS.   In general, true!—but she——
DIEGO.   Our lives reflect
The light of our surroundings.   What are
    here?—
Accursèd customs that mistrust the soul,
Ay, robe its every feature in their rags,
Draped all to hint unshapeliness beneath.
Away with earthly habits that can hide
God's image framed within!]

    Enter—Left—the MONK, JUAN PEREZ,
    another MONK, *the officer* SANCHEZ,
    and several SOLDIERS.

COLUMBUS (*looking toward the* MONK).   Why,
    who are these?
PEREZ (*to* COLUMBUS).
    God greet you friends.
COLUMBUS.   His messengers are welcome.
PEREZ.   And doubly so if from Jerusalem?
COLUMBUS.   The holy city?
PEREZ.   Yes.   The grand Soldan
Of Egypt sent us.

COLUMBUS. With a message?

PEREZ. Yes.
　He vows, in case the Spaniard will not stay
　This war against the Moor, to rouse the East,
　Pull down all Christian churches, and beneath
　Entomb their worshipers.

COLUMBUS. He thinks this threat
　Will influence Ferdinand?

SANCHEZ. It should not.

SOLDIER. No.

COLUMBUS. But must the faithful suffer?

PEREZ. They do now.
　At each pretext oppressed, reviled, and robbed
　Of property and freedom, flayed and hung,
　And heaven knows what; for it gets most of
　　them.

[SANCHEZ. That should not be.

PEREZ. Ah, when what should be is,
　What is will be beyond this earth.

SANCHEZ. When once
　Old Spain's white line of ships have tailed for
　　good
　This flying kite here of the Moor, and cleared
　The blue about us, there should rest no ship
　Not steered to right our brethren there.

SOLDIER. Not one.

PEREZ (*to* SANCHEZ). Would you go?

SANCHEZ. Ay, I would.

PEREZ. The time may come——

SANCHEZ (*to* SOLDIERS).

  Meanwhile, the Moor! Now, to your sta-
    tions— march.]

  *Exeunt—Left—*SANCHEZ *and* SOLDIERS.

DIEGO (*glancing at the* MONKS, *and speaking
    aside to* COLUMBUS).

  They seek the king—might speak for you, not
    so?

COLUMBUS (*to* DIEGO). They might.

  (*To the* MONKS.) Would you not rest with
    us to-night?

PEREZ. We thank you—and your name?

    (*The* MONKS *and* DIEGO, *as* COLUMBUS
      gestures to them, enter the tent of
      COLUMBUS *and sit.* COLUMBUS *sits
      on the log to the left of his tent with
      his back to the rear.*)

COLUMBUS.   Columbus.

PEREZ.   Oh!

    Have heard of you.

COLUMBUS.   Heard good?

PEREZ.   Why—

COLUMBUS.   Ah, have not.

  I understand. The silence of the good

  Damns more than bad men's curses. Yet
    my aims

  Are one with yours—to speed the truth to
    all.

  But "all" means more than most men deem.

PEREZ. The wise
Aim not beyond their reach.

COLUMBUS. The faithful aim
Wherever they are called.

PEREZ. You heard the call
Just made?

COLUMBUS. And not a breast could out-thrill
mine
With indignation at the tale.

PEREZ. It failed
To stir your lip to pledges.

COLUMBUS. When heaven crowns
My present plan——

PEREZ. You will be like your mates,—
Ennobled, rich, and found a family.

COLUMBUS. My western mission is for Christ
alone.
Pray heaven with me that I fulfill it; then
I vow to live a life like yours, and more—
To give it to this Eastern mission. See—
(*drawing his sword and showing the cross form-
ing its hilt.*)
This cross—it aims the sword I wield!—will
find
No final rest, till waved above the crescent.

PEREZ. You seem a holy man.

COLUMBUS. Nay, none is that.
When men seem holy do not think of
them,

But of the cause that has affected them.

Exit—Left Rear—the Sentry *guarding the
gateway, apparently called away.*

Enter—Left Center, from the gateway—
Beatrix. *She comes forward stealthily
and touches* Columbus *on his back,
then withdraws toward the Right Rear,
behind his tent.*

(Columbus *rises, looking back and around as if
for* Beatrix.)

Perez (*to the other* Monk).   He seems inspired
by purposes well worth
Regard.

Columbus (*to* Diego).   Diego, will you guide
our friends
Across the pathway to our other tent?—
One waits here who has business with me.

Exeunt—Right—through the tent of Columbus, Diego *and the two* Monks.

Enter—Right—from behind the same tent,
Beatrix

Columbus.   You, Beatrix? and here?—this
time of night?
[Have you forgot?   Your father——

Beatrix.   Is a bird,
Flown southward, wrong, forgetting for a time
The winter whence it fled?

Columbus.   But there are ways——]

Beatrix.   I am not welcome then?

COLUMBUS. Oh no—not that—
   [But unexpected.
BEATRIX. I have heard you say
   Good fortune would be so.
COLUMBUS. You bring it, then?]
BEATRIX. One door ajar to it. These worthy
      friars,
   Just in your tent, I hear, will see the king.
   They might commend you.
COLUMBUS. Yes, I thank you.
BEATRIX. Well?
COLUMBUS. More?
BEATRIX. You seem cold.
COLUMBUS. The night is.
BEATRIX. I am not.
COLUMBUS. No, no, forgive me.
BEATRIX. I have more to say.
   The Dona Bobadilla——
COLUMBUS. Your old foe?
BEATRIX. New friend; for your sake made and
      kept a friend
   [By courtesies limbering my stiff limbs of pride
   Till limp and limping as humility.
COLUMBUS. But really——
BEATRIX. Really, when one's inward sense
   Of mastership outweighs an outward show
   Of servitude, why, one but serves herself.]
   This Dona Bobadilla has in view
   To urge your claims upon the queen.

13

COLUMBUS. She has?—
What is it makes a woman serve as you
A mere enthusiast without success?

BEATRIX. No need were there to serve one with
success.

COLUMBUS. But failure——

BEATRIX. Shows a spirit as it is.
It throws one's manhood into full relief,
Stript of all circumstance and accident.

COLUMBUS. This heart of mine were heavy
were it not
Made light and bright by eyes that can detect,
Beneath all veils disguising what it is,
Its one sole virtue.—You forget that all
The world is full of brains, and all the brains
Of whims, and all that gives the whims more
worth
Than blood that churns them up to con-
sciousness,
Is that they leave the brain and live in deeds.
Mine have not done this yet.

BEATRIX (*sitting on the log to the left of the tent
of Columbus, and in doing so, letting the
shawl that she has worn fall from her
on to the ground behind the log. Columbus stands at the right, and after a little
while sits beside her*).
The deed that best
Proves each man's workmanship is what he is.

If God be the eternal, he who shows
Eternal perseverance falls not far
From fellow-craft with Him.

COLUMBUS. You, like a myth,
Are not inspired, but yet inspiring; not
Religion, but could make a man religious.

BEATRIX. You speak in figures.

COLUMBUS. We all live in them.

BEATRIX. What then?

COLUMBUS. Why, they are beautiful.

BEATRIX. And this
Gives life its beauty?

COLUMBUS. Ay, and interest.
For every time a spirit veiled in them
Reveals itself, why, it anticipates
The resurrection of the soul, not so?
And that brings heaven.

BEATRIX. Then to reveal myself——

COLUMBUS. Is very much in such a world as
this—
When owning so much that is worth revealing.

BEATRIX. You jest.

COLUMBUS. I am in earnest. When one needs
More strength of spirit, nothing save a spirit
Can ever give it. You have given me
yours.

BEATRIX. In truth I have. Not seldom I have
thought
That I could lose my soul to give it you.

COLUMBUS.   Thank God, a brother's love need
      not accept
   The sacrifice.—But—should we linger here?
   Your——
BEATRIX.   Well?
COLUMBUS.   Your relatives—
BEATRIX.   Of flesh, or soul?
   I care but for the latter.   You——
COLUMBUS.   But yet
   Their reasons are the world's.   We live in
      Spain.
   You are—
BEATRIX.   A virgin, yes, but were I *the*——
COLUMBUS.   Do not say that—
BEATRIX.   I could imagine times
   When one I know would seem divine.
COLUMBUS.   Wait, wait!—
   How near together heaven and hell may be!
BEATRIX.   Yes; only earth and earthly thinking
      make
   It possible for sense to deem them two.
   Throne God in hell, all heaven would burst the
      gates
   And dream of blessèd rest, though every foot
   Were sea'd upon a prostrate seething devil.

> *Enter—Right—from behind Columbus' tent
> —the* MOOR.   *He looks at* COLUMBUS
> *and* BEATRIX *then begins to draw
> toward himself her shawl that lies*

> *on the ground behind her.* COLUMBUS
> *looks back. The* MOOR *draws away*
> *and wraps the shawl about himself.*
> COLUMBUS *rises.*)

BEATRIX.   Some one was listening?

COLUMBUS.   Yes—keep still.

> *Exit—Left Center—through the gateway—*
> *the* MOOR.   COLUMBUS *sees him.*

                                   I see
A form.   It disappeared there through the
   gate.

BEATRIX.   My shawl on?

COLUMBUS.   Yes.

BEATRIX.   Why, all the ladies' tents—
   The queen's—are reached through that.   I
   follow.

COLUMBUS.   No—
A thief,—assassin, may be.   No, let me—
      (*advancing toward the gateway.*)

BEATRIX (*stopping him*).   Be thought a cul-
   prit?—never!

COLUMBUS (*handing her a dirk.*)   Then take this,
And call me.   I will keep in hearing.—God!
I cannot bear to let you go.

BEATRIX.   I must.

> *Exit—Left Center—through the gateway—*
> BEATRIX *with the dirk in hand.*
> *Enter—Right—through* COLUMBUS'   *tent—*
> DIEGO.

COLUMBUS (*to* DIEGO).   You must have over-
      heard?

DIEGO.   I did—in part.

[COLUMBUS. How brave in her! Yet what
      could one expect!

How brave in her to let me know her love!

And what unnatural, unmanned man am I,

Who does not, will not dare, return it her!

Strange mixture life is of the right and
      wrong!

Should one be good, or kind? and which is
      which?

How much that seems in line for both is
      but

A ray that falls to form a pathway here

From the rent forms of clouds beyond our
      reach

Which, while they let the light in, bring the
      storm!]

      (*Distant Voices are heard calling.*)

Hark, hark!—What is it that they call?—

DISTANT VOICE.   A Moor!

COLUMBUS.   (*Shouting*) A Moor! (*to* DIEGO)
      You rouse the Camp!

   Exit—Left Center—through the gateway—
      COLUMBUS.

      Enter—Left Rear—the SENTRY.

DIEGO (*shouting*). A Moor! A Moor!

      *Exit—Left—*DIEGO.

Enter—Left Front—and Exeunt—Left Center,
*through the gateway—*SANCHEZ *and* SOL-
DIERS.

VOICES (*from within the gateway*).
Ay, ay, take this and that.

*Enter—from the Gateway—*SANCHEZ, COLUMBUS,
and SOLDIERS *dragging the* MOOR.

SANCHEZ. Here—drag him out!
Is dead already—Humph!—is limp enough
To make a rug of! Let him lie!

Enter—Left Rear—other SOLDIERS, *the officer*
GUTIERREZ *and the* KING.

GUTIERREZ. The King.
(*All salute. The* KING *looks at the* MOOR.)

KING. Who is he?

SANCHEZ. An assassin—sought the queen—
Got by the guard.

KING. He did not reach her?

SANCHEZ. No.
(*pointing to* COLUMBUS).
Well nigh! He tracked him in, and thwarted
him.

KING (*to* COLUMBUS). Ay, ay! Your name?

COLUMBUS. Columbus.

KING (*to all*). Now to rest.
(*to* COLUMBUS.)
But you may come with me—Would see you
further.

Exeunt—Left Center—through the gateway—

King, Gutierrez, *and* Columbus.
Exeunt at other entrances, all except the
Sentry.

CURTAIN

Scene Second.—*Council Chamber in the Do-*
minican Convent of St. Stephen at Salamanca.
Wood paneling in ceiling and walls. A long
table in the Rear with chairs beside it and at
the rear. Entrances at the Right and Left.
        *Enter—Left—*Zalora *and* Fernandez.

Fernandez.   All here?

Zalora.   Oh yes.   One must obey the king.

Fernandez.   He must suppose the times ahead
        are dark.

Zalora.   How so?

Fernandez.   In giving us this *pastime* here.

Zalora.   We have our holy days and holidays.
    I sometimes wonder which are holier.

Fernandez.   What, what! and you a priest?

Zalora.   An old one—yes.
    Like other earthly things, our lives move on
    Half light, half shadow, and with me
    The shadows came in youth.

Fernandez.   Your brilliancy
    Developed late, eh? like a day when foggy—
    Or lightning from a cloud.   But you are right.
    This life is like a bladder-air-ball.   If
    You press its youth-side in, you, by-and-by,

Will bulge its age-side out; and, say, does
that
Make preachers, eh? sensational? You should
know.

ZALORA. You think sensations are acquired?

Enter—Right—St. ANGEL and PEREZ and exchange greetings with FERNANDEZ and ZALORA.

FERNANDEZ. I know
A soul that squeals well, is a soul well squeezed.
Sensation is the stepson of depression.
You step on——

ZALORA. Oh, go to!—that spoils the form.

ST. ANGEL. What form?

FERNANDEZ (*to* ST. ANGEL). Why, of a ball.
(*To* ZALORA) Not so?—Tell why
These balls—our children's balls—are like a
bishop.

PEREZ (*laughing and pointing to* ZALORA).
Because, like him, they usually are *round?*

ST. ANGEL. And sometimes, though not always,
holy, eh?

ZALORA (*good-naturedly*).
Why point your wit with personality?

ST. ANGEL. Oh never, when the person is
around.
But now the child's ball?—

FERNANDEZ. Why, the *bawl* is made
(*brings his hands down as if ordaining, and also
striking a blow.*)

By laying on of hands.
> (*All laugh.*)

> *Enter—Right—*MENDOZA *and* TALAVERA.
> *Enter—Left—*ARANA, FONSECA, BREVIESCA
> *and others. All in, or entering, the*
> *hall exchange greetings.*

TALAVERA (*to* FERNANDEZ). What were you
doing?

FERNANDEZ. Our duty here—ordaining nonsense. [You
Should know. You sent for us.

ZALORA.   And why for me?
Am I an expert on insanity?

FERNANDEZ (*to* ZALORA). Oh no, your place is
on beyond that.

ZALORA.   How?

FERNANDEZ. Beyond an *x*pert is a *y-z*-pert.

ZALORA. Quite low down in the alphabet of
wit!

FERNANDEZ. I know—the *last* of it—just
where you *shoe* it.

FONSECA (*to* ARANA *in another part of the hall*).
But think—the danger.

ARANA.   He will never sail!

FONSECA. Not that I mean, but in his theories.
You know they contradict the church.

ARANA.   If this
Be true—

FONSECA. It is,—is very serious.

FERNANDEZ (*to* FONSECA).

   And what of that? I say the best of physics
   For seriousness is laughter. Where is bile,
   Well tickled throats will throw it up.

FONSECA.   To fool

   With fools is feeding folly.

FERNANDEZ.   Feed a fool

   On folly, and he grows so fat, you think,
   That soon all wisdom's world that he would
      sit on,
   Would it not die itself, must make him
      diet?

FONSECA. Oh, cease your jesting!

FERNANDEZ.   To have gravity,

   We ought to have grave work to do.

FONSECA.   We have,

   As a commission sitting on Columbus.]

       All begin to take places around the table,
       though not yet to sit. TALAVERA *goes to*
       the central seat behind it, MENDOZA
       to his right, and ST. ANGEL *and* PEREZ
       to the right of MENDOZA. FONSECA,
       BREVIESCA, ARANA, ZALORA *and*
       FERNANDEZ *are at* TALAVERA'S *Left.*
       Others go where there are places.

[FERNANDEZ.   (*aside to* ZALORA *alone.*) He

   thinks an old hen, even, doing that,
   Should hatch out something.

ZALORA.   Wait now. You will find

Enough old hens here to bring forth, at least,
What they will think worth while their
    cackling over.
St. Angel (*who overhears* Zalora, *to* Perez).
    Instead of hens, I think that I should call
    them
    Birds of *another's feather*—birds of *prey*.
Perez.   In *praying* they do priest's work.
St. Angel.   Yes; in that—
    And making mortals humble.   One with aught
    To plume himself on, will not go unplucked.
    But see—the victim.]
                *Enter—Right—*Columbus.
Talavera (*to those in the chamber*).
                          Friends, the Mariner.
            (*to* Columbus *and all.*)
    I think that you have met before.
        (Columbus *and all exchange greetings.*)
                                [And now
    We get to work.]
            The others sit. Talavera *motions to*
                Columbus *to do the same, which he*
.   *does at the extreme Right.*
            [Where thought appeals to thought,
    The only sovereign is the wisest word,
    Which sometimes is the last word;—any
        way,
    Is always of the spirit, and needs not
    Accoutrements and courtesies of form

To prove its prestige. We can waive them,
    then,
And let the spirit prompt us as it may.]
       (*turning to* COLUMBUS.)
They say you wish to have a fleet and men,
And outfit, too, involving much expense.
What reasons have you?

COLUMBUS.   To extend the sway
Of Spain and Christianity in lands
Where now they are not known.

TALAVERA.   That wish is ours.
What proof have you, though, that these
    lands exist?

COLUMBUS. Reports of mariners—authority—
The nature of the world.

TALAVERA.   Do these off-set
The dangers?

COLUMBUS.   Which ones?

ARANA.   Like the boiling waves
Of Africa, and giants on the shores.

COLUMBUS. Mere fables, all! Why, I myself
    have sailed
To Guinea, past where these were said to be.
[And have you never heard of Eudoxus
Of Cyzicus, who left Arabia
And reached Gibraltar! how too from Gibral-
    tar
The Carthaginian Hanno, sailing back,
Came to Arabia?

FONSECA.   All pagan lies!

COLUMBUS.   A statement that confutes a
    general faith
  At risk of reputation; yet meantime
  Confirms our natural reasoning, seldom lies.
  Who would have said this, had it not been
    true?
  Yet that it should be, what more natural?

ZALORA.   But sailing east is not the same as
    west.

COLUMBUS.   Enough is known to warrant even
    that.

FERNANDEZ.   St. Brandan and the seven cities,
    yes!
  But these have always melted into clouds
  To those who sought them.

COLUMBUS.   Other lands are told of.

MENDOZA.   Atlantis, eh?

COLUMBUS.   Yes, and Antilla too,
  Well known to Carthage, Aristotle says.
  And many a modern vessel has been driven
  Where shores have been descried by accident
  And other signs of——

FONSECA.   Desert islands.

COLUMBUS.   No.]
  Vicenti, twenty score of leagues beyond
  The Cape St. Vincent, came on floating wood
  Carved by men's hands.

ZALORA.   Ay, from some other ship.

COLUMBUS. Then lost in many places. Wood
    carved thus
  Was found by my own brother-in-law, Correo.
  And plants and trees too drift thus from the
    west.
FONSECA. Washed there, washed back.
COLUMBUS. No, different in kind
  From any in the East. They found besides
  Two men's forms cast upon the isle of Flores,
  With features not at all like people here.
ARANA. And what of that?
COLUMBUS. The men—not only they—
  The trees, the plants, were like in kind to those
  Described by Polo and by Mandeville
  As found in those great lands of Gengis Khan
  And Prester John, far in the Indies.
ARANA. They
  Were east, not west.
COLUMBUS. Just so, both east and west.
FERNANDEZ. What, what?
BREVIESCA (*to* FERNANDEZ). You see——
COLUMBUS. It seems a contradiction.
  It could not, did you think the world were
    round.
[FONSECA (*laughing*). No, never, no!
ARANA. No, never!
ZALORA (*to* COLUMBUS *sarcastically*). You are
    right.
COLUMBUS. There is authority for thinking this.

ARANA.   For fancying it, yes; or anything.

COLUMBUS.   But Aristotle, Seneca and Pliny
Say one can sail from Cadiz to the Indies.

TALAVERA.   Yet wait.   Besides this, is it not
a fact
That they too calculated three years' time,—
Enough to starve a ship's crew ten times
over——
Before her cruise could compass it?

COLUMBUS.   Some did;
Yet, judging by the globe of Ptolemy,
Compared with one by Marinus of Tyre,
A third of it alone rests unexplored,—
Eight hours of twenty-four.   You measure
this.
It seems not more than seven hundred leagues.

FONSECA.   You measure it?—The whole of it
is fancy.

ARANA.   Yes;—not a ray of reason in it!

FONSECA.   No.]

ARANA (*to* COLUMBUS).   And, if the world were
round—what, then, forsooth?—
Could sail around it, without tumbling off?

FONSECA (*to* ZALORA).   Ay, or without the
water's tumbling off?

ARANA.   Same thing!

FERNANDEZ (*good-naturedly to* COLUMBUS).
I think that you must be the man
That once I heard of, though I never saw him.

Who wants to turn the whole world upside-
    down——

FONSECA.   Where roots of trees bear leaves, and
    rain spurts up.

BREVIESCA.   Oh, he would feel at home there—
    let him go!

His head feels upside-down without the going.

FERNANDEZ.   You wait and hear the whole tale.
    They examined

The feet of those they found at Flores; not so?

ZALORA.   They did?

FERNANDEZ.   Oh, yes! and found them shaped
    like spiders',

Made to walk up like this.

          (*gesturing with his hands.*)

[BREVIESCA.   Like those one sees

Clawed on a pictured devil.

FONSECA.   If he sail,

He soon may see them too upon a reàl one.

TALAVERA.   Severe!

FONSECA.   I mean it; ay, I speak the truth.

The holy father, St. Augustine, shows it:

Men formed like this—to walk thus upside-
    down—

Could not be sons of Adam.   Did they live,

It would upset our whole historic base

Of Christian faith.

ARANA.   Just so!

FONSECA.   To argue it

14

At all, grant it conceivable—involves
Clear heresy.

ZALORA.   Hear, hear!

ARANA.   Quite right!

BREVIESCA.   Ay, ay.

COLUMBUS.   But are you sure these men are not
     like us?

FONSECA.   Humph, you would practice many
     years before
You walked with your heels up.

COLUMBUS.   But there, as here,
The earth may seem to be below one.

ARANA.   Ah!
We grant to fancy, man, a certain flight—
Have witnessed one to-day. But do you
     dream
Her wings could turn us all to flies
Without our knowing it?

COLUMBUS.   There may be laws
Of nature past our understanding.

BREVIESCA.   Yes.
He means that when we lose our under-
     standing—
Has had experience of that—why then——]

TALAVERA.   Come, no more nonsense, gentle-
     men.

ZALORA (*rising*).   No more?
Time to adjourn then, eh?   Is nothing else
Before the house.

COLUMBUS (*rising to address* ZALORA).

        In such a case as this,
 In which none know the truth——
FONSECA (*rising*).   Your pardon, but
 The Scripture says: "He stretcheth out the
  heavens"—
 How?—like a ball?—No, no; but "like a
  tent."
 You dare throw doubt upon the word of Him
 Who framed creation?
COLUMBUS.   What you quote is but
 A figure.
FONSECA.   Fiction?
COLUMBUS.   Figure—not the same.
[BREVIESCA. Accuse of figuring—Him who
  knows the end
 From the beginning—all the sum at once?
 He does not figure up. He counts the whole.
TALAVERA (*to* BREVIESCA). Oh, you mistake
  his meaning!
BREVIESCA (*looking around incredulously*).
         What?
FERNANDEZ (*to* BREVIESCA).   Yes, yes.]
COLUMBUS. Were one upon the other side the
  globe,
 The heavens might seem as like a tent as here.
FONSECA. They only might? The Scripture
  says they do.
 You make it doubtful?

BREVIESCA.   Heretic!

ARANA.   Too true!

COLUMBUS.   My one desire, the purpose of my
      life
   Is to become an earthly instrument
   Through which the Scriptures may become
      fulfilled,
   That all the ends of earth—they are ends
      now—
   Be brought together with one Lord and God.

FONSECA.   What good would this do, if His
      word were false?

COLUMBUS (*in surprise*).   You think I doubt it.

FONSECA.   We have heard you term
   Its affirmations figures, argue down—
   And that with pagan proofs—the fathers.
      Truth
   Can never change.

COLUMBUS.   We can.

FONSECA.   And change it?

COLUMBUS.   Change
   Its bearings for us.   Truth is of the heaven:
   The mind regarding it is of the earth.
   [The one is infinite, the other finite:
   The one expressed in light itself, the other
   In forms that but reflect light; and the truth,
   Made such but by reflection, cannot flash
   An equal ray to every view-point.

SEVERAL.   Oh!]

COLUMBUS. Give blind men sight. At first
their new-viewed sun
Will stand still in the heaven. But give them
time,
That sun will set and rise. Then give them
space,
Lift them a thousand miles above the soil,
It may do neither.

ARANA. Dangerous doctrine that!

FONSECA (*to* COLUMBUS). No truth then, eh?

COLUMBUS. Yes; truth enough for all.
But truth expressed is coin to use, not hoard.
For when it bears the stamp of times too
old,
It loses current value.

FONSECA. Hear that! hear!
Why, that blasphemes tradition!

BREVIESCA. Just as if
Antiquity itself did not prove truth!

COLUMBUS. The moonlight guides us, if we
have no sun.
But forms that loom at midnight lie to those
Who know them in the day; and in the day
No judgment of the distance can be true
Except for him who pushes on to reach it.

[FONSECA. Hold! Hold! Enough of this!
There is a law
That ought to be enforced here.

ARANA. We shall see!

COLUMBUS.   The world will see in time that I am
    right.
  No theory spun for concepts immature
  Can ever fit their full maturity.]
        Enter—Right—an ATTENDANT.
TALAVERA (*rising*).   A moment, gentlemen.
          (*to the* ATTENDANT.)   What is it?
ATTENDANT.   Sire,
  The royal courier.
TALAVERA.   Ah, has come so soon?
          (*to all.*)
  Then for to-day our conference must end.
       (*All who are sitting rise.*)
COLUMBUS (*to* TALAVERA).
  And I withdraw?
TALAVERA (*bowing in assent and adieu to* COLUM-
    BUS).   We thank you for your candor.
(COLUMBUS *bows to all the council, and the council
        to him.*)
*Exeunt—Right —*COLUMBUS *and* ATTENDANT,
      showing him out.
FONSECA (*moving with the others toward the Left*).
  But we must see we have no more of it.
FERNANDEZ (*to* ZALORA, TALAVERA *and* MEN-
    DOZA, *who are walking behind* FONSECA,
    ARANA, BREVIESCA *and others*).
  A spark in hayloft! bull in porcelain!
  Will bring the whole church crackling round
    us yet.

*Exeunt—Left—*F<small>ONSECA</small>, A<small>RANA</small>, B<small>REVIESCA</small>
and others.

M<small>ENDOZA</small> (*to* F<small>ERNANDEZ</small>).
But racy as a bull fight!

F<small>ERNANDEZ</small>. In the which
The bull did some tall tossing.

Exeunt—Left—First M<small>ENDOZA</small>, *then* Z<small>ALORA</small>,
T<small>ALAVERA</small> *and* F<small>ERNANDEZ</small>.

P<small>EREZ</small> (*to* S<small>T</small>. A<small>NGEL</small>). Did you hear?—
Strange words for him!

S<small>T</small>. A<small>NGEL</small>. No; I have always found
The light mind is the bright mind. Wit and
wits
Are twins; without the other each is lacking.

*Exeunt—Right—*S<small>T</small>. A<small>NGEL</small> *and all others.*

———

S<small>CENE</small> T<small>HIRD</small>.—*Exterior of the Convent of La
Rabida, near the little seaport of Palos, in
Andalusia, in Spain. Backing, a wall, behind
which are hills, trees, and a distant sea-view.
At the right, a gateway opening into the Convent.
At the left, trees. Entrances at the Right Rear,
behind the Convent; Right, further forward,
through a gateway opening into the Convent;
Left Rear and Front through trees.*

*Enter—Right Rear—*B<small>EATRIX</small>, *a* M<small>AID</small>, *and*
D<small>IEGO</small> *in out-door costumes.*

B<small>EATRIX</small>. I could not keep him back.

DIEGO. You tried to block
His pathway, eh? but he looked over you—
Beyond you?

BEATRIX. Humph! poor treatment from a
friend!

DIEGO. And you would fill his whole horizon
then?

BEATRIX. Why—in a friend——

DIEGO. Is easy, yes; make friends
Of little souls. Humph! they are common.

BEATRIX (*offended*). What?

DIEGO. A spirit's measure is its outlook. Find
A man horizoned by the whole broad world,
Who sees it all in all, he stands a son
Of God!—is here to do his Father's work;
And you should join in it, or not join him.

BEATRIX. Why should he go to France?—no
sailors there!

DIEGO. A soul when conscious of the highest
mission
Is always on the wing.

BEATRIX. You know our king
Gave weight to what he argued, promised
ships?

DIEGO. But would not place my brother in
command.

BEATRIX. Far safer so!

DIEGO. For whom?

BEATRIX. Your brother.

DIEGO. What?—
　You talked of his own safety to my brother?
BEATRIX. Why, he had done his duty, sown
　　the seed;
　Then why not leave the rest to Providence?
DIEGO. Fling seed to seas, or bid it root in
　　winds;
　But do not trust your thoughts to Providence.
　Their soil is in humanity, nor there
　Spring, grow, or ripen without husbandry.
BEATRIX. He talked and argued——
DIEGO. Oh, to talk the truth
　Is easy as to breathe. To live the truth,
　And, mailed in its pure radiance, burn to
　　black
　The shade its white heat severs, needs a
　　strength
　To suffer hatred and inspire to love,
　Half hell's, half heaven's, and wholly Christ's.
[BEATRIX. And yet
　If others go——
DIEGO. So far off is the goal,
　And so unseen, that all but faith will fail;
　And this they lack.
BEATRIX. But yet, you told him, too,
　You thought it vain to leave here.
DIEGO. Feared it vain.
　But you, you urged him to submit, not sail,
　Nor push his claims upon the king.

BEATRIX.   Of course.

DIEGO.   Poor, lonely man!

BEATRIX.   His own fault—would not have
A soul go with him.

DIEGO.   Why should he?   To minds
In which the spirit so subdues the sense,
A lack of sympathy itself is absence.

BEATRIX.   But you will join him?

DIEGO.   Like a faithful slave
Whom word, not thought, commands.

BEATRIX.   Why should not I go?

DIEGO.   You could not live contented with a
          man
With no home either for himself or you.
He must have told you this.

BEATRIX.   Home seems a state,
Not place.

DIEGO.   A state of happiness, and that
He knows he could not give you.]

BEATRIX.   Do you think
That we shall see him here?

DIEGO.   Why yes, I think
That they will find him; if so, bring him back.
He would not miss a meeting with the queen.

BEATRIX.   You say she lunches with the monks
          to-day?

DIEGO.   I heard so, yes—
          (*pointing toward the Left Rear.*)
                    And look you—she is coming.

BEATRIX.   I have some faith in her.
DIEGO.   Faith always waits
On perfect womanhood.   Show men a form
Whose outward symmetry of nature frames
A symmetry of soul, whose pure-hued face
Complexions pureness of the character,
Whose clear sweet accents outlet clear, sweet
      thought,
Whose burning eyes flash flame from kindled
      love,
And all whose yielding gracefulness of mien
But fitly robes all grace-moved sympathy,—
Ay, find a soul whose outward beauty shields
But brighter beauty of the blade within
By what seems merely ornament,—to her
All men will yield a spirit's loyalty.
The fairy-goddess of the world of fact,
Dream-sister of the brotherhood of deed,
An angel minister as well as queen,
The splendor of her station lifts her high
But like the sun that she may light us all.

Enter—Left Rear—the QUEEN *and* ATTENDANTS,
            among them ST. ANGEL.

            *Enter—at the same time—at the Right
            through the convent's gateway,—*
            MONKS, *among them* PEREZ, *behind
            them* SANCHEZ *and* COLUMBUS.

PEREZ (*to the* QUEEN *to whom all do reverence*).
   We feel much honored by your presence.

QUEEN.　　　　　　　　　　　　Nay,
　You are the ministers of higher power.
　The honor comes to me.

BEATRIX (*to* DIEGO *in the rear*).
　　　　　　　　　Look there—your brother.

DIEGO.　So they have found him.

BEATRIX.　　　　　Hark—they speak of him.

PEREZ.　Your majesty, your couriers have re-
　　　turned.
　They found the Mariner.

QUEEN.　　　　　　Yes, and where?

PEREZ.　　　　　　　　　　　Far up
　The mountains, just beside the boundary.

QUEEN.　Alone?

PEREZ.　　　　Alone.
　　　(*introducing* COLUMBUS.)　The Mariner.
　　　(COLUMBUS *salutes the* QUEEN.)

QUEEN (*to* COLUMBUS).　　　　As I hoped.
　And you were leaving us?

COLUMBUS.　　　　　I was.

QUEEN.　　　　　　　　　　Why so?

COLUMBUS.　I have an aim in life.
　　　'BEATRIX, *in her gestures towards* DIEGO,
　　　　to which she tries to attract the attention
　　　　of COLUMBUS, *expresses disapproval*
　　　　of his answers which follow here.)

QUEEN.　　　　　　　I thought the king
　Had promised ships.

COLUMBUS.　　　　He had.

QUEEN. And officers.

COLUMBUS. Not those for such an undertaking.

QUEEN. You
Can go with them.

COLUMBUS. Your pardon, but—I beg—
Excuse me.

QUEEN. Why?

COLUMBUS. I have no time to waste.

QUEEN. To waste?

COLUMBUS. Full eighteen years ago I first
Made known my plan. I am no longer
young.

QUEEN. Why, ships and men, and you to sail
with them!

COLUMBUS. Sail off, sail back—I have no time
to waste.

QUEEN. You think they would not persevere?

COLUMBUS. The goal
Is not of their discerning.—Why should they
Be thought the ones to bring it to the light?

QUEEN. But they——

COLUMBUS. To them it seems a madman's
whim,
A thing to flout;—to me the one conception
Of all that is most rational and holy.
Which, then, would give his life that it might
live?

QUEEN. Why, we had hopes that none would
need do that.

COLUMBUS.   And hopes well based; yet any man
     who sails
  Across that unknown sea must have far more
  Than enterprise, experience, caution, skill,
  Knowledge of sail and compass, wind and
     star.
  The soul must be embarked upon the voyage
  With aims outreaching all that but concern
  The narrow limits of this earthly life.
QUEEN.   How few such men! Where would
     you find your crew?
COLUMBUS.   Wherever minds are subject to
     ideas.
QUEEN.   And where is that?—You judge men by
     yourself.
COLUMBUS.   I would not dare to boast such
     difference,
  Or so humiliate my humanity,
  As to presume it possible that aims
  Inspiring my own soul, if rightly urged,
  Would not inspire, too, many another.
QUEEN.   Yes,
  I can believe it, with yourself to urge them.
  And were you given command, would you
     collect
  A crew and sail with them?
COLUMBUS.   No man can reach
  A problem's right solution, if he fail
  To calculate aright the means.

QUEEN. Of course—
　And that——
COLUMBUS. Has not been done in this case.
QUEEN. No?—
　What more would you require?
COLUMBUS. Ten times the sum
　That has been promised.
QUEEN. Ten times?—ten times that
　Is not in all the treasury.
COLUMBUS. I would give
　The whole I have—both property and life.
SANCHEZ. And I.
QUEEN. You would?—Yet rich!
SANCHEZ. I would.
DIEGO (*coming forward and bowing before the*
　　　QUEEN). And I,
　Though I have nothing—only what you see.
ST. ANGEL. Your Majesty, with men like these,
　　　preparing
　To root their very spirits out from earth,
　That they may thus transplant them where the
　　　world
　Will reap a richer fruitage, what were Spain,
　Were she to grudge a void from which were
　　　scraped
　A paltry heap of gold! All were too mean
　To pedestal aright the lasting fame
　That would be hers, did they attain their
　　　end

QUEEN.   How true!—and yet the royal treas-
        ury——
ST. ANGEL.   Are there no treasures elsewhere
        than in that?
QUEEN (*hesitating a moment*).
    There are.   If I be queen, let me be queen
    Of Spain's rich spirit as of Spain's rich soil.
    I will—there is a treasure.—What to Spain
    Are her most precious treasures, that star most
    The crown that they surround with living
        light?
    Mere jewels, think you?—Nay, not these, but
        men.
    And if I give the one to gain the other, who
    Could strike a better bargain?   Ay, I will—
    I pledge you the crown jewels of Castile.
    I pledge you the commandership.   Enough!
    When ready, you shall go.
COLUMBUS (*falling on his knees before her*).
                        God bless the queen.
    (*The others fall on their knees beside* COLUMBUS.)

CURTAIN.   END OF ACT II.

ACT THIRD.

SCENE FIRST.—*A street in Palos de Moguer, in Andalusia. Backing, a distant harbor, with ships. At the Right, a porch before the house of* BEATRIX. *At the Left, other houses. Entrances, Right Rear, behind the house of* BEATRIX; *Right, farther forward, through a door opening from this house onto the porch in front of it; Right Front, through the street in front of this house; Left Rear and Front, through streets.*

(*The rising curtain reveals* COLUMBUS *and* BEATRIX, *standing on or near the porch.*)

COLUMBUS.   Now I must off, and see the ships.
        You know
    How long I have been gone.

BEATRIX.   You met the queen?

COLUMBUS. And king, and got their last instructions.

BEATRIX.   Oh,
    I cannot bear to have you sail!

COLUMBUS.   Nor I
    To leave you.

BEATRIX.   Yet——

[COLUMBUS.   I must.

BEATRIX.   Oh, yes, you must!

COLUMBUS.   Our lives are finite, but the aims of life

Are infinite, and crowd on every side.

Whate'er we strive to reach, in thought, in deed,

At last, some one aim surely tips the scales;

As it has weight, its rivals are thrown up.

BEATRIX.   Yes, even she who loves you.

COLUMBUS.   I had hoped,

Now that my project seems, at last, afloat,

That your soul would be buoyant as is mine.

BEATRIX.   Yes, yes, but yet can it be worth the price?

COLUMBUS.   I know your meaning,—loss of life, perhaps,

And all for which some prize life,—ease and love.

But, ah, who would not feel it is worth this? —

And others go with me who think the same.

BEATRIX.   Some call them fools.

COLUMBUS.   Some?—where?

BEATRIX.   In all the streets.

COLUMBUS.   Here?

BEATRIX.   Yes.

COLUMBUS.   They are fools, if this life be all;

And fools, if they but claim that it is all.

For, risking dangers thick as mid-sea-mists

In war, in wave, men's deeds outdo their
  words,
And prove they serve a grander sovereignty,
Whose realms outreach all death-lines.

BEATRIX.   Is it these
You seek in that cloud-circled, storm-set sea?
Ah, how can I let them out-price your life?—
Or how can you?]

COLUMBUS.   So often I have told you!—
What moves me seems beyond all conscious
  thought;
Seems like the lure that leads the summer bird
Southward when comes the fall. It is enough,
It is my destiny. I weigh it well,
And find it rational; yet why I first
Conceived it as I do, I cannot tell.

  *Enter—Left—*DIEGO *and a* COMPANION.

DIEGO (*to his* COMPANION *as he looks at* BEATRIX).
Like all the other women in the town,
Is leagued to keep him back, eh? It is not
In nature that a man obey a woman.
And human ways, when not in nature, bode
Inhuman tampering somewhere. He should
  know
That none can turn to *she* the pronoun *he*
Without an *s* that puts a hiss before it.

   *Exit—Left—*COMPANION.
    (*to* COLUMBUS.)

My brother?

Columbus (*to* Diego). Ay?

Diego. Have business (Diego *and* Beatrix
  bow to each other).

Columbus. I know it—(*to* Beatrix),
  Will find you later. Now, you will excuse me.
  Exit—Right—into her house, Beatrix.

Diego. You should have come before. That
  woman's gowns
  Are always clinging to you—look as if
  She thought to make a woman of yourself.
  Confound their sex!

Columbus. Not all now! There are some——

Diego. Some men too; but in all of Spain, not
  six
  To man your vessels of their own free will.
  Why not?—Because not fit to go with you.
  How many women think you fit for it?

[Columbus. Be not so hard on them.

Diego. No, they are soft,
  More soft than cats, and mew, too, ay, and
  scratch.
  Have seen their blisters! ay, have seen a man
  Whose very soul had been scratched out by
  one.

Columbus. You talk as if you feared for me.

Diego. I fear
  For all the expedition. Have you heard
  The news?

Columbus. What is it?

DIEGO. Nothing that is good.

COLUMBUS. The ships are——

DIEGO. Floating. You may thank the guards.
The crews have all deserted.

COLUMBUS. What?

DIEGO. As if
The howlings of their wives and mothers here
About their ears, could bring them less of hell
Than howlings of the wind upon the sea!

COLUMBUS. The women have persuaded them to break
Their word with us?

DIEGO. Why, yes. Who else would, eh?
What woman ever cared about her word,—
Her own word or her husband's? Bless her jaws!
They have so many words, why care for one word?]

COLUMBUS. Oh, waive the women! Is it true the crews
Have all deserted?

DIEGO. Almost all.

COLUMBUS. But yet
The government——

DIEGO. Yes, they have sent around
Arresting some, imprisoning others. You
Will have your crew; for they have found a source
Beyond exhausting.

COLUMBUS.   What is that?
DIEGO.   The jail,
  Which, like an Arab-shirt turned inside out,
  Will shake its lice upon you.
COLUMBUS.   That, at least,
  Will give us men.
DIEGO.   If you can call them men,
  [These creatures, whom a life-long fear of light
  Has trained for treachery stabbing in the
        dark;
  Sneaks, too irresolute and indolent
  To push by worthy means to worthy ends.
  But I would trust in waves adrift for hell
  As much as in a rudder held by knaves.]
  What can you ever do with such as these
  When three months out at sea?
COLUMBUS.   I shall depend
  Upon my officers.
DIEGO.   You know them then?
  You never know a coward soul till cowed
  By gusts out-winding his own self-conceit;
  And garbs they guise in, never cloud the air
  In time for us to brace the fence they fell.
  I would that I were going with you.
COLUMBUS.   No;
  All that we settled.   One should stay behind
  To guard our interests here.
            *Enter—Left—*GUTIERREZ.
DIEGO.   And will be needed

Far more than you could guess. This officer
Will tell you,—is the one has been in charge.

COLUMBUS. (*to* GUTIERREZ *as they exchange
salutes.*)
The ships are safe and ready?

GUTIERREZ. Guarded, Senior,
All night, all day. Some men here took an oath,
Perhaps you know, to scuttle them.

COLUMBUS. They did?
But they have not succeeded.

GUTIERREZ. No, of course.
We always guard a ship, when once impressed
For royal services, like treasure. Still
They came within an inch of it.

COLUMBUS. How so?

GUTIERREZ. We thought that Breviesca was
your friend.

COLUMBUS. Quite otherwise, I fear.

GUTIERREZ. And I, but yet,
As agent of Fonseca, Bishop of——

COLUMBUS. O, worse and worse! The bishop,
I believe,
Would be assured that only truth had tri-
umphed,
If I and all the crew were drowned.

GUTIERREZ. Ah, so?
Well, they have tried it.

COLUMBUS. What?

GUTIERREZ. To have you drowned.

COLUMBUS.   You mean?—

GUTIERREZ.   Tried to corrupt the calkers.

COLUMBUS.   No!—
  Are sure of that?

GUTIERREZ.   I overheard.

COLUMBUS.   Good God!—
  This man Breviesca?

GUTIERREZ.   It was he.

COLUMBUS.   And you?——

GUTIERREZ. We turned the calkers off; and
        had a task
  Impressing other.   That performed, we put
  A soldier back of every one to calk
  His pores with steel unless he calked the
        ships'.

COLUMBUS.   They now are ready?

GUTIERREZ.   All things ready, Senior.

COLUMBUS.   We sail to-morrow, then.

GUTIERREZ.   Meantime, perhaps—
  Your pardon—you will hold yourself unseen?

COLUMBUS.   Why so?

GUTIERREZ.   To save a conflict with the mob.

COLUMBUS.   You mean that——

GUTIERREZ. They might keep you here by
        force;
  [Or sacrifice your life, and readily,
  To save their friends,—the friends they deem
        are doomed.

DIEGO.   Why, very victims burning at the stake

Could never cause a cloud more black than seems
To hang above the town to-day.]

COLUMBUS (*to* GUTIERREZ).   I see,
Your hint has value.   I will join you soon.

*Exit—Left—*GUTIERREZ, *after saluting.* COL-
UMBUS *continues to* DIEGO.

So so!   You note what influenced Beatrix.

[DIEGO.   Of course.   A man but in his public
thought
Antiphonals the public sentiment.
A woman does it in her private thought;
And woe to lovers who dare say their say
Without a little clique that, echoing it,
Can make it seem, at least, a little public.

COLUMBUS.   But can you blame her—

DIEGO.   Trend to fashion?   No.
You flaunt the flag of fashion in a crowd
And, in the bee-line of their rush to tail
Its leading, one could pick the women out
Without their having skirts on.]

COLUMBUS.   I must send
For Pinzon.   He awaits me at his home.

DIEGO.   Let me go.

COLUMBUS.   Thanks, and say that I must wait,
And meet him at the ships.   Find Perez too,
And tell him that we sail at dawn, and wish
The sacrament.   You say that we will use
The little chapel there beside the dock.

DIEGO.   I will.

COLUMBUS.   And I go too—

(*looking toward the left, then at the house of*
                    BEATRIX.)   And yet I ought
  To say a word more here.   When courtesy
  And caution balance in the scales, the heart
  Is kinder than the head, if not more wise.
                *Exit—Right Front—*DIEGO.

*Enter—Right Rear—*BREVIESCA,   *accompanied
          by a* CITIZEN.

BREVIESCA (*stepping between* COLUMBUS *and the
      house of* BEATRIX).

  Good day.

COLUMBUS.   Ah! Senior Breviesca!

BREVIESCA.   I
  Would speak to you.

COLUMBUS.   You have your wish.

BREVIESCA.   I bring
  An invitation from the bishop.

COLUMBUS.   Which—
  Fonseca?

BREVIESCA.   Yes.

COLUMBUS.   And where is he?

BREVIESCA.   Why, at
  The monastery.

COLUMBUS.   On the other side
  The town, not so?—What would he with
      me?

BREVIESCA.   Talk

About the mission that the church has
    planned.

COLUMBUS. These matters have been all ar-
    ranged.

BREVIESCA.   But he
  Would see you.

COLUMBUS.   He can see me at my ship.

BREVIESCA.   His work prevents.

COLUMBUS.   Then give him my regrets.

BREVIESCA.   But he demands your presence.

COLUMBUS.   I am not
  Within his jurisdiction.

[CITIZEN.   Ho! hear that.

COLUMBUS. My work was ordered by the
    queen.

BREVIESCA.   And mine
  Was ordered by the bishop. Will you come?

COLUMBUS. My answer has been given.

CITIZEN.   Frightened eh?—
  Aha!—would get behind the soldiers there.
  (*pointing toward the ships and harbor at the Left*).

COLUMBUS. A man who lives for others, not
    for self,
  Has little fear for self; yet care for them
  May give him caution. I have weighty
    reasons
  For keeping eyes upon the ships.

CITIZEN (*sarcastically and looking significantly
    at* BREVIESCA). Oh, yes!]

BREVIESCA (*approaching* COLUMBUS *as if to lay his hand on him*).

Say, will you go with us?—I think you will.

COLUMBUS (*knocking* BREVIESCA *down*).

Yes, yes, when down there with you, then I will.

*Enter—Left Rear—*GUTIERREZ *with two* SOLDIERS.

*Enter—Right Front—*DIEGO.

*Exit—Right Rear—*CITIZEN.

DIEGO.   What is it?

COLUMBUS.   I am practicing, you see—
On criminals.—That man there set a trap.
But it takes two to make a trap work.   He,
He was a genius, this man, played both rôles.
He set it and was caught in it.

*Exit—Right Rear—*BREVIESCA, *crawling anxiously away.*

DIEGO *and* GUTIERREZ *start to follow and arrest him.* COLUMBUS *motions them back with his hand.* No, no!

DIEGO.   And you, my brother?   Such a patient man?

COLUMBUS.   Oh, patient! When a fire has been kept in
For eighteen years, blame not its blazing out.
Thank God it did not wholly blast the fool
Whose fumbling fouled it—thought it had no life.

The villain! if I only could be sure
He would be better for the punishment!
DIEGO. You go now to the ships?
COLUMBUS.   Yes, very soon.
GUTIERREZ. Shall I go with you?
COLUMBUS (*ascending the porch of the house of*
      BEATRIX).   Wait here if you choose.
But yet, of all men taught the lesson, I
By this time, should have learned to go
   alone.
                *Exit—Right Front—*DIEGO.
*Exit—Right—through the porch—*COLUMBUS.
GUTIERREZ *motions to the soldiers as if setting
      a guard about the house of* BEATRIX.

———

SCENE SECOND.—*The deck of the ship of* COL-
   UMBUS. *Backing, sky and sea; at first, invisible
   because it is night; later visible, as at sunrise and,
   if thought best, representing, in a panorama, a
   gradual approach of the ships to shore, the
   scenery moving from Left to Right. At the
   Right is a cabin; above it, a box for the pilot
   and a platform on which sailors can stand. At
   the Left, apparently near the bow of the vessel
   is a hatchway into the ship's hold. On the deck
   are masts, sails, ropes and other things that will
   readily suggest themselves.
   Entrances, at the Right, into the cabin, and on to*

*the platform above it, also on to the deck; at the
Left, into the hatchway, and on to the deck.*

   Roldan *appears near the bow of the ship,*
   Escobar *beside him, and* Pintor *nearer
   the cabin.   Other* Sailors *also are present.*

Roldan (*looking off through the dark*).   Oh, I am
 sick of this!

Pintor.   And I.

Escobar.   You wait.
 Another storm will make you sicker still.

[Pintor.   If it would only sicken him.

Roldan.   Make him
 Throw up, eh?

Pintor.   Yes, throw up the voyage.

Escobar.   That
 Will come in time.   But when it comes, my
  lad,
 The ship will throw up us too.

Pintor.   I know now
 How fish feel when they see the water boil,
 Just when we drop them in alive.

Escobar.   Are not
 More out their element than we are here,
 With these few planks between—then purga-
  tory.

Pintor.   Nor any more sure, either, to be
 cooked.]

Roldan.   What means it all?—those weeks
 without a stir

Amid the waves, and then those heavy swells
Without a stir amid the winds?

ESCOBAR.   What means it?—
Why, like enough our ship is near the place
Where all the waters pour down hill.

ROLDAN.   You mean
The edge?

ESCOBAR.   Why not?—In streams you always
     find
Smooth, rapid water, waves, and then the
     plunge.

ROLDAN.   Is quiet now.

ESCOBAR.   So is a cataract
Just where it nears the brink.

ROLDAN.   The holy dame!
Do you believe?—

ESCOBAR.   There must have been some cause.
What was it?   There was not a wind.

PINTOR.   And when
There was, ten times to one time it blew west.
No wind like that will ever speed us home.

ESCOBAR.   And what wind think you will, or
     can?

ROLDAN.   Or can?

ESCOBAR.   Humph! let him keep on here, a day
     or two,
These floating weeds will hold us like a vise.

ROLDAN.   He calls them signs of land.

ESCOBAR.   Oh, yes, of land!—

That fatal land afloat in fatal seas
Entrapping in their meshes all the ships
That dare to venture near.

ROLDAN (*looking for approval to* PINTOR *and
    other* SAILORS, *who nod to him in con-
    firmation of what he says.*)

                                    Yes, we have heard—

ESCOBAR.   You have?—Then you are all a set of
    fools.

[PINTOR.   I know it; but it never was our
    fault.

ESCOBAR.   Not?—Whose?

PINTOR.   The government's.   It forced us here.

ESCOBAR.   We were not kept here by it.   What
    does that

Is one man's will, and he a lunatic.

ROLDAN.   How did he ever gain the ear of
    Spain?

ESCOBAR.   By talking.   Most men's thoughts
    are led, you know,

In trains of their own talking.   Talk them
    down,

They lose their leader.   Keep on talking
    then,

They find in you another.   Any sound

You choose to make, they take for sense.
    Why not?

That course has grown to be their habit.

PINTOR.   Oh,

Yet not through talk or thought he deals with
us,
But force.

ESCOBAR. And he will find before he dies
That men accept one's estimate of them.
If he esteem them thinkers, give them thought,
They turn to him like thinking beings; but
If he esteem them brutes, and give them
force,
They turn upon him like a brute.

ROLDAN. Should we,
Ourselves?

ESCOBAR. Why not?—if he deserve it?

ROLDAN. But
If we should mutiny, and then go home—

ESCOBAR. The choice is not between this place
and home;
No, but the bottom of the sea and land.
And other lands are fertile as are Spain's.

ROLDAN. You own no wife and children!

ESCOBAR. Humph, that means
My life is not behind me, but before—
With precious little left of it, and this—
How much is time here worth, if in it
all
We live but slaves, and never know of good
times?
The man who squeezes these all out our
life—

16

Wrings our last sweat-drop out to serve himself,—
He has——

PINTOR.   A vampire's care for us.

ESCOBAR.   What he
  Cares for is notoriety, which means
  The bulge of contrast.   Crush and hush your
    kind,
  And you are seen and heard.]

PINTOR.   What right has he
  To lord and offset Genoese mastership
  By making slaves of Spaniards?

ROLDAN.   That was what
  They asked at home!

ESCOBAR.   What they will ask again,
  If we sail home without him.

PINTOR.   .   That they will.
  What man of station in the land would not
  Be glad to hear that he had failed?

ESCOBAR.   And all
  The rest will see that those who sailed beyond
  All others on a sea like this, have done
  The whole that Spain could ask.

ROLDAN.   And still——

ESCOBAR.   As if
  It were not right, when in a madman's hands,
  To use our reason, and resist him.

PINTOR.   Yes,
  A man should use his reason.   Are we brutes?

[ESCOBAR. No;—worse than brutes when he
      comes. Brutes, at times,
  To save their lives, will turn upon a man.
  But we—five score to one, but all afraid
  To call our souls our own. Let him appear,
  We fly like cry-girls from a buzzing bug
  One touch could crush in no time.
ROLDAN.   But the court
  Has clothed him with authority.
ESCOBAR.   Mere sheep
  Would not be driven by another sheep
  Though clothed in bear-skin, could they only
      hear
  His old familiar bleat.
ROLDAN.   And yet you know
  He has the power——
ESCOBAR.   Because we give it him,
  Who whine,—whine merely like a set of babes,
  Too weak to lift a finger for ourselves.
ROLDAN.   The King——
ESCOBAR.   Is all divine! I grant it; ay,
  What else could ever pick out, plying but
  A random sword, and prick and pin in place
  As many Spanish cowards as are here?]
ROLDAN. Man, you will have us hung for
      murder yet.
ESCOBAR. Oh, there is many a way to kill a cat.
  The best I know is drowning. Nights are
      dark.

And one may slip against a man, and he,
When slipped against, may stumble over-
　　board.
If so, he drowns—but how?—he drowns
　　himself.

ROLDAN.　Hark!—He is coming!—Down—and
　　clear from this.

　　　　*Exeunt—Left, into the Hatchway—*ROL-
　　　　　　DAN, PINTOR *and* ESCOBAR.

*Enter—Right, from the Cabin—*COLUMBUS *and*
　　　　BARTHOLOMEW.

COLUMBUS (*to* BARTHOLOMEW).

He comes on plotting.—That is plain enough.
How form and face—mere garments that they
　　are—
Will twist and wrinkle to a touch of thought!—
Fools!—Yet without fools, where were sover-
　　eignty
For wise men?—they would find it harder
　　work
To do earth's thinking for it; harder work
To string the nerves that center in one's brain
Through all the mass, and rein it to one's
　　will.—
Can I do this with these men? or must I,
I who have given all these years to it,
Ay, and my young love too, my life, my all,—
Must I turn back?—I will not, though they
　　kill me. (*looking at a paper in his hand.*)

These figures give seven hundred fifty leagues.
How wise to make my false log for the crew!
That log has passed six hundred; but without it
I might have had more trouble.   In the time
I served King Renier, and went off to take
The galley Fernandina; and my crew,
In fright to hear two ships were guarding her,
Had turned our helm, and thought we flew away;
Ah, how I steered straight for her in the night!
And fought her at the dawn!—So act I here.
We men who think have duties due our kind.
One duty is, to block their finding out
What are our thoughts.   Yes, they may learn too much.
The truth is not a plaything for a babe.
Truth is a gem, and sometimes needs encasing.
Yet, if we sail on long, the day will come
When our true distance will be known.—
      What then?
What then?

VOICES (*from the hatchway*).   He shall turn
      back!   He shall!   Will make him.

COLUMBUS.   Hark! hark!—turn back?   They
      dare speak out like that?
Oh, what a cruel destiny is mine
To unfulfillment doom'd, if I do not
What even heaven itself has never done,—

Give patience to a world of restlessness!
Oh, God, I think I serve thee.   Give me power
To calm these minds, as Christ could calm the
    sea.

*Enter—Left, from the hatchway—*ESCOBAR, ROL-
DAN, PINTOR; *and from other Entrances, Right
and Left,* SANCHEZ, GUTIERREZ *and others.*
Well, what is wrong?

ESCOBAR.   We came to tell you, Senior,
We think it time that we turn back.

COLUMBUS.   Turn back?
A strange idea that!

SEVERAL.   Oh, strange!

COLUMBUS.   Why, yes,
With what we saw to-day—the herbs and
    flowers.

PINTOR.   Humph! they were seen before,

COLUMBUS.   But not the same—
Not fresh and green; and then the small shore-
    fish
And birds too, birds of kinds that never sleep,
Nor light, except on land—the singing birds
That perched upon our mast.

ESCOBAR.   If there were land—
Three times it has been called—we now have
    passed it.

COLUMBUS.   We may be in a bay.

ESCOBAR.   You would not steer
As Captain Pinzon wished.

COLUMBUS. The birds all flew
This other way. I thought them flying home.
PINTOR. We are not birds.
ESCOBAR. Are going home though.
ROLDAN. Yes.
COLUMBUS. A pleasant swim! The ship is
     going on.
SEVERAL. No, no.
COLUMBUS. Why, men, you said the same
     before.
Have you forgot how many of you cried,
Ay, cried, in fear of burning skies above
The Teneriffe volcano?—and I said
It would not harm you. Did it? Then shot
     by
Those meteors; and I said they too would pass.
Did I mistake? Then tireless western winds;
But east winds turned them. Then a glassy
     sea;
But billows broke it. Then came signs of
     land;
And now they multiply, as I had hoped.
If right so far, then I have earned your trust.
ESCOBAR. Ugh! Those are old tales now.
SEVERAL. Yes.
COLUMBUS. Let them be so.
The land toward which we sail is not unknown;
Those who have seen it say, that all the gold
In all of Europe grouped and fused to make

A single mass, would hardly form one cliff
Of endless mountain ranges that are there.

ROLDAN.   Hear that now!

COLUMBUS.   They would be enough to make
A lord, at home, of every one of you
Without the title; but, think you, the court,
The courtiers, would not wish you this besides?
You, who had burned through unknown dark-
    ness here
More brilliantly than comets through the
    sky?——
I mean it, for the trail you leave behind
Will write in deathless light around the world
The endless glory of our Christian Spain.

ROLDAN and OTHERS.   Yes, yes.

ESCOBAR.   No, no, come on!
(*moving toward* COLUMBUS, *and urging others to do
        the same*).

PINTOR (*to* ROLDAN *and those who hold back*).
                        Ay, you are pledged.
Lay hands upon him.   Make him yield.

ESCOBAR *approaches* COLUMBUS. *He and*
    BARTHOLOMEW *draw their swords.*

COLUMBUS (*to* ESCOBAR).   Stand back.
I represent the king.

ESCOBAR.   And we your slaves?

COLUMBUS.   Far better so than slaves to one
        another.
Lay hands on me, not I alone will have

A score of masters. Look you to your mates.
You pledged yourselves to stand together?
      What?—
Have you, or you, no foe in all this crew?
And now you place your life in that foe's
      hands?
When all he needs to raise himself in Spain
Is telling truth—no more—Humph! will he
      not tell?
Ay, kill me, drown me, I shall be avenged.
When bad men band, then traitors fill the
      camp;
And, if a fair foe fail, the foul will not,
For in that fight are God and devil both.

ROLDAN. Humph! I must not be found here.
PINTOR. (*leaving the mutineers.*)   No, nor I.
COLUMBUS (*to* BARTHOLOMEW). At last the tide
      has turned. Heaven help me now.
            (*to the sailors.*)
I thought that I had officers and men
Too manly to see one man stand alone,—
That some would stand beside me. Was I
      wrong?

SANCHEZ.   No.
GUTIERREZ.   No.

      (ROLDAN *and those with him come beside*
            SANCHEZ *and* GUTIERREZ. *They ap-
            proach* COLUMBUS. ESCOBAR *falls
            back.*)

COLUMBUS.   I thank you, men.   I hoped
    as much.
  And now—why you are my brave crew again;—
  Have been so brave, I could not bear to think
  That you could fail of perfect victory—
  Here, too, almost in sight.   How you would
    feel
  When, after that next voyage—which now
    we know
  That some one else would make, did we go
    home—
  You saw the wreaths and wealth that you alone
  Had really won, deck other's heads and hands!
SANCHEZ.   Well asked!
ROLDAN.   Ay, ay.
COLUMBUS.   You had forgotten this.
  Well, now let us forget what just has happened.
  You know, men, that the same ship holds us
    all;
  And all that comes to you must come to me.
ROLDAN.   It must.
COLUMBUS.   Then let the matter rest.   Enough!
  Now to your places.

       *Exeunt—Left—into the hatchway—*Es-
        cobar, ROLDAN, PINTOR *and others;*
        *On deck, Right—*SANCHEZ; *Left—*
        GUTIERREZ.   COLUMBUS *continues*
       to BARTHOLOMEW.

                One more crisis passed!

How many further?—Lord, how long! how
    long! (*He looks off over the sea.*)
Because a soul will gaze at darkness thus,
It does not prove he sees—mere habit. Ah!
    (*A slightly moving light appears in the
        back distance at the Left; i.e., in the
        direction in which the ship is sailing;
        and another steady light at the Right.*)
COLUMBUS (*looking at the Left light*). What light
    is that?
BARTHOLOMEW. It cannot be the Pinta's?—
    (*looking at the Right light*).
  No; it sails there.
COLUMBUS.   And yet, I thought—why yes;
    (*looking farther to the Right*).
  The Nina is behind too.
BARTHOLOMEW.   Then that there?—
    (*pointing to the Left light.*)
COLUMBUS. It cannot be a star! Are we
    deceived? (*beckoning to the Left Rear.*)
  Don Gutierrez, come and help us, please.
    *Enter—Left Rear—*DON GUTIERREZ.
      (*all salute.*)
COLUMBUS (*pointing toward the Left light*).
  Can you see anything off here?
GUTIERREZ.   Why yes—
  The Pinta.
COLUMBUS (*pointing to the Right light*). No; is
    there.

GUTIERREZ.   Humph! so it is.
    The Nina is ahead, then?

BARTHOLOMEW (*pointing to the Right again*).
    No, look back.

GUTIERREZ.   Yet some ship's light.

COLUMBUS.   It could not be a star?

GUTIERREZ.   How could it be?

COLUMBUS.   The Inspector there: ask him.
    Inspector?
    (*Calling to some one beyond the Right Front*).
    *Enter—Right Front—*SANCHEZ *and salutes.*

SANCHEZ.   Senior?

COLUMBUS (*pointing to the Left light*)
                        Can you see that light?

SANCHEZ.   Where?

COLUMBUS.   There, beyond the Pinta's.

SANCHEZ.   Yes. I thought
    The Nina was behind us.

COLUMBUS (*pointing to the Right light*).·
                        So she is.

SANCHEZ.   What? can another ship have sailed
    off here?

COLUMBUS.   Another ship, eh? Watch it further.

GUTIERREZ.   Why,——
    I think it moves.

SANCHEZ.   It does!

COLUMBUS.   Not up and down
    As if on waves, but to and fro?

GUTIERREZ.   Just so!

COLUMBUS. And some long distance to and fro.
    (*The light makes this motion.*)
SANCHEZ.   Shall call
  The others?
COLUMBUS.   No, not yet—no false alarm!
GUTIERREZ. You think it land?
COLUMBUS (*nodding*).   Inhabited by men.
GUTIERREZ. By men?—Good God!
BARTHOLOMEW.   Yes, you may well say good.
GUTIERREZ. I think I see what seems a line
    of surf.
COLUMBUS. Perhaps. If so, the Pinta nears it.
    Wait!
  Is almost daybreak. We shall hear her gun.
SANCHEZ. Your order that a false report would
    stop
  The starter's chance for the discovery-prize
  Will keep the signal back till all are sure.
COLUMBUS. Best so! If blind men all were
    born blind, none
  Were cursed by losing sight. In nights like this,
  Not unawakened hope I dread, as much
  As wakening disappointment.
    (*The report of a gun is heard.*)
                  What? so soon?
SANCHEZ. It must be true!
COLUMBUS.   No doubt of it!
GUTIERREZ.   No, none.
    (*The scene is gradually becoming brighter*

*with the approaching dawn. Voices
of the* SAILORS *are heard.*)

COLUMBUS. The sailors! I must go now.
You receive them;
And wait till I return. An hour as grand
As this one should be welcomed fittingly.

Exit—Right—into the cabin, COLUMBUS.

Enter—Left—from the hold, ESCOBAR, ROLDAN,
PINTOR, *and others.*

Enter—Right—others.

(ROLDAN *rushes to the Left, and gazes towards
where the light was first seen.*)

ESCOBAR. A false report, of course!

PINTOR. Of course, but then——

ROLDAN. Good heavens, it is true!

ESCOBAR. True?

ROLDAN. There is land.

ESCOBAR. It cannot be.

ROLDAN. It is. Look there.

PINTOR (*contemptuously, after looking not exactly
where* ROLDAN *points*). A cloud.

ROLDAN. Cloud? No. As clear as daylight,
man. Dry land.

ESCOBAR. It is, hurrah!

PINTOR. You think so?

ESCOBAR. Are you blind?
Is no mistake, it is land!
(*to the other* SAILORS).
Boys, hurrah!

SAILORS. Land, land!

ROLDAN. No doubt of it!

SAILORS. Hurrah!

(*They embrace each other and make wild demonstrations of delight.*)

ESCOBAR (*looking toward the Cabin Entrance— and calling aloud*).

The admiral!

ROLDAN. Three cheers!

PINTOR. The admiral!

ROLDAN. He does not know it yet?

SANCHEZ. Trust him for that.

SAILORS (*shouting*).

The admiral! Hurrah! The admiral!

SANCHEZ. "All hail the Queen," now. That will fetch him. Sing.

(*All remove their caps and chant the following*):

ALL HAIL THE QUEEN.[1]

> All hail the Queen.
> No thrills can fill the lover's breast
> For that first love he loves the best,
> Like ours that throb to each appeal
> Of her in whom, enthroned above

[1] "The crew were now assembled on the decks of the several ships, to return thanks to God for their prosperous voyage, and their happy discovery of land, chanting the Salve Regina and other anthems. Such was the solemn manner in which Columbus celebrated all his discoveries." (Irving's *Columbus:* Book VI., Chap. I.)

The nation's heart, we see, we feel
   The symbol of the sway we love,
   The while we hail our Queen.

   All hail the Queen.
No cause can rouse the soul of strife
In men who war for child and wife,
Like ours that, where her battles be,
   Know not of rest until above
The foe that falls, enthroned we see
   The symbol of the sway we love,
   The while we hail our Queen.

   All hail the Queen.
No loyalty can make a son
Show what a mother's love has done,
Like ours who press through land and sea,
   Our one reward to find above
Our gains that show what man can be,
   The symbol of the sway we love.
   The while we hail our Queen.

(*While this song is being sung, the scenery
     at the back of the stage moves from
     Left to Right, thus representing the
     gradual approach of the ship to land.
     Before the music ceases,* COLUMBUS
     *appears in full uniform on the platform
     at the Right above the cabin. He is
     clothed in scarlet. Behind him stands
     a standard-bearer holding aloft the
     royal standard, and on either side of
     this, two others hold the banners of*

> *the enterprise, emblazoned with a*
> *green cross flanked by the letters F and*
> *Y, the initials of Fernando and Isabel.*
> (*Irving's Columbus. Book* IV., *Chap.*
> I., *also Book* VI., *Chap.* I.)

ROLDAN (*catching sight of* COLUMBUS).

See there!

ESCOBAR. Ah, there he is.

SAILORS. Hurrah! hurrah!

ESCOBAR (*shouting to* COLUMBUS). Ay, you were
right—were right!

ROLDAN. As he is always!

ESCOBAR. I told you so.

ROLDAN (*aside to* ESCOBAR).

You did?—What time was that?

PINTOR. The Admiral forever!

ROLDAN (*aside to* PINTOR). Ay, since when?
(*shouting aloud.*)

Let him remember who have been his friends.

ESCOBAR. Ay, that he will.

ROLDAN. We knew you would succeed.

PINTOR. The greatest hour that Spain has ever
known.

ESCOBAR. Gained through the greatest man
that Spain has had.
(*to the* SAILORS.)

Here, swear him your allegiance. Down,
men, down.

(*All fall on their knees before* COLUMBUS.)

17

COLUMBUS.   I thank you, men, both for my-
  self and those
Who sent us forth; and join with you to swear
Allegiance to our sovereigns—more than this,
  (*pointing to the cross upon the banner*),
To that far higher Power that they too serve
Whose emblem is inscribed upon our banner.
In that we conquer.   When we disembark
Our hands will plant the cross just where we land.
And now—you seem exultant—I confess
To awe like that which Moses must have felt
When God's own hand had touched him as it
  passed.
I cannot stand—nay, let me kneel with you
With praise, thanksgiving, and new-vowed
  devotion.
  (*They all kneel beneath the standard, and
   while the scenery, moving behind,
   represents the approach to land, after
   a few moments of silence, except for
   the music of the orchestra, they chant
   the following*):

  O God of all things living,
   Our Sovereign, Saviour, Guide,
  All gifts are of Thy giving,
   All gains by Thee supplied.
    The stars that make
    High hopes awake
  But beacon what Thou seëst.

The stroke and stress
That earn success
Are but what Thou decreëst.
O God of all things living,
Our Sovereign, Saviour, Guide,
All gifts are of Thy giving,
All gains by Thee supplied.

O God, all good bestowing
On souls that seek Thy way,
Our hearts, with joy o'erflowing,
Give thanks to Thee to-day.
In all the past
Whose blessings last,
Thy presence fills the story;
And all the gleams
That gild our dreams
Obtain from Thee their glory.
O God, all good bestowing
On souls that seek Thy way,
Our hearts with joy o'erflowing,
Give thanks to Thee to-day.

CURTAIN.   END OF ACT III.

ACT FOURTH.

[SCENE FIRST.—*Reception room in a house in Spain.*

> *Entrances—Right and Left.*
> *Enter—Left—*BEATRIX.
> *Enter—Right—*COLUMBUS *and* DIEGO.

BEATRIX.   Returned?   Thank God!

COLUMBUS.   Yes, God alone could do it.
    (*to* DIEGO, *as voices are heard from without.*)
    In pity for me, Diego, send them off;
    And say that I to-night will tell them all.

> *Exit—Right—*DIEGO.
> (*to* BEATRIX.)

    How fares our son, Fernando?

BEATRIX.   Grown and strong.
    Is out just now—will not be back till noon.
    I thought you coming when I heard the noise.

COLUMBUS.   Ah, yes, as I remember, when I
        left,
    I roused a noise too.

BEATRIX.   You have roused one now
    That all the world will hear.

COLUMBUS.   You never praise

A wind, because it makes the sea-waves roar:
It may be empty, and it may do harm.
A man should judge men's noises at their
  worth.

BEATRIX. To think I ever joined with them
  against you!

COLUMBUS. Why, what were woman's nature,
  void of fine
Susceptibility on edge to play
Society's deft weather-vane?   You know
Society is like the atmosphere:
Is always round us, and is all alike,—
All warm in sunshine and all chill in storm.
And you—you did not see me at the time,
Surrounded by my friends, but foes.

BEATRIX.   If you
Had heard the talk!

COLUMBUS.   I heard too much of it.

BEATRIX.   You found the land though!

COLUMBUS.   Yes, and such a land!

BEATRIX.   As fair as this?

COLUMBUS.   A land of endless May,
And set in seas transparent as their skies;
Where every kind of spice, grain, fruit and
  flower
Teems in green valleys that need not be tilled,
All crowned on high by mounts, whose gold
  and gems
Lie on the surface.

BEATRIX.   And belong to you!—
What joy to feel that now it all is over!

COLUMBUS. All never will be over in this world.
The great care passes, but trails lesser cares
That aggregate no less of worry.

BEATRIX.   True;
But when the land was found——

COLUMBUS.   One ship was wrecked;
And twice returning, too, we all seemed lost.
If so, the whole would have been lost that now
Is found.

BEATRIX.   And then?

COLUMBUS.   I vowed a pilgrimage,
Wrote out our story.   Like the wine it was,
I sealed it in a cask, and let it float.

BEATRIX. But reached the land!

COLUMBUS.   Yes, first at the Azores
As wet as fish, too.   That was why, perhaps,
The Portuguese there spread their nets for us,
And not their tables.

BEATRIX.   Nets?

COLUMBUS.   To trap us, yes.

BEATRIX. But why?

COLUMBUS. To get our charts, resail our course,
And claim the credit of it.

BEATRIX.   They could not
Have been successful.

COLUMBUS.   Not if we had lived.

BEATRIX. But yet——

COLUMBUS. No but! Our ship was driven then
  To Portugal itself—by accident,
    Of course: a storm came on—and there the
      court
  Were soft as cats are, when they play with
    mice.
  The fur, though, did not wholly glove the claw,
  Nor cloak a plot to murder us. It failed.
  Instead, Francisco de Almeida sails,
  With secret orders from the envious court,
  To cross the sea, and make our gain his own.
BEATRIX. But Spain will right you, give you
    titles?—fame?——
COLUMBUS. You rate them first?
BEATRIX. But wealth will come with them.
COLUMBUS. If I had worked for these, I had
    not lived
  The life I have.
BEATRIX. If you have not worked for them
  In part, at least, you are not what I thought.
COLUMBUS. How so?
BEATRIX. You mean that you could tamely
    waive
  Your rights—your children's too—to fame
    and wealth?
COLUMBUS. I see—I had not thought.
BEATRIX. Oh, yes; a mind
  May be so wholly filled with its own thoughts,
  They crowd out thoughts for others.

COLUMBUS.   Think you so?
  I must correct the fault.
BEATRIX.   You now have time.
  How sweet to settle down upon your honors!
COLUMBUS.   What, what?—You think I am
      prepared for that?
BEATRIX.   You are not young.
COLUMBUS.   No; fifty-eight.
BEATRIX.   Not strong.
COLUMBUS.   To-day there came a letter from
      the sovereigns.
  It begs my presence to prepare with them
  A second expedition.
BEATRIX.   You to lead it?—
  You will?
COLUMBUS.   Why not?
BEATRIX.   Why, you have earned your rest.
COLUMBUS.   From whence?—I do not feel it
      given me here.
      (*placing his hand on his heart.*)
BEATRIX.   Are not content yet?—What an
      appetite
  Has man's ambition! all that gluts to-day
  But bringing greater hunger for the morrow;
  A fire consuming all it feeds upon,
  Still flaming upward and beyond it all.
COLUMBUS.   True!—but of more than you apply
      it to,—
  Of those desires that are but of the soul.

I strove to find the Indies.   Are they found?
To plant the cross in all those lands; and yet
Great lands wait undiscovered.

BEATRIX.   Other ships
Are sure to sail and reach them.

COLUMBUS.   Ay, they may.
But all that I can know is that the call
Has come to me.

BEATRIX.   Well, well, if you say must,
Perhaps it must be.   Still—if you be needed—
You think you are—mark one thing: you can
      make
Your own terms with the sovereigns.
            *Enter—Right—*DIEGO.

COLUMBUS.   What?

BEATRIX.   Your terms—
Demand your rights, and mine—your son's
      and mine.

Enter — Left —a   MAID *who speaks aside to*
                  BEATRIX.

DIEGO (*aside to* COLUMBUS).   Ah, nothing like
      a she-hand, skill'd in needles,
To prick man's vanity, and gown the hurt
In vain disguises!   When unselfish zeal
Demands investment in the mail of force,
He that of old had spirit to inspire
Swings but a sword that cleaves a scar for
      greed.
      (*to* BEATRIX *who is looking toward him.*)

As rich must he be as a king ere long.

That ought to satisfy you.

(*to* COLUMBUS, *referring to the crowd outside the
          house.*)   Yes, I sent

Them off.

BEATRIX (*to the two men, as she turns from talking
          to the* MAID).   Excuse me for a moment.

> BEATRIX *bows to* COLUMBUS *and* DIEGO,
> *and they bow to her. As* BEATRIX
> *turns away,* DIEGO *continues to talk
> aside to* COLUMBUS, *shaking his head
> as if disapprovingly.*

*Exeunt—Left—*BEATRIX *and* MAID.

DIEGO (*to* COLUMBUS, *as if continuing a conversa-
          tion*).

Will waive that then.—Now tell me of the
          people.

COLUMBUS.   A noble race, who live there in a
          state

Almost of Paradise, their wants but few;

And nature so profuse—I tell you truth—

They neither toil nor spin.

DIEGO.   Nor spin?   Why how

About their clothing?

COLUMBUS.   Is not needed.

DIEGO.   What?

COLUMBUS.   Oh, you get used to that!

DIEGO.   Then how about—

Their character?

COLUMBUS.   Is not so much a thing
  Of clothes as Europeans think, perhaps.
DIEGO.   But then——
COLUMBUS.   The Turks keep faces veiled; turn
      all
  The body into private parts—what for?
  If ill-desire be fruit of thinking, germed
  In curiosity, to clear away
  Some underbrush, and let in light might help
  To blight the marsh-weed, and reveal, besides
  Part of the beauty that brought bliss to Eden.
DIEGO.   You mean——
COLUMBUS.   That nothing like a length of robe,
  Material in substance and suggestion,
  Can stole an anti-spirit-ministry.
  It bags what heaven made that the world may
      deem
  The bag well baited for a game of hell.
DIEGO.   You talk in riddles.
COLUMBUS.   Read a page or two
  From human nature, they are solved.   Out
      there,
  Except with chiefs—it is the same, you know,
  With our high classes—people live in pairs,
  As birds do; and, myself, I saw no hint
  Of lust or competition.   They all seem
  To love their neighbors as themselves, and
      own
  All things in common.   Why, to us they gave

Whatever we could ask; and often too
Without the dimmest prospect of return.

DIEGO.   They welcomed you?

COLUMBUS.   They thought us fresh from heaven:
  Our flesh was fair; that wide, wild sea our
      slave.
  Oh, what a race to be made Christians of!

DIEGO.   What for?

COLUMBUS.   Why, only give such men reli-
      gion——

DIEGO.   With lives of love, and welcoming
      guests from heaven—
  Where would you find much more in Christian
      Spain?

COLUMBUS.   Well, but——

DIEGO.   Precisely what I mean—a butt.

COLUMBUS.   You always will be butting some
      thing.

DIEGO.   Yes,
  A family trait with both of us, I think.
  Were I a man of action like yourself,
  I might not doubt but do.

COLUMBUS.   Not undo, eh?—
  You mean you doubt my statements?

DIEGO.   Hardly that,
  But I was thinking——

COLUMBUS.   Thinking has its dangers.

DIEGO.   Yes, but for it I should have been a
      priest.

At present, am confessor but to you.
And my advice is,—not to say to others
What you have said to me.

COLUMBUS. Why?

DIEGO. It would make
The world suspect you.

COLUMBUS. How?—and what?

DIEGO. Why, say,
Your faith.

COLUMBUS. Impossible! God knows—they
know—
The purpose of my life.—

DIEGO. Your life! But faith—
Seems not to-day a thing of life, but talk;
And God—He has not much to do with it.
A man of faith, is one whose faith in those
To whom he talks will make him talk their
thoughts.
None here will think that what you say can
be.

COLUMBUS. Not even you?

DIEGO. Why, yes,—but yes and no.
The power that makes imagination burst
Through limits of our world, as you have
done,
To find this new world, makes it pass beyond
them.
The glories of that sunset-land may all
Be in the land you saw, or in the sky.

COLUMBUS.   I see your meaning.

*Enter—Left—*BEATRIX.

DIEGO.   If your mounts of gold too
  Do not come tumbling very speedily
  To fill the itching lap of Spain, why then,
  We know who will be blamed.

COLUMBUS.   Oh, but they will!

BEATRIX.   Now, gentlemen, if you will walk in
        here (*motioning toward the Left,*)
  A luncheon waits: and I have news for you,
  Both bright and black.

COLUMBUS. Humph!—nothing bright can come,
  But brings beside it something in the shade.

BEATRIX.   The court, so Dona Bobadilla writes,
  Will welcome you in state at Barcelona.

DIEGO.   Well, that is bright.   Now tell us what
        is black?

BEATRIX.   That Pinzon's crew has reached
        Bayonne; and there
  The man has claimed your honors as his
  own.

COLUMBUS.   What perfidy!—Would make us all
        turn back
  Before we found the land, and after that
  A claim like this!

DIEGO.   To herald his delight
  In what he made you do!—Yet not surprising!
  The train of genius marshals everywhere
  Distrust before success, and envy after.

*Exeunt—Right—*BEATRIX, COLUMBUS *and* DIEGO.]

———

SCENE SECOND.—*A temporary Pavilion, erected in front of the royal residence at Barcelona. In the extreme background, beyond an open place, is the exterior of the house of Cardinal Mendoza. In front of this house, are awnings or curtains, which, at the conclusion of* SCENE SECOND, *are to be lifted or drawn aside in order to prepare for* SCENE THIRD. *To the Right are parts of the Palace, to the Left are pillars supporting the Pavilion. Within the Pavilion, is an elevated platform on which are four throne chairs.*

Entrances:—Right Rear—into the open place beyond the Palace; Right Front—in front of the Palace; Left Rear—open place beyond the Pavilion; Left, farther forward—between the pillars of the Pavilion; and Left Front—at the side of the Pavilion.

The curtain rising reveals the KING *and* QUEEN *and* PRINCE JUAN, *seated upon the throne, attended by the dignitaries of their court and the principal nobility of* Castile, Valentia, Catalonia *and* Aragon; *also* GONZALEZ, ARANA, FONSECA, BREVIESCA *and others. The royal choir are at the extreme Left Front, and*

*spectators of the more common sort at the Right
and in the Rear.   All seem enthusiastic.*
*Music by orchestra and choir, with the following
words:*

HAIL TO THE HERO, HOME FROM STRIFE.

Hail to the hero, home from strife,
Pride of our hearts and hope of our life,
Hail to his glancing crest and plume,
Flashed like lightning into the gloom.
Hail to the grit that, when borne from view,
Out of the darkness brought him through,
Sprout of the slough-pit, bud of the thorn,
    After the night
    The light of the morn.
Crown him with flowers and cull them bright,
Crown him, the man of the land's delight.

Hail to the hero, home from strife,
Pride of our hearts and hope of our life.
Hail to the ring of the voice that taught
Drumming and roaring the rhythm of thought.
Hail to the tone that could change to a cheer
Groan and shriek of a startled fear,
Hushing to rills the flood that whirred,
    Chorusing night
    With songs of the bird.
Shout him a welcome, and shout with might,
Shout for the man of the land's delight.

*Enter—Right Rear—during the song, the following
procession:*
    First come SOLDIERS *who march across the*

stage to the Left Rear—then halt, turn toward the audience, and stand on guard at the Rear. Following the soldiers, surrounded by a brilliant throng of Spanish cavaliers, comes COLUMBUS. *He is on horseback, but dismounts at the entrance of the pavilion and enters it. As he does so, the* KING, QUEEN *and* PRINCE *rise to welcome him.* COLUMBUS *kneels, the* KING *instantly takes his hand and motions to him to seat himself as they do on the slightly elevated platform. He is the only one besides the* KING, QUEEN *and* PRINCE *who is seated.*

While the KING, QUEEN, *and* COLUMBUS *continue to talk, there come men bearing various kinds of parrots together with stuffed birds and animals of unknown species and rare plants supposed to be of precious qualities. A display is also made of Indian coronets, bracelets, and other decorations of gold. Last of all come Indians brought from America. They are painted according to their savage fashion, and decorated with their national ornaments. As those who are in the procession approach the*

pavilion, each in turn salutes the
KING *and* QUEEN, *who remain sitting
as also does* COLUMBUS.
(*See Irving's* COLUMBUS: *Book* V.,
Chapter VI.)
*Enter—Right Front—*DIEGO *and* BEATRIX, *and
stand watching the ceremonies.*
KING (*just as* COLUMBUS *seats himself beside
him*).
  Well done, thou good and faithful servant.
QUEEN.   Yes,
  The land was where you said it was.
COLUMBUS.   Not more
  Than eighty leagues from where I reckoned it.
QUEEN.   A rich land too?
COLUMBUS (*motioning to the attendants who in
marching past exhibit, as he mentions them,
the different objects which they are carrying*).
            You see what we have brought:—
  These birds and animals unknown to Spain,
  All promising vast wealth in plumes and furs;
  These trees and plants that grow like reeds in
        swamps,
  And covered thick as leaves with ready food;
  These aromatic herbs, in which all forms
  Of sickness find a sure and natural cure;
  This gold that lies upon the soil like dust,
  Or else like pebbles tumbling from the cliffs,
  And easily moulded into ornaments;

These pearls and gems that line the river-beds;
And these brave people, sons of God like us,
With generous natures and compliant wills,
Who met us kneeling, as we knelt on shore,
With reverent souls prepared by heaven itself
To welcome us as heavenly messengers;
And who to be made whole in holiness
Need but the cleansing water of the church.
Are these not eloquent beyond the power
Of mortal lips?

QUEEN.   They are.

KING.   They are.

ALL.   Yes, yes.

[COLUMBUS.   But what that land contains is in
      supply
As far beyond the treasure here, as is
A whole vast continent beyond the store
That can be packed in one small vessel.   Yes,
That realm of boundless wealth in rock and
      soil
And boundless progress for the state and soul,
Past all that human fancy can conceive,
Lies there, embed in crystal seas and skies,
A wondrous gift, fresh from the hand of God,
As if untarnished by the touch of man,
Awaiting your most Christian Majesties.]

KING (*standing, as all do*).   Give God the praise.

PEOPLE.   Thank God.   Amen, amen.

KING (*to* COLUMBUS, *who when addressed,*

descends from the platform). You hear
the people and their whole-souled thanks.
We but fulfill their wishes, crowning you
With every proof of royal approbation.
We now decree that, through all time hence-
forth,
You shall be known as Admiral, Viceroy,
And, if once more you cross the sea for us,
Commander-General of all armaments,
And Governor of all realms awaiting there,
The bearer of the royal seal, with power
To name your own successor and to will
Your own inheritance; and evermore
These arms here are decreed your family.

*Enter—Left Rear—an attendant bearing
a banner in which the royal arms, the
castle and lion, are quartered with a
group of islands surrounded by waves
and under them the motto:*
"*To Castile and Leon
Columbus gave a new world.*"

(*See Irving's* COLUMBUS : *Book* V., *Chapter* VII.)

DIEGO (*at the extreme Right Front—to* BEATRIX).
You think he needed all those titles?

BEATRIX.   Why?

DIEGO.   I think they sound like you.

BEATRIX.   Well, what of that?
He ought to make his own terms with the
sovereigns,—

Demand his rights, and mine—my son's and
    mine.

DIEGO. When hunting sometimes, I have
    found that birds

Of brightest plumage are the soonest shot.

This is a world where many men go hunting.

KING (*continuing to* COLUMBUS).

And more than this: of all the ships in Spain

We authorize your choice of which you will,

With power to force each captain, pilot, crew,

Or owner of a vessel, arms or stores,

To do your bidding; and besides we pledge

Two-thirds of all the royal revenues

Derived from our church tithes, and all that
    comes

From confiscating all the property

Of all the Jews, whom now, to yield us this,

We banish from our realm.

PEOPLE (*with fervor and exultation*).

                 God bless the king!

FONSECA. God bless your Christian Majesties!

OTHERS.   God bless!

[COLUMBUS. You do me honor, overmuch, I
    fear.

And I too would give praise where all is due;

And that with deeds, not words. In view, this
    day,

Of all the wealth that, with the power you
    give,

Is destined now to come to me, I vow
To raise and arm, inside of twice four years,
Four thousand horse and twice as many foot,
And just as many more in five years more,
To drive to death the heathen Saracen
And wrest from him the Holy Sepulchre.

PEOPLE.   Oh, God! we thank thee!

OTHERS.   Glory to the Lord!]

KING.   Now let us, all together, seek the
        church,
    And praise Him, as is meet for these vast
        boons
    Vouchsafed to Christian Spain, there to con-
        vert (*motioning toward the* INDIANS.)
    By holy baptism these heathen souls.

ARANA (*to* FONSECA, *exultingly*).
    The day begins when all the earth and all
    Its wealth shall be converted unto us.

*Exeunt—Left—*KING, QUEEN, PRINCE, COLUM-
        BUS, *Courtiers, Indians, etc.*

    *Exeunt—Right—*DIEGO, BEATRIX *and others.*
(*While the rest are leaving the choir chant as
            follows:*)

        Oh soul, what earthly crown
        Is bright as his renown
            Whose tireless race
        Outruns the world's too halting pace,
        To reach beyond the things men heed
        That which they know not of, but need!

> Oh soul, what man can be
> As near to Christ as he
> Who looks to life
> Not first for fame and last for strife;
> But shuns no loss nor pain that brings
> The world to new and better things!

Exeunt—Left—Choir.

Awnings in front of the house of Mendoza *rise revealing Scene Third.*

————

Scene Third:—*Interior of a banqueting hall in the house of* Mendoza. *A table crosses the stage at the Rear. Behind it in the Center, on a seat slightly raised above the rest, is* Columbus. *At the right end of the table is* Mendoza: *at the left end,* Fonseca *and* Breviesca. *Others arranged as suits convenience.*

Breviesca (*to* Fonseca).

What native here has ever yet received
Such royal honors?—Why, the sovereigns both
Stood up to greet him, hesitated, too,
To let him kneel, and sat him in their presence.

Fonseca.   He sat, too, on the throne.

Breviesca.   I never saw
A Spainard treated thus.

Fonseca.   He takes it all
As if his due.

BREVIESCA.   Wait!—let me put him down—
In thought, at least.

(*to* COLUMBUS, *who sits playing with an egg on
the table.*)
                    Say, Admiral, do you think
If you had not made this discovery
That no one else in Spain here could have done
        it?

COLUMBUS.   That seems a new idea.

MENDOZA.   So it is.

COLUMBUS.   I never asked myself about that
        yet—
Oh, by the way, can any of you here
Make this thing stand on end?

        (GONZALEZ, BREVIESCA *and* FONSECA *be-
        gin to experiment, as do others, with
        eggs lying on the table near them.*)

FONSECA.   An egg?

COLUMBUS.   An egg.

MENDOZA.   Can it be done?

COLUMBUS.   Why, yes, you try it.

MENDOZA (*trying*).   No;
    I give it up.

FONSECA.   And I.

COLUMBUS (*to* BREVIESCA).
                    You give it up?

BREVIESCA.   I fail to see how—

COLUMBUS (*setting the egg down on its small
        end with enough force to break the shell*

and make it stand). Now you see it—
    there!
MENDOZA. Oh!
BREVIESCA. That is nothing!
COLUMBUS. Yes, like other things,
Is easy enough, when once you see it done.
            (*Laughter.*)

CURTAIN. END OF ACT IV.

ACT FIFTH.

SCENE FIRST:—*A camp on the Island of His-paniola, Backing, a clearing, amid woods with thick forests in the distance. At the Right and Left, trees; at the Left near the Front, the hut of* COLUMBUS. *Entrances at the Right—Rear, and Front—between trees; at the Left—Rear, behind the hut of* COLUMBUS; *farther forward, opening into this hut; and Front, between trees. Enter—Right Rear—*ESCOBAR *and* GAMEZ.

ESCOBAR. Ojeda, when his boats were on the coast,
Said that at home the Admiral's cause was lost.
Our notes have reached there. They have learned at last,
How Spaniards, ay, and Spanish nobles too,
Are lorded over by this foreigner.

GAMEZ. And now he has been superseded?

ESCOBAR.   Yes,
By Bobadilla.

GAMEZ.   Who is he?

ESCOBAR.   Enough,
If but a Spaniard.

GAMEZ. Strange, though, all the same!
[ESCOBAR. I hear Breviesca and his bishop there,
  Who was Fonseca, now rule everything;
  That they it was, who got the crown to give
  Ojeda all the Admiral's charts and half
  His rights too; and would grant indulgences
  Without a stint if they could have their way
  To any here who struck him down.
GAMEZ. Why so?]
ESCOBAR. You never heard about his impu-
      dence,
  When brought before the bishops, years ago?
GAMEZ. At Salamanca, yes; but he was right.
ESCOBAR. Or how he knocked down Breviesca,
      when
  Fonseca's messenger?—Besides, who wants
  To blacken Spain with shade from Genoa?
  Well, Bobadilla's men have come; and when
  His troopers flash in sight here, why, these eyes
  That have been straining so to see them come
  Will scratch some blinks to cure their vision's
      itching.

Enter—Right Front—an old INDIAN, *and advances
    toward* ESCOBAR, *who addresses him.*

  Humph! Who are you, old cove?—What?—
      Clear the air.
  Stand off a white man's shadow.
INDIAN. Me would see
  The Admiral.

Escobar.   Use your eyes then.   Are you blind?

Indian.   Me thought you know——

*Enter—Left Rear—*Columbus, *and listens.*

Escobar.   What right had you to think?
    And if we know, is it our business
    To do your errands for you?

(Indian, *seeing* Columbus, *passes toward the
                Left Rear.*)

Gamez (*laughingly to* Escobar).   Settled him.

Columbus (*to* Indian).
    What now?

Indian (*to* Columbus).
                    Me wants to see you.

Columbus (*motioning toward his cabin*).
                                Yes, but wait
    In there a moment, please.

Exit—Left—into the hut of Columbus, *the* Indian.
        Columbus *goes on to* Escobar.
                        It would be wise
    To keep the red-men friends; and friendship's
        light
    Reflects but what is kindled in ourselves.
    Extinguish it within, and soon without
    We find our world in darkness.—Now, to
        work.
    [The trenches must be dug, and no delay.
    They threaten an attack.

Gamez.   Am I a man
    For work like that?

COLUMBUS.　　　　Like what?

ESCOBAR.　　　　　　　The work that lets
These common laborers wipe their dirty paws
Upon one's coat.

COLUMBUS.　　　　Then take it off.

GAMEZ.　　　　　　　　Ay, ay;
And grovel at their level.

COLUMBUS.　　　　　Does your rank
Depend upon your coat?—pray heaven that
　　you
Be born again, a new man and a true one.

GAMEZ.　You did not promise this work, when
　　we sailed.

COLUMBUS.　The Spaniards had not shown their
　　lust and greed,
Defiled the native women, killed the men,
And, sent in squadrons to preserve the peace,
All grasping for the whole of all they saw,
Beset their comrades like a set of bulls
Becrimsoned with each other's gore.　Mere
　　brutes!
No wonder they have disenchanted thus
The people who at first believed them gods.
Now get you gone—no waiting!

　　　　(COLUMBUS *turns toward his hut.*)

ESCOBAR (*to* GAMEZ, *shaking his fist at* COLUM-
　　BUS's *back*).　　　　　　Yes, until
We get you gone, which will not take us long.]

　　*Exeunt—Right—*GAMEZ *and* ESCOBAR.

COLUMBUS (*going to his cabin and motioning the
            INDIAN to come out.*)
  Well now, my friend, what is it?
INDIAN.   White man kill
  Our men and steal our women.
COLUMBUS.   Yes—and I?
INDIAN.   Kill white man.
COLUMBUS.   What?
*Enter—Left Rear—*BARTHOLOMEW, *and stands
            by* COLUMBUS.
INDIAN.   We Injun call you men
  Great-Spirit-men.   Poor Injun when he die,
  When bad go here, when good go there.
            (*pointing first down and then up.*)
COLUMBUS.   What, you—
  You Indians think this?
BARTHOLOMEW.   I shall write that home.
  Is more than some there seem to think.
COLUMBUS.   It is.
            (*to* INDIAN.)
  And what of that, my friend?
INDIAN.   White-spirit-chief
  Send bad men here and good men there.
            (*pointing first down and then up.*)
COLUMBUS.   I see—
  Put down the bad, put up the good. Quite right!
  And I will try to learn the lesson, friend.
INDIAN (*pointing in a half-frightened way toward
      the Right*).

Bad man come there.

> (BARTHOLOMEW *steps toward the Right*.)

COLUMBUS. Humph, humph, please leave us
then;

And wait in here again.

> (*motioning toward his hut.*)

Exit—Left—into the hut, INDIAN. COLUMBUS
turns toward BARTHOLOMEW.

Whom have we coming?

BARTHOLOMEW. A crowd of captives—women,
as I think.

The men with them are Roldan's.

COLUMBUS. Only force

Can deal with them;—are all old criminals.

Suppose you bring a guard here.

BARTHOLOMEW. Yes, I will.

> *Exit—Left—*BARTHOLOMEW.
> *Enter—Right—*PINTOR.

COLUMBUS (*to* PINTOR). Back, Pintor?—Who
are with you?

PINTOR. Household gods.

COLUMBUS. Whose are they?

PINTOR. Ours.

COLUMBUS. Oh, yours?—how came they yours?

PINTOR. By right of conquest.

COLUMBUS. What?

PINTOR. We killed their men.

COLUMBUS. And left them widows?

PINTOR. No; we made them brides.

We thought this kinder than to leave them
    widows.

COLUMBUS.   Law-breakers!

PINTOR.   Pugh! with all that you have seized,
    Made slaves of, sent to Spain and sold——

COLUMBUS.   But they were captives from our
    foes.

> *Enter—Left—*BARTHOLOMEW, GUTIERREZ
> *and a guard who cross the stage at the*
> *back, and march forward between*
> PINTOR *and the Right Side.*

PINTOR.   Well I
    Take any man who flushes red all over,
    As they do when I meet them, for a foe.

COLUMBUS.   The slaves we sent to Spain were
    taken there
    To be made Christians of.

PINTOR.   And so with us—
    Nice Christians, too; for we shall have them
    washed
    And not made slaves, but take them to our
    homes,
    And let them lead a free and easy life.

[COLUMBUS.   You fail to see the danger? Why,
    their tribe
    Will massacre us all; if not, your vices
    Will bring you hell here, even while you live.

PINTOR.   You know my story—was condemned
    to death—

For nothing, though—and then the court
   decreed,
Instead of this, that I should come out here;
And if I make it hell, it seems to me,
In hell is where they want me.]

COLUMBUS (*to* GUTIERREZ).   Take this man,
   Remove his arms, and march him to the
      works.

(*To* PINTOR.)

Hereafter keep a hold upon your tongue.

[PINTOR.   Ay, Senior; but be not so hard on
   me.
This land needs peopling.]

*Exit—Left—*GUTIERREZ *and* SOLDIERS *with*
PINTOR.

[BARTHOLOMEW.   And will need it more,
If Spain send more of those vile wretches here.
We all may be killed off.

COLUMBUS.   And rightly so.

BARTHOLOMEW.   Had I my way, a brute forever
      kicking
Against the law should go in bit and bridle;
Ay, ay, to see a surgeon too.   A touch
Of horse-play—there were cuttings that would
   cure him
And all his kind.   The best should let their
   land
Be peopled only by the best.

COLUMBUS.   That might

19

Be wise; but where, pray, would you find the
    best?]
No man can tell which curse a country most;—
Its gentlemen who feel above all work;
Or workmen so far down they feel beneath
All obligation to be gentlemen.
As for the first, heaven grant they soon find
    out
That this new world is not a place for
    them.
As for the second, if we plan no way
To keep them on the other side the sea,
Farewell to all the good we hope for here.
       [*Enter—Left—*GUTIERREZ.
What now?

GUTIERREZ (*handing* COLUMBUS *a note*).

  We found this when we searched him.

COLUMBUS.   Ay?

  It seems not mine.

GUTIERREZ.   Perhaps it might be well

  For you to read it.

COLUMBUS (*reading it*).

          So?—I will. Why, why?
        (*to* BARTHOLOMEW.)

  Bartholomew, a new conspiracy!

BARTHOLOMEW.   But that man could not write.

COLUMBUS.   Oh no; not he!

  He merely carries it from one who can.

      (*handing the note to* BARTHOLOMEW.)

This time, it seems the high and low will meet,
And we, between them, will be crushed.

BARTHOLOMEW (*threateningly*). Perhaps.

COLUMBUS. It speaks about another fleet in
port.
I thought the treachery that had given my
charts
And right to govern islands west of here
To Pinzon and Ojeda was enough.
This tells of one who claims a jurisdiction
In our own island.

BARTHOLOMEW. Bobadilla, yes.
What will you do?

COLUMBUS. Divide and conquer.
(*To* GUTIERREZ.) Here!

GUTIERREZ. Ay, ay.

COLUMBUS. To chains with all those named in
this.
(*handing* GUTIERREZ *the note.*)
The most should be at home now. Be alert.
*Exit—Left—*GUTIERREZ.
(*to* BARTHOLOMEW.)
Bartholomew, the rest of those condemned
For sharing in that last conspiracy,
Whom our too willing clemency had spared,
Should be brought out to-day and shot.

BARTHOLOMEW. But then——

COLUMBUS. I see no other way. When mercy
fails

The cause is lost that does not call on justice.]
(*Noises outside.*)
What noise is that—a riot?

BARTHOLOMEW (*who with* COLUMBUS *looks toward
the Right*).   No;—are cheers.

COLUMBUS.   You make them out?

BARTHOLOMEW.   Why, all the town is there!
And look—our prisoners too!

COLUMBUS.   What—those condemned
To death?

BARTHOLOMEW.   Ay, ay; and have the leader-
ship;
And with them—can it be?—it is! there come
The San Domingo traitors.

COLUMBUS.   Is that so?
(*looking toward the Left.*)
Here, here!

*Enter—Left—*GUTIERREZ *with the* SOLDIERS.
Ay, steady now.   Stand there.   On guard.

BARTHOLOMEW (*still looking toward the Right*).
They halt, consulting.—What? Can that
be he?—
Velasquez, our sub-treasurer!   Not so?
Juan de Travierra, too!

COLUMBUS.   How strange!
Why, they were friends—and yet——

BARTHOLOMEW.   Have left the rest—
Are coming here.

COLUMBUS.   Alone?

BARTHOLOMEW. I think so.

COLUMBUS. Yes.—

[But how to solve now what it means!—Can
you?

BARTHOLOMEW. Who could?—The others have
begun to follow.

COLUMBUS. Aha! They think that these will
seem our friends;

And make an opening through which all can
enter.

What keener point could treachery find to
edge

Its wedge of enmity, than long-tried friendship? (*to the* GUARD.)

Make ready.—Wait.]

> *Enter—Right—*VELASQUEZ *and another
> officer. They bow and* COLUMBUS
> *addresses them.*

Well, have you business here?

VELASQUEZ. We have been sent——

COLUMBUS. True men are never sent
By their inferior. They will face him down;
And not turn tail like driven beasts of burden.

VELASQUEZ. You do not know our message.

COLUMBUS. One may judge
A message from its messengers. I see
A crowd of common criminals. Were they
Set free by you, yourselves are criminals.

VELASQUEZ. Your pardon; but——

[COLUMBUS.   You should have asked for that
    Before you freed your pals there. No one
        here
    Has any right to pardon men but me.
VELASQUEZ.   But you mistake——]
COLUMBUS.   I am the Viceroy.
    Traitors to him are traitors to the king.
VELASQUEZ.   You may not be this now.
COLUMBUS.   What mean you?
VELASQUEZ (*handing him an official paper of
        which he holds many*).   Here,
    Is from the court.
COLUMBUS (*taking and reading it*).

                    An outrage! Yet but gives
    This Bobadilla—who? and what is he?—
    Authority to make investigations.
    Insulting!—There is here no grant
    For freeing captives that have been con‑
        demned.
VELASQUEZ (*handing* COLUMBUS *another roll*).
    They sent another paper.
COLUMBUS (*receiving and reading it*).

                    That I yield
    All arms and ships and royal property—
    Yes, yes, if the investigation warrants—
    It will not though.
VELASQUEZ.   Ah, but he says it does.
COLUMBUS.   It does? Why, I have never seen
        this man.

VELASQUEZ.   He has investigated.——

COLUMBUS.   What?

VELASQUEZ.   Your papers.

COLUMBUS.   My papers?—Which and where?

VELASQUEZ.   Those in your house.

COLUMBUS.   He entered that?

VELASQUEZ.   He lives there.

COLUMBUS.   In my house?—
And reads my private papers?

VELASQUEZ.   They were found,
While carrying out his other orders.

COLUMBUS.   More?

VELASQUEZ (*handing other papers to* COLUMBUS).
Yes, these.

COLUMBUS (*receiving and reading them*).

              That I should pay all wages due
With all arrears for royal services—
What then?

VELASQUEZ.   He takes them from your prop-
              erty.

COLUMBUS.   Without a word to me?—Why this
              means ruin!
And who decides the claims?—a man without
The means or inclination, as it seems,
To know the truth?—whose first official act
Is making friends by setting traitors free?
And violating both the laws of Spain
And common courtesy?—It is too much.
Away, and tell him I defy him.   Say,

With all the rabble that are back of him,
Enough are here yet that are loyal still
To Spain and me, to crush one traitor more.
VELASQUEZ.　I fear the loyal must be all against
　　you.
　　　　　(*handing* COLUMBUS *another paper.*)
Read this:—a royal patent that invests
This Bobadilla with all power and right
Of governing these islands.
COLUMBUS (*looking at the paper*).　Royal seals?
It cannot be—but yet—
　　(*handing the paper to* BARTHOLOMEW.)
　　　　　　　　　Can it be true?
I knew that we had enemies; but not
That they could be so powerful.
BARTHOLOMEW.　　　　　Shall we fight?
COLUMBUS.　It might be useless; and it must be
　　wise
To keep the right, when with us, with us yet.
No; let us yield.　My brother, there are times
When wrongs are great that they may be
　　perceived,
And emphasize the need of their redress.
　[(*turning to* GUTIERREZ *and the* GUARD.)
My men, this royal patent takes from me
The government; bestows what powers were
　　mine
On Bobadilla.　All the loyalty
Once shown to me, for which my gratitude

Will always thank you, now belongs to him.

GUTIERREZ.   No, never.

GUARD.   No.]

*Enter—Right—*SANCHEZ, SOLDIERS, ESCOBAR,
            GAMEZ *and a rabble.*
            *Enter—Left—*PINTOR.

[COLUMBUS.   It seems the sovereign's will.
Help me by sharing with me what I bear.
                  (*to* VELASQUEZ.)
Inform the governor we await his wishes.]

VELASQUEZ.   There is another order.

COLUMBUS.   Eh?

VELASQUEZ.   Is with
   This officer.   (*gesturing toward* SANCHEZ.)

SANCHEZ (*advancing slowly toward* COLUMBUS).
                  My orders—not desire.

COLUMBUS.   Am I to die for serving Spain so
   well?

SANCHEZ (*to both* COLUMBUS *and* BARTHOLOMEW).
   Not that—Your swords.

COLUMBUS (*as he and* BARTHOLOMEW *give up
      their swords, as does also* GUTIERREZ).
            But worse than that!—What next?

SANCHEZ (*motioning to a* SOLDIER *who brings
      forward some handcuffs.*)
   I act but for the court.

COLUMBUS.   Are those for me?
   What crime have I committed?

SANCHEZ.   I know none.

COLUMBUS. I said I would submit. You
    doubt my word?
Or courage?—or persistency?—or what?
SANCHEZ. You must return to Spain.
COLUMBUS.   In chains?—Who dares
  To place them on me?
      (*looking at* SANCHEZ *and his* GUARD.)
SANCHEZ (*hesitating and looking around*).
               There are large rewards
  For him that does it. They are offered.—
    Speak. (*to* COLUMBUS.)
  We all are friends, you see.
PINTOR. (*taking the handcuffs.*) Not all; not all!
  Here, let me have them, boys—am used to
    them.
  A fair man gives what he receives, not so?
        (*puts them on* COLUMBUS.)
  Here, curse you! Now fall overboard, and
    these
  Will sink you, as we meant to, years ago.
(*turning to* BARTHOLOMEW *and fastening another
           pair on him.*)
  Now you too.
RABBLE.   Ho, ho, ho!
COLUMBUS (*to* BARTHOLOMEW). Bartholomew,
  A single bracelet is enough, men think,
  To show a common gratitude. But we,
  Why, we have two! They think their debt
  To us a doubled one! How it will thrill

Ambition in the future sons of Spain
To learn what badges of true servitude
Await the souls that serve her best.   We, we
Who made of Spain the Empress of the West,
Have weightier honors waiting us,—to be
The slaves that, crushed to earth, will pedestal
The towering contrast of her sovereignty.
*Exeunt—Left—*Sanchez, *his* Soldiers, Colum-
bus *and* Bartholomew.
*Exeunt—Left and Right—*Omnes.

———

Scene Second:—*A room belonging to a house in
Seville.   Near the Left entrance a chair or two
and a sofa with one end raised on which to rest
the head.*

Entrances—at the Right—and Left.
(*Enter—Right—*Diego *and* Beatrix.)

Diego.   You must not talk about his poverty.
Beatrix.   Why not?
Diego.   Will kill him.
Beatrix.   I am nursing him.
Diego.   Yes, all that grows toward death.
Beatrix.   If he had been
Content,—had left the land to others, when
Once found——
Diego.   What?   Can a mother leave her child,
When born—no more?   Far less the land he
sought,

Than those grand hopes that he had based on
　　it
　　As a foundation.
BEATRIX.　　　　These he might have watched
　　As well at home here.
DIEGO.　　　　　　　Why, I thought it you
　　Who urged him on to wealth.　The wealth
　　　　was there.
　　And how about those titles?　All of them
　　Were labels not of use unless he sailed.
BEATRIX.　Why did he use them arbitrarily?
DIEGO.　Less use than their possession gave
　　offense.
　　Besides, we men are trained in government
　　As well as manners.　And the curse of force
　　Is that its own mean methods keep alive
　　Its first excuse for being.　Tyranny
　　May make of chaos order; but, when throned,
　　Knows not a subject that is not a slave.
　　Would one of those o'er whom my brother
　　　　ruled,
　　Have bent the knee to an authority
　　Not ermined in the old familiar guise
　　Of arbitrariness?
BEATRIX.　　　　Had he conceived
　　How all would end!
DIEGO.　　　　　It could not be conceived.
BEATRIX.　But you conceived it.
DIEGO.　　　　　　　　　I?

BEATRIX. Why yes. You spake
Of envy sure to follow.

DIEGO. Did I so?——

[BEATRIX. And it came true—as often so with
you—
Not that I like you better for it, though.

DIEGO. My words come true, eh?—One might
think they would;
So few regard them! It is one sure test
Of prophets that they prophesy in vain.

BEATRIX. You might have urged your brother——

DIEGO. Oh, not I!
I never urge myself.

BEATRIX. But when you know——

DIEGO. Imagine only—not the same as know-
ing!
Imagination dreams: its dreams anon
May leap Time's processes, or keen-eyed, spy
The end from the beginning. Yet such
dreams
Come but to him so stirred in sympathy
With nature's courses, or inspired in aim
For nature's goals, or swept on by its force,
That sheer inertia of the soul outspeeds
The pace of grosser matter.

BEATRIX. And to you
At times——

DIEGO. The times come seldom. Ay, not oft

Do fancy's flowers foretoken fruit; not oft
Is ripe fruit laden on the limbs that bloom
Most brilliant with the flowers.—Yet have I
    seen it,—
Imagination imaging true life,
Life true to all its images; and then
I found a seer, earth's rarest product.

BEATRIX.   That
Is what some say that you are.

DIEGO.   To be true
To life, when all the men that have life doubt
    me
I ought to join with them, and doubt myself.

BEATRIX.   In that you are not like your brother.

DIEGO.   No;
With him quick action follows on the thought.
With me come only talk, and then more
    thought.
He mounts to find success.   I prophesy—
Perhaps; but where success is, at my best,
Am only of the crowds that cheer it.
        (*looking to the Left.*)   Here
He comes, poor man—his faithful sons too.
    How
I love them for their faithfulness!   Alas,
How fast he fails!   If there were once a time
We feared he might be wrecked, a time has
    come
When his firm spirit reels, the prey of waves

Far worse than waves that sweep the sea
    alone.
Such havoc has fierce envy wrought in him,
What wonder if soon nature, in revolt,
Should doff the guise this world has torn to
    rags
And give him something richer?]

> *Enter—Left—*COLUMBUS, *attended by his
> two sons,* YOUNG DIEGO, *a man, and*
> FERNANDO, *a youth.* COLUMBUS
> *with help is seated on the sofa.* DIEGO
> *continues to* COLUMBUS.

                         Well, what news?

COLUMBUS. A new world has been found of
    boundless wealth;
And he who found it, finds himself a beggar.
A king and queen were throned o'er that new
    world.
Who throned them there, they seized and
    bound in chains.

DIEGO. Oh, yes; but then the chains were taken
    off.

COLUMBUS. A nation has been made the first
    on earth.
Who made it this, for this deed has been made
The last in all that nation—not one shred
Of all his property, or power, or rank,
Stripped by injustice from him, when well
    proved

To be injustice, has been given back.
His name he leaves dishonored, and his heirs
Inherit nakedness.

BEATRIX.   Yes, that is it.
You see if he——

DIEGO (*gesturing violently to silence* BEATRIX).
          Not now.   The time will come——

BEATRIX (*aside to* DIEGO).
Oh, when you prophesy I always fear
That you will prophesy some ill of me.

          *Exit—Right—*BEATRIX.

DIEGO (*to* COLUMBUS).
Nay; nothing now can dim your well-earned
          fame.

COLUMBUS.   A man who gave his life for what to
          all
Appeared impossible, attained it, then
Found charts and notes that told the story,
          stolen,
And that which was his own discovery,
Called not by his own name but by another's.

DIEGO.   Yes, it is very strange.

COLUMBUS.   So very strange
It seems that when I think it can be true,
I pause to listen for the morning bells
To wake me from a dream.

DIEGO.   It is a dream.
The force that keeps eternal worth from light
Is but of time—a thing short-lived.

COLUMBUS. I know—
  Were it not for my children.——
YOUNG DIEGO. They are proud
  Of one who, all his life-time, has kept faith
  With his own soul, however left alone.
COLUMBUS. Alone, and yet not lonely. Be one true
  To his own mission, he is in the ranks
  With all that move toward all good ends that wait. (*looking at his sons.*)
  And but for you—think not I lived my life
  To beg men for a badge to brag about!
  Enough, if I have been an influence.
DIEGO. Ay, that is all that God is.
COLUMBUS. God?
DIEGO. Yes, God.
  What voice, or face, or form, or robe, or crown,
  Or throne attests His Presence? Who can trust
  And serve mere outward, sensuous things like these,
  And not be, all through life—ay, out of it
  And even after death—a slave to sense,
  No brother of the Christ, no son of God?
(COLUMBUS *suddenly falls back upon the sofa.*)
FERNANDO. See—he is fainting!
YOUNG DIEGO. Help him!
DIEGO. What is this?
  Why, Christopher!
  20

(*To the sons as they bend over* Columbus.)
                              Go, call a doctor—priest!
          Exeunt—Left—the two sons.
Columbus (*reviving and pointing toward the
          center of stage*).

The new world—you must watch it—it will
          grow.

Hark—there are words I hear—and look—
          Felipa!

O Lord, to thy hands I commit my spirit.
          (Columbus *sinks in death supported by*
              Diego, *who does not seem to notice
              what follows, being wholly absorbed
              in attending to* Columbus.)

———

Scene Third:—*The curtain forming the back of
    Scene Second rises disclosing at the Left the
    same convent chapel and wall that occupy that
    place in Act First, Scene First.   The convent
    wall, however, extends across the stage to the
    Right, and the whole Scene is backed by a dis-
    tant view of a fertile, cultivated, and populous
    country,   including   mountains   and   valleys,
    rivers spanned by bridges, and low lands filled
    with   towns   and   cities,—all representing the
    present   condition   of   the   western   continent.
    Near the entrance of the chapel, stands* Felipa,
    gazing toward this land, while, by a choir unseen

*within the chapel, the same hymn is chanted as
that with which the drama opens, as follows:*

O Life divine, from thee there springs
   All good that germs and grows;
Thy Light behind the sunlight brings
   The harvests to their close.

O, Life divine, thou art the source,
   Of truth within the soul;
Thou art the guide through all the course
   That leads it to its goal.

O, Life divine, what soul succeeds
   In aught on earth but he
Who moves as all desires and deeds
   Are lured and led by thee.

CURTAIN.

CECIL THE SEER.

CECIL THE SEER.

INTRODUCTION.

To determine aright the relations that should exist between form and spirit is to solve the most important, perhaps, of human problems. Ideally, of course, the one should be a perfect expression of the other; but, in this world, nothing is ideal or perfect; and in nothing is the fact more clearly exemplified than in the frequent failure of a form to represent that which, apparently, it exists for the sole purpose of representing. To recognize, and, so far as possible, to remedy this condition, are primal obligations of intelligence; and this fact justifies the extensive treatment of the subject which has characterized the literature of all periods. Such treatment, however, cannot go to the bottom of its possibilities without considering relations that are distinctively religious; for it is religion that most imperatively demands that the form be a truthful expression of the spirit. But forms which, as in the Second Act of the following drama, are to be turned inside out in order to reveal their inadequacies, must, of themselves, be forms in connection with which such inadequacies are unexpected. Otherwise the whole portrayal will be too commonplace to warrant attention. It will be perceived, therefore, that the selection of religious characters for the drama was justified by the requirements of the theme; and also that the use which is made of these characters is not intended to discredit religion as a whole. Indeed, only those can recognize the full significance of the presentation who also recognize that the incongruities indicated are not of ordinary occurrence.

Again, the suggestions derivable from a subject like that

treated in Cecil the Seer, in order to appear generally applicable, need to be drawn from a general survey of all the possibilities of form ; and it is for this reason, and not because of a desire to disparage any particular form, that such religious characters were selected as are typical of the remotest extremes of the narrow and the broad in theory and of formalism and non-conformity in practice. The inconsistencies suggested do not arise because any one form of religion invariably tends to self-deception, but because, in certain circumstances, all or any forms may tend in this direction. A sufficient motive for portraying the fact is that only in the degree in which a man has a practical recognition of it can he exercise that discernment, or be controlled by that principle, which should characterize the spiritual life.

With reference to the Second Act of the drama, it may not be out of place to say that the underlying conception of it is in strict accordance with human experience. Not a few, but many, who, through accident or disease, have, for a comparatively long period, lost consciousness, and have again been restored to it, have borne witness that, while in the subconscious state, their minds seem to have been employed in developing exclusively the last thought impressed upon them before passing into the state. In unfolding the details necessitated by this general conception, it is enough to say that it would not have been in accordance with the practice of the author had he not carefully and consistently sought to conform them to that which is most universal in the testimony given by those supposed to be in such states, or in corresponding ones produced in accordance with what are termed psychic methods. How much absolute truth one is justified in assigning to testimony thus obtained—from that of Swedenborg downward—no one, perhaps, can decide with authority ; but there must be some reason why the general tendencies of the statements made—as applied to things reported as heard or seen, not to the testifier's explanations of them—virtually

coincide. The suggestion that there may be such a reason is
enough to make a man pause and think, and to do this
whether he surmise that the testimony, because coming through
the subconscious, reveals the results of extraneous revelation,
or only because, coming from the subconscious, it reveals the
results of universal intuition. It is true, too, that at the end
of many years of pausing and thinking, he may not have been
able to make out beyond dispute the source of that which he
is considering ; but one thing he can always do, and from the
very first : He can compare the import of that which is
received with the results, in his own mind, of a combination
of previous information, spiritual insight, and rational inference. Whatever, in its general outlines, coincides with these
results will have for him, and must have—his mind cannot
prevent it—the authority of truth. But exactly the same may
be affirmed of statements which have the authority of truth
when communicated through the forms of poetry. Could
there be given any better reason—or excuse if needed—for
letting the thought of this drama be borne on as a result of
yoking together the poetic and the psychic ?

PLACE AND TIME.

ACT FIRST : In a Southern "Border State" of the American Union, a little before the War for Secession. An evening party at the home of the Cecils. *Scene :* A large hall with glimpses beyond it of a parlor and a porch.

ACT SECOND : *Scenes First and Third :* Interior of a sick chamber. *Scene Second :* A grove representing the surroundings of a dream or trance.

ACT THIRD : In a Northern "Border State" just at the opening of the War for Secession. *Scene First :* The interior of the home of Freeman and Celia; *Scene Second :* A village green in front of Freeman's house, at one side of which the porch of his house is visible.

Is this a revelation?

               Ay, to those
Who heed the truth behind the words I use;
And yet for those who heed this truth themselves
I do not need to term it revelation.

                       Cecil the Seer, II, 2.

               All life on earth
Is girt with warfare, where the light of heaven
That brings each new day's liberty and truth
Contends with darkness, and there is no peace.
Our very bodies are but phantoms formed
Of that same darkness that we must oppose,
And we must fight, if nothing else, ourselves.

                          Idem, III, 2.

CHARACTERS.

CECIL.   Professor in a College, a Candidate for the
                highest Judicial Office of the State, to
                be appointed by its Governor and con-
                firmed by its Senate. Also a particular
                friend and the instructor of Celia.

KRAFT.   Head Politician of the ruling party of the
                State, and a particular friend of Madam
                Cecil. Celia has been the adopted
                daughter of his deceased wife.

FREEMAN.   A young Law Student, friend of Cecil and
                Celia, and in love with Faith Hycher.

BLAVER.   Religious Exhorter, and Head of the Pro-
                hibition party of the State. Particular
                friend of Miss Primwood.

FATHER HYCHER. Head of the Church party of the State
                who wish to obtain a division of the
                School Fund. Uncle of Faith Hycher,
                and particular friend of Widow Hycher,
                his sister-in-law.

LOWE.   A Quaker, representing a syndicate of rail-
                way monopolists who are pushing a plan
                for appropriating and improving a part
                of the chief city of the State.

JEM.   A colored servant.

317

CELIA.	Adopted daughter of deceased wife of Kraft. Pupil and particular friend of Cecil; also friend of Freeman.
MADAM CECIL.	Wife of Cecil, particular friend of Kraft.
FAITH HYCHER.	In love with Freeman, niece of Father Hycher and step-daughter of Widow Hycher.
MISS PRIMWOOD.	Principal of a Female Seminary, particular friend of Blaver.
WIDOW HYCHER.	Step-mother of Faith Hycher, particular friend of her brother-in-law, Father Hycher.
MADAM LOWE.	Quakeress, wife of Lowe.
MILLY.	A colored servant.

A PHYSICIAN, CHORISTERS, PROMENADERS, DANCERS, POPULACE, RUFFIANS, DETECTIVES, MILITIA, AND GENTLEMEN.

CECIL THE SEER.

ACT FIRST.

SCENE: *An evening party at the home of the Cecils. A parlor with windows at the back where hang long heavy curtains. Backing at the Right, extending diagonally across the stage, a wide doorway, beyond which is a glimpse of another large room. Further forward on the Right, a small table about which are chairs and, nearby, an alcove containing an apparently half hidden sofa. Backing at the Left, extending diagonally across the stage, a wide doorway, beyond which is a glimpse of another room.*

ENTRANCES: *Right and Left, through doorways, at both sides and in both the Rear and the Front.*

The rising curtain reveals FREEMAN *and* FATHER HYCHER *sitting in the alcove, and couples walking to and fro.*

FATHER HYCHER. My standards are the standards of the world.

FREEMAN. I know it.

FATHER H. You were questioning——

FREEMAN. Their truth.

[FATHER H. (*slowly and sarcastically*).

Your name is Freeman.

FREEMAN. It defines me, yes.

FATHER H. You think fidelity to man can grow
From germs of infidelity to God?

You think that questioning the forms men most

Esteem, proves high esteem for men themselves?

You think in one that weds, or vows to wed,
To love a third one proves true love for all?

FREEMAN. That all depends on what he does.

FATHER H. And that?

FREEMAN. On what he is. Why ask these things of me?—
And here?

FATHER H. Why should I not? We see so much
In scenes like this!

FREEMAN. Oh no!—You mean so little.]
The forms we see are puppets of a play,

A dull play too! Though seek what pulls the string,

No longer is it dull. A button breaks,

A veil falls off——

FATHER H. Too bad to hope for that!

FREEMAN. Too bad, if lives be bad! If not,
    too good!
  Some things that on the outside seem profane,
  Upon the inside may be sacred.
FATHER H.   Ah?
FREEMAN.   The converse too is true.
FATHER H. (*haughtily*). You mean to say?—
          (*Music starts.*)
FREEMAN (*rising, as does* FATHER HYCHER).
  That all should watch the play, and not forget
  That they themselves are part of it.
FATHER H.   Oh, yes.
Exit—Right Front—after bowing to Freeman,
      FATHER H. (FREEMAN *sits, then,*
      rising, moves toward the Left. Part of
      the following chorus is sung to the
      accompaniment of a piano apparently
      in the rooms beyond the Left Rear.
      During the singing certain of those
      upon the stage, or entering from its
      various entrances, dance to the music.)

  We live but for bubbles, and those who know
  The way of the world their bubbles will blow.
  Ay, all but whose doings are fated to be
  No more than are drops in an infinite sea,
  Will blow them, and show them, till, by and by,
  They fill and float to the air on high;
  Hoho! hoho! and the world will thus
  Know how big a bubble can come from us.

We live but for bubbles that grow and glow
The bigger and brighter the more we blow;
And, borne on the breath of the breeze around
Wherever the tides of the time are bound,
There is nothing of earth or of heaven in sight
But they image it all in a rainbow light;
Hoho! hoho! and the world will thus
Know how bright a bubble can come from us.

We live but for bubbles a-dance in the blast,
But who can tell how long they will last?
So swell your cheeks, and puff, and fan,
And make the most of them while you can,
For if ever the breath in them fail, they will pop,
And only the drizzles to dry as they drop;
Hoho! hoho! and the world will thus
Be done with the bubbles that come from us.

> *Enter—Left Rear—during the singing,*
> FAITH. *She meets* FREEMAN *and,*
> *after a time, they sit in the alcove at*
> *the Right.*
> *Exeunt—at different Entrances—the dan-*
> *cers or singers.*

FAITH.   This night seems like a *fête* in fairy-
land.
 That singing proves it so.   I like to see
 Our Cecil circled by the people singing.
FREEMAN.   You note its meaning then?
FAITH.   What?
FREEMAN.   Cecil-worship.

[FAITH.　And worship is the interest men pay
　　For worth when they can get it—justly due
　　To men of principle.
FREEMAN.　　　　　　　And how of women?—
　　This Madam Cecil is the priestess here.
　　The fee is hers; and he, the puppet-idol.]
FAITH.　How so?
FREEMAN.　Our state is lacking a Chief Justice.
FAITH.　And what of that?
FREEMAN.　　　　　　　　His is a high position.
　　[She, who is always looking upward, sees it.
FAITH.　That may be; but you spoke of worship.
FREEMAN.　　　　　　　　　　　　　Why,]
　　If any idol's niche be tenantless,
　　The one all worship is the one all want there.
FAITH.　Oh yes!—and Madam Cecil——
FREEMAN.　　　　　　　　　Drawing hither
　　The undirected flow of current thought,
　　Though little rills, may find them, all together,
　　Enough to float the bark of her ambition.
　　You see this house—and she herself—are
　　　　gems.
　　For setting, gems need gold.　Her husband
　　　　earns
　　By teaching in the college, at the most,
　　No gold to spare; and, even did she hope,
　　From her own managing, no perquisites——
[FAITH.　What perquisites?
FREEMAN.　　　　　The kind that make us call

A public man "His Honor," lest the world
Might fail to recognize it, if not labeled.]

FAITH. Will Cecil get the place?

FREEMAN. The governor
May nominate him; but the senators
Can scarcely be expected to confirm,
Without some reason not upon the surface,
A man so young and inexperienced.

FAITH. But he is worthy of it.

FREEMAN What is worth
With those that she will try to get to push
him?
Their favors must be paid for. Most have
suits
They sue for in the law-courts. Think you
Cecil,
An upright, downright and straightforward
nature,
Will twist and smirk with twenty different
faces
The twenty different ways that these would
have him?

FAITH. It were a brilliant chance!

FREEMAN. Yes, far too brilliant
For moths to meet with, and escape a scorching.
No wick-light dazzles him. He knows the
sun.

FAITH (*looking toward the Left*).
Look—Madam Cecil now—

Freeman (*rising*).   And angels too,
 They say, draw near us when we talk of them.
Faith (*also rising*).   With her comes Kraft.
Freeman.   The ruler of his party,—
 Controls the governor.
Faith.   Ah!   And Cecil, then,—
 Are he and Kraft such friends?
Freeman.   No; she and Kraft,
 A man whom she so floods with flattery
 That his half drowned, asphyxied reason raves
 Past all resisting her.   Beside this too,
 He means, they say, to seat that son of his
 In Cecil's present chair.   Your men that rule,
 When others hold the place that they would
  fill,
 Tramp an inferior, and push off an equal;
 But if some scheme they basely brew be
  spoiled
 By one above them,—they are left no option;
 But, like a cover, they must lift him higher.
 So, by their very righteousness, you see
 The righteous force their foes to do them
  justice.
  *Exeunt—Right Front—*Freeman *and* Faith.
 *Enter—Left Rear—*Kraft *with* Madam Cecil.
Madam C.   Your charming son—
Kraft.   Gains charms from you who say that—
Madam C.   And with his noble brow, and eyes,
  and manners—

KRAFT.   Yes; he is like his—mother.

MADAM C.   Why, my friend,
His mien, his manner are as like to yours,
As ever were the echoes of a wood
To singing of a woodsman.

KRAFT.   Oh, you flatter!

[MADAM C. And pardon, if I add both have
    their music.

KRAFT.   No, no; but Madam Cecil, you do
    flatter!

MADAM C.   Not half so much, my good friend,
    as your mirror,
When you but face—

KRAFT (*looking at her intently*).

                    And find it very bright?—
But now, about my son: I think—I think—

MADAM C.   What I think. Do we ever dis-
    agree?]

KRAFT.   I wish your husband could be led—

MADAM C.   You think
He cannot then?

KRAFT.   Why that depends—

MADAM C.   On whom?—
A good judge is a man whose judgments you
Approve.

KRAFT (*bowing to her*).   Thanks for your interest.

*Enter—Left—*MR. BLAVER *with* MISS PRIM-
                    WOOD.

MADAM C.   (*continuing to* KRAFT).   Why that

Becomes me,—does it not?—Have you not
    said
I always do, as well as wear, the thing
That seems becoming?—and the principal
(*touching* KRAFT *with her fan; then pointing it
    toward herself.*)
Should always draw its interest.   Not so?—
(*turning to speak to* MISS PRIMWOOD *and* BLAVER,
    who carries a pamphlet in his hand.)
Miss Primwood, ah! Good-evening—You too,
    Deacon:
(*All bow.*   KRAFT *talks aside to* MISS PRIMWOOD.
    MADAM CECIL *continues to* BLAVER,
    tapping his pamphlet with her fan.)
We read your little prohibition tracts.
BLAVER. Yes?—Thanks.—Yet, as you say,
    they are but little.
MADAM C.   The littlest diamond in this ring I
    wear
Is better for my humble, human use,
Than a whole world of dust whirled in a star
Set in an orbit out beyond my reach.
BLAVER.   If, in some humble way, my tracts do
    good—
MADAM C.   The littlest bird-track, sometimes,
    in the sand
May make one think of wings flown out of sight.
BLAVER.   If only mine would—wings of progress,
    wings—

MADAM C.   Ah, but your cause is right.

BLAVER.   Yes, all our pleas
　Are based upon religion.   Yet you know
　The lower courts are hostile.

　*Exeunt—Left—*MISS PRIMWOOD *and* KRAFT.

MADAM C.   Right must win.

[BLAVER.   You think so?—The professor too?—

MADAM C. (*assuming an air of disparagement*).

　　　　　　　　　Come, come;
　No man should anchor trust in such as he,
　Why your opponents never——

BLAVER (*eagerly*).   Would support him?—
　They never would?

MADAM C.   How could they?   Do you know,
　That only last night, when some friends were
　　here
　And talking of the governorship, he said
　Our next might be a prohibitionist.

BLAVER (*greatly pleased, rubbing his hands*).
　Is that so?   Really!—Is that so?   Why,
　　why!—]

　*Enter—Right Rear—*FATHER HYCHER *with*
　　　　WIDOW HYCHER.

MADAM C. (*noticing them*).   But there comes
　　Father Hycher—
　　　　(*insinuatingly to* BLAVER.)
　　　　　　　　Do you think
　A man, religious truly, will not win
　When battling for a cause that is religious?

(MADAM C. *and* BLAVER *bow to* FATHER
H. *and* WIDOW HYCHER. BLAVER
talks aside to WIDOW H. *and, with
her, presently, exits at the Left—*
MADAM C. *continues talking to*
FATHER HYCHER.)

You act like saints we read of in the legends,
With holy air about them. As you enter,
Our thoughts turn toward religion.

FATHER H.   Ah?—with mine!—
I saw you at the church, the other day.

MADAM C. I heard the Father was to preach—

FATHER H.   And came?—

MADAM C. To be a worshipper.

FATHER H.   You think perhaps,
That we make less of preaching than of praise.

MADAM C. Now, honestly, I do admire your
    form.

FATHER H. I like to see you give it counte-
    nance.
But, really, Madam Cecil, you are right.
We must have form;—all eyes, ears, crave it so.
The only question, as I say, is this—
Which form is *the*——

MADAM C.   The form the most emphatic,
One might call *the* form.

FATHER H.   Right, just right again!—
In schools, asylums, prisons, everywhere
That faith should be impressed——

MADAM C.   There one should use
 The most impressive form.
FATHER H.   Why, why, how strange!
 Just what I told your husband!
MADAM C. (*laughing significantly*).   You have
      learned
   A woman's thoughts are echoes; and she echoes
   The thoughts that have been nearest his
      heart too
   To whom she stands the nearest.
FATHER H.   No—but I—
   How could I think my words had had such
      weight?
MADAM C.   Words are a currency that owe their
      worth
   Less to their substance, often, than their
      source.
[FATHER H.   Your husband, then, you think——
MADAM C. (*with an implied suggestion*).
                          A man that knows
   Enough to judge a beaker by its brand.]
FATHER H.   I did not think I had such influence.
MADAM C.   Nor does the sun.   It never thinks
      at all;
   Yet keeps the whole world whirling—by its
      light?—
   No, no,—by its position.
*Enter—Right Rear—*FREEMAN *and* FAITH, *pres-*
      ently seating themselves in the alcove.

FATHER H.   If the courts
  Had only sense to recognize the wrong
  Of taxing our schools to support a rule
  From which our own religion is ruled out—

MADAM C. And on your side are many sena-
      tors?—
  And they confirm the judges?

FATHER H.   What of that?

MADAM C. Why, Father, sometimes I have
      played at whist;
  And when my partner holds the cards that
      win——

FATHER H. (*to* MADAM C.).
  What then?

MADAM C. Then I play low—play whist.

FATHER H.   Ha! ha!
     *Enter—Left Front—*LOWE *carrying a map-*
     like plan of streets, parks, etc. Other
     GENTLEMEN *enter with him. All*
     surround MADAM C.
     *Exit—Left—*FATHER HYCHER.

[FREEMAN (*to* FAITH).
  See Madam Cecil. How her ribboned form
  Bends o'er the black coats!—like a bow of
    promise
  Above thick cloud-banks. Each one thinks
    he sees
  Those of his own cloth fly at Cecil's bid-
    ding

  Like crows where grows but shall not grow a
    harvest.
  Oh, to be popular, just let one be
  Abulge with promise, pledging everything.
  Till time present him his protested bills,
  The world will fawn and paw him like a cur
  To do his bidding. Promise is a flea:
  It makes us itch; but fools us, would we catch
    it.]

MADAM C. (*looking over* LOWE's *plans*).
  This line here is the river bank,—not so?

LOWE. And here the railway; and the park is
    here,
  And here the church (*pointing*).

MADAM C.   The church?

LOWE.   You know with me
  Religion is the chief consideration.

MADAM C. I know; but yet a Friend—?

LOWE.   The company
  Are world's folk,—will not build a meeting.
    So
  We would not quarrel with them: we build
    this.

MADAM C. Yes. How considerate!

[LOWE.   I wish to be so.

MADAM C. But no one lives here yet?

LOWE.   In time some will.

MADAM C. And, for their future good, you
    build the church?

LOWE.   Yet some do not approve.]

MADAM C.   Is there much doubt
Of your success?

LOWE.   Oh no—not if the courts
Remove the injunction of the district's owners.

MADAM C. But that will follow. As my
husband says,
The corner stones of monumental deeds
Must always crush some worms; and plans
like these (*laughing good-naturedly*)
Are monumental—even in their size!
We ought to find a table for them here.
          (*gesturing toward the Left.*)
          Exeunt—Left—MADAM C., LOWE *and
          other* GENTLEMEN.

FREEMAN (*to* FAITH).
This is a swindle shrewdest of them all,—
A syndicate that steals the river-bank;
Then taxes doubly those they steal it from
[For what is left them.   But the abuse is old.
Where thrived ambition yet, but strove to build
Itself a monument by heaping up
That which, when lost, made hollow all about
it!
How many castles I have seen in Europe,
Where every graceful touch in breadth and
height
That formed the great hall's pride, seemed
underlined

As if by shadowy finger-prints of force.
That snatched all from the hamlet at its base!]
But look you—there is Cecil, and with Celia.
      (*pointing toward the Left Rear*.)
How indiscreet his kindness toward that ward
Of Kraft!—Kraft who could make him judge, and who
Abhors her, treats her like a slave, they say.

FAITH. Why so?

FREEMAN.   He has his reasons.

FAITH (*rising*).   Do you know them?
  (FREEMAN *rising and shrugging his shoulders*.)
Some say that you admired her once.

FREEMAN.   I did.
  Before my eyes met you——

FAITH.   This never can be.
My uncle's honor and mine own are pledged.

FREEMAN. But honor helping none and harm-
    ing self,
Need never serve the body of a vow
From which the life to which it vowed has
    flown.

*Exeunt—Right Front—*FAITH *and* FREEMAN.

  *Enter—Left Rear—*CELIA *and* CECIL.

CECIL. Must leave off study, Celia?

CELIA.   So it seems.

CECIL. To be their brightest, minds need
    burnishing;
And earth needs all the light that we can give it.

CELIA. I know—were I not so opposed—were
    I
Not, say, a woman. What can woman do?
CECIL. Do, Celia, do?
CELIA.   Why, yes—what starts with her?
CECIL. No matter what. Men sow the seed,
    you think.
How could it grow, were it to find no soil?
You know the crystal globes clairvoyants
    look in,
And think they see as heaven sees then?—
    Some women
Have crystal souls. One faces them to find
His thoughts divine, himself akin to God.
CELIA. If that be woman's nature——
CECIL.   It is not,
Till polished in the friction of the schools,
Which some think needless; but where wo-
    man's mind
Has never been made bright, the thoughts of
    men
Will never flash for it.
[CELIA.   The sun may find
Its image in the dullest pool.
CECIL.   To be
Too modest, is to lag behind, and not
Keep step with God's advancing lines.
CELIA.   My trouble
Is caused by lines prescribed by men. A soul

That swerves from these in either thought
    or deed
They treat as traitor both to them and God.

CECIL. Of course!—If they can group them-
    selves with God
They may appear more lordlike to the souls
That they desire to lord it over.—But
How is it you have come to learn of this?—
What lines of thought or deed have you been
    breaking?

CELIA. I may have been at fault—I had a
    dream—

CECIL. And you were blamed for dreaming?

CELIA.   No; I told it.

CECIL. Another Joseph!—indiscreet, I see.
You should have known we all at heart are
    Tartars;
And value most the beauty of the spirit,
When, like the Tartar's daughter, it is veiled.—
But now, this dream,—why not let me too
    judge it?

CELIA. My dream awoke a whim. I said I
    thought
That, if a soul must live hereafter, why,
It must have lived before.—You know the
    Christ
Did not rebuke those who confessed they
    thought
Elias had returned; but, in an age

When all believed he might return, confirmed
 them.
And then our creed—Where can it come to
 pass,—
The body's resurrection?
CECIL.   Where?
CELIA.   Where but
In that new earth of Hebrew prophecies?—
Which would have but misled, had those that
 heard
Not had it in their power themselves to be
Restored to life in that restored estate.
CECIL. The state of Adam, do you mean, and
 Eve?—
From which men fell away?]
CELIA.   I sometimes think
The sources of men's thoughts—and deeds,
 as well—
Are far, far back of all they meet with now,—
In previous lives from which the present
 grow;
And men are born to what they bring them-
 selves.
CECIL. You seem to make life hard to under-
 stand.
CELIA. No; I explain it; for, if I myself
Had been an Eve, my suffering now were just.
CECIL. Your suffering now?—so great?—What
 is it?—How?—

22

CELIA. I must find some one—let me tell it
     you:
  To him, whose wife, ere death, was more to me
  Than mother, I am naught.
CECIL.   But others prize you.
CELIA. The rarest jewel might be cheaply
     bartered
  By one who did not prize it.
CECIL.   Bartered?—You?——
CELIA. Note my complexion—who think you
     my mother?—
CECIL. What, what?—Kraft never claimed you
     as a slave?
CELIA. Nor will, perhaps; but he has threatened
     it;
  And even the suggestion of this here—
CECIL. But why suggest it?
CELIA.   I alone have seen
  The writings that were left him by his wife,—
  Her wish to free her slaves——
CECIL.   Oh, what a worm
  Is greed for gold! Did ever human fruitage
  Turn into rot but this greed gnawed the
     core?—
  Was there a will? (CELIA *nods slightly.*)
            You are in danger, yes.
CELIA. A wretch has come, as vile as he is ugly;
  And if I were the charmer of a snake,
  I could not shrink from touch more horrible.

CECIL.   And what of him?

CELIA.   Why, I must go with him;
  Indeed, have been forbidden to come here.

CECIL.   To-night?

CELIA.   To-night.

CECIL.   Must marry him?

CELIA.   Nay, worse.
  He needs, or says he needs, a housekeeper.

CECIL.   Why, Celia, this is monstrous! By
        what means
  Would Kraft enforce his will?

CELIA.   By force itself;
  And what he deems my ignorance.

CECIL.   Tell me, child,
  Has Kraft good reasons?

CELIA.   If he have?

CECIL.   Why, then
  [By your white soul, and by the work of Christ,
  Howe'er they storm, although with thunder-
        bolts
  As thick as bristling blades in bayonet charges]
  I stand between you and the coming danger.

CELIA.   I thank you, friend; but no; your race
        is mine.
  But one needs time to prove it.

CECIL.   Who meanwhile
  Will guard you?

CELIA.   Yes—who will?

CECIL.   That son of Kraft?

CELIA. He?—Such a villain, that his daintiest act
  Of kindness is a counterfeited coin
  With which he chaffers and intends to cheat!
  If I were drowning, I would spurn to grasp
  His hand, if it would draw me near himself.
  Better to die at once, when washed and clean,
  Than catch contagion and live on defiled.
CECIL. You must remain at my house.
       *Enter—Left Rear—*KRAFT.
KRAFT.   Celia here?
CELIA (*noticing* KRAFT).
  I—I—have an engagement. I must go.
       *Exit—Left Front—*CELIA.
KRAFT (*to* CECIL).
  I interrupt you. She was——
CECIL (*to* KRAFT).   Telling me
  That you desire to have her drop her studies.
KRAFT. Well, she must win her bread.
CECIL.   Quite true; but how?
KRAFT. Humph!—my affair!
CECIL.   Why, no; not wholly,—is it?
  Let me relieve you of the charge of her.
  And take it on myself. In two years' time,
  When once she gets to teaching, she can pay
    me.
KRAFT (*sarcastically*). Perhaps; but, by the
    way, now that you speak
  Of teaching, there is no one named, I think,
  For your professorship, in case you leave it.

CECIL. I have not left it yet.

KRAFT. You may do so.
If not, too, there are more professorships;
And I—I have a son.

CECIL. I see. No doubt
His claims would have fair hearing.

KRAFT. But if you
Could recommend him——

CECIL. That would pass for little;
I know so little of him.

KRAFT. But your word——

CECIL. Would, like a bank-note, quickly lose
its worth
Were nothing stored behind it, to make true
The storage it bespeaks.

[KRAFT. Humph! I have found
The men most praised for judgment are the
men
Most echoing others' judgments. Thus, for-
sooth,
They make their own appear approved by all.

CECIL. Not so with me! Has he experience
In teaching?

KRAFT. He has knowledge.

CECIL. For a teacher,
A knowledge of mere books does not suffice;
He needs a knowledge too of human nature;
And sympathy, to make his teaching welcome:
And fire, to make it felt; and tact and skill.

To aim and temper it for others' needs;
And modesty to keep his own acquirements
In strict-held servitude to their demands,
And dignity that comes from honoring truth,
To crown its bondman as the student's
     master.
What think you? Has he these?

KRAFT.   Has had no chance
   To show——

CECIL. Then why not test him where a failure
   Would not be trumpeted? A man's best
     friend
   Will bid him wait for honor till he earn it.
   Amid earth's envious crush of frenzied greed,
   It is no kindness, pushing to the front
   One who is not a leader. Zealous forms
   That crowd him there, may tramp him under
     foot.

KRAFT.   I will remember
   What you have said.]

Enter—Left Front—a GENTLEMAN *beckoning
          to* KRAFT.

*Exeunt—Left Front—*GENTLEMAN *and* KRAFT,
          after bowing to CECIL.

          *Enter—Right Front—*FREEMAN.

CECIL (*to* FREEMAN). I hear Kraft has a son.

FREEMAN. And I am more unfortunate—
   have met him.

[CECIL. He wants to rise in life.

FREEMAN.   In politics,—
  What low souls like because enabling them
  To worm themselves to slimy eminence
  Without abandoning the dirt they gloat in.]
    *Exeunt—Left Rear—*FREEMAN *and* CECIL.
    Dance music. Enter at the different en-
        trances, dancers in couples or in sets.
        At last, those nearest the Left beckon
        to the others, and all, as if suddenly
        called away, exeunt at the Left En-
        trances.
    *Enter—Right Rear—*JEM, *carrying a tray*
        with plates and refreshments on it.
        He looks at the dancers, then meeting
        MILLY, *he places the tray on the table*
        near the alcove.
    *Enter—Right Front—*MILLY, *carrying a*
        tray with glasses containing iced tea.
        She too places her tray on the table.
JEM *looks at the departing dancers and at*
        MILLY).
MILLY. De white folks leave deir shadders.
JEM (*stretching his hand to take* MILLY'S).
                  Heah! come heah!
MILLY (*drawing back her hand*).
  No, no, yer don't.
JEM (*looking sharply at her hand, which she keeps*
    clenched).   Now tell me what yer got
  In dat black hollah dah.

MILLY (*jerking her hand away*).

Jes' what yer hasn't.

JEM.   Come, come, now, Milly.   Lawd ob all
de stahs!

Dis heah's a patch ob his own pitchy sky,
   An' hol's a stah in dah.   Whose am it, hey?
MILLY.   Whose?   Mine.
JEM.   Yer'll catch it—libin' deed o' darkness!
MILLY (*throwing breast-pin from one hand into
   the other*).

Dey'll hab to catch dis fust.

JEM.   Come, yer knows, Milly,
   Dat I'll not gib yer way.   Say, whar'd yer get
   it?
MILLY.   Why, on de floah.
JEM.   Who drapt it off 'um den?
MILLY.   De folks dat owes us twenty times as
   much

As dat 'll fetch us.

(*shaking the breast-pin at* JEM.)

[JEM.   Ah, dat's right.
MILLY (*putting the breast-pin in her pocket*).

Yes, Laud!

An' doin' right.
JEM.   All 'cep' dat yer aint dancin'.
   (JEM *makes motions as if dancing.*)
   Heah, now, heah an' heah!
MILLY.   Now, Jem, yer wait.
JEM.   What fur?

MILLY.   'Case dey'll fine out.

JEM.   Ugh, dey can't see us.

MILLY.   Ole missus 's allers houndin' roun', yer
      knows,
  To fine de niggah.]
    (*moving and gesturing toward the alcove.*)
          Dah.   Set down.
          (MILLY *sits in the alcove.*)

JEM (*looking at the refreshments*).   An' take
  De crum dat's fallen fro' de rich man's table?—
  Dat'm scripter.   (JEM *sits.*)
          Look heah, Milly.

MILLY.   What's ter see?

JEM.   Dis dahky's lips would like anoder cake.
      (*puckering lips, as if to kiss her.*)

MILLY.   Oh, yer go home.

JEM.   No; it am cold out dah.

MILLY.   Den let it shake yer! yer got one wife
      now.

JEM.   Not one! De las' 'un, Dinah, 'm sold, yer
      know—
  Gone like de dark cloud when de night am
      come.
  I'll nebah see her moah.

MILLY.   Jem, dat am sad.

JEM.   An' yer don't reckon dis Jem's meant ter
      be
  A gem widout a settin'?

MILLY.   Dah's de white folks.

Enter — Left Rear — BLAVER *and* MISS
    PRIMWOOD—MILLY *and* JEM *rise,*
    taking their trays.

[JEM.   Well, dey don't reckon so nuther.

MILLY.   What dey reckons,
    Dey show by sellin' Dinah.

JEM.   What yer reckon——

MILLY.   Is all de number ob yer wives!
            (*bowing to* JEM.)

JEM.   Yer can't.]

*Exeunt—Right Front—*MILLY *and* JEM *hurriedly.*

MISS PRIMWOOD (*catching a glimpse of them, and
            holding up her hands*).

None have religion, none—I tell you none.

Men are not solemnized as once they were.

BLAVER.   No, they are sodomized. You say
        you saw

In Cecil's hand, a reddish-colored dram?

MISS PRIMWOOD.   It might have been——

BLAVER.   To those who saw it drunk
    It looked, at least, like liquor. He was not
    Avoiding the appearances of evil,
    [Is not the man I thought—no proper mate
    For Madam Cecil. She——

MISS PRIMWOOD.   You think so, eh?—
    Men never will know women.   This is
        hers—
    Her party—making those not thirsty drink,
    And eat, too, with no appetite,—and dance,

When prudence knows, they ought to be in
   bed.]
    *Enter—Right—*MILLY, *carrying a tray
        containing a reddish-colored liquid in
        glasses. She stops before* BLAVER.

BLAVER (*to* MILLY).
  Ah,—what is this?
MILLY.   Iced tea.
BLAVER   Why, that will be
  Refreshing, very!—Here! (*pointing to the chairs
  near the table*). Iced tea!
        (*To* MILLY.) Yes, yes.
    (BLAVER *and* MISS P. *sit at the table.
      MILLY places two glasses of the red-
      dish-colored liquid before them.*)
BLAVER (*continuing the interrupted conversation*).
  Where none wish levity, affairs like this
  Create it. I have known most sober men
  Grow indiscreet—(*tasting the tea.*)
        This is good, yes—and make
  All that they pray for seem ridiculous.
Enter—Left and Right—couples walking together.
      *Exit—Left—*MILLY.
*Enter—Right—*JEM *carrying a tray on which
  are plates containing refreshments to eat.*
MISS PRIMWOOD (*looking in disapprobation at
  the couples*).
  And scenes like this, too, cater to flirtation—
    (*looking at two elderly people together.*)

In them so old, too, they should be above it.

> (MISS PRIMWOOD'S *spoon that she has been
>   using, falls to the floor.*— BLAVER
>   *hands* MISS P. *his spoon that he has
>   not used, at the same time picking up*
>   MISS P's. *spoon and significantly plac-
>   ing it in his own cup.*)

BLAVER.   Precisely!

MISS P.   Yes, at times, it makes me feel—

BLAVER (*who evidently has lost the connection of
          thought*).

Flirtation makes you feel?

MISS P. (*in evident disgust*).   Oh no; not that!

> (JEM *stands before them with his tray.*)

BLAVER (*noticing* JEM, *and taking the plates from
           his tray for* MISS P. *and himself, as if
           thinking* MISS P. *referred to these*).

Oh yes, I see!

MISS P. (*disliking his inference with reference to
           the meaning of her former words*).

No, no!

BLAVER (*referring to the plates*).   Not take them?

MISS P.   These?

Oh yes, I thank you.—You mistook my
meaning.

I sometimes think that none should feel at all.

*Exit—Right—*JEM.

*Exeunt—Right and Left—the promenading
          Couple*s.

BLAVER. No, in flirtation none should feel at
    all.
MISS P. No, no, no! not in that—in anything.
    If none would feel, none would have dis-
      content;
    And that would cure all evils of the time.
[BLAVER. Yes, that is true. Why, even small
      boys now,
    Must have small beer——
MISS P.   For that will pop, you know!
    Will make a noise! explode monotony!]
    Our slaves now even hint of earning wages;
    And girls, once clad in bonnets and in slippers,
    Now strut in hats and boots.
BLAVER.   And where, strut where?
MISS P. Well put, well put, my friend! They
      strut for schools
    In which they study, think and talk like boys.
[BLAVER. And times that do not like a cackling
      hen,
    And seek to fill their coops with fowl that crow,
    Will not get many eggs.
MISS P.   No, no; will not!—
    Think what a scandal, if our highest courts——
BLAVER. Should not court women of the high-
      est kind.
MISS P. Precisely; and o'errule th' iniquity
    That gives free entrance into men's resorts
    Of maids——

BLAVER. That in your school are prized like
jewels!]

(BLAVER *and* MISS P. *continue their conversation
aside.*)

*Enter—Left Rear—*CECIL *and* FATHER HYCHER.

CECIL. Yes, Father Hycher; but you know our
laws

Have never recognized the churches thus.

FATHER H. But we have rights—

CECIL. To change the laws you have,
But not to break them.

FATHER H. Did one merely waive
The letter of the law, what could be harmed?

*Enter—Left Rear—*FREEMAN.

CECIL. One's conscience, if he went against
the law,—

One's heed of right,—a fact, I take it, Father,
You ought to see.

FATHER H. I do not see it so;
And if I did, above it I could see
A higher law.

*Exit—Left Rear—*FATHER H.

[CECIL (*to* FREEMAN).

Humph, humph! we live to learn.
It seems that even formalists like him
Can see some spirit through a form; but
what?—

One time upon a mountain top, I saw
My own shape magnified on clouds about me.

How many men in earth's high places find,
Looming on clouds of false regard about them,
False forms of self, distorted in their size!
To waken such to their own true position,
Thank heaven for precipices! When they fall,
Their views of God and self, turned upside
    down,
    May bring, at last, conversion.]

(CECIL *and* FREEMAN *move toward the right near*
      where BLAVER *and* MISS P. *are sitting.*
      Both rise.)

MISS P.   Oh, Professor,
    Professor Cecil, how your ears must burn!
    You know the rumors that are in the wind.

CECIL (*bowing and motioning them to be seated*).
    Trust not in words with wind alone to back
      them.
    Nothing is quite so empty as the sky
    Behind a blow, when once it has blown by.

MISS P.   That does for you to say; but you two
    friends, (*bowing to* BLAVER.)
    Your judgment, (*bowing to* CECIL.)
            and your judgments, when they rule
    Our civil, social, educational ways,
    Will put a close to some things.

CECIL.   To their life?

MISS P.   How you enjoy a joke!—You read,
    not so? (*gesturing toward* BLAVER.)
    The deacon's latest work?

CECIL.   To tell the truth,
   I have not yet——
MISS P.   So little interest?—
CECIL.   Of course the question has two sides——
BLAVER (*aside to* FREEMAN).   Two sides?—
   It has but one.   I see—he is not with us.
MISS P.   The great book of the age!
BLAVER (*to* MISS P).   You flatter me.
              (*to* CECIL).
   [She likes my essay, since, on general grounds,
   As I detail the duties of the state,
   I argue prohibition by the whole
   Of all things detrimental to the part,
   Applying this, not only to the cause
   To which my life is pledged, but with this, too,
   To questions like the giving of instruction
   To slaves, and free tuition to poor whites,
   And throwing open to our girls and women
   The State schools, not the ones to train their
       sex.
   It is my proving of this latter point
   Enlists her praise, whose long—
    (MISS P. *straightens up and draws back.*)
              no, I mean wide—
   Whose wide experience, as the principal
   Of our first female college, seals her right
   To criticise all efforts of the State
   To train our girls in different schools from
       hers.

CECIL (*in good-natured banter*).
    Ah, yes, I see.   The same boat floats you both.
    You pull together.   Friends are worth the
        having
    Who best can serve themselves when serving
        us.]

MISS P. Oh, you must read his book!—will
    like it too;
    If but for what it says of slaves and women.

CECIL. You class the two together? I should
    not.

FREEMAN. (*aside to* CECIL). How women love
    their fetters!—Best, perhaps!
    They make sweet slaves, but very bitter
        masters.

            *Exit—Right—*FREEMAN.

MISS P. You would not open then our college
    doors
    To women?

CECIL.   Why not?

MISS P.   Why, our boys and girls
    Might think of love!

CECIL.   That would be no new thing;
    And, being wont to walk in love, when young,
    They might be much less prone to fall in love,
    In ways not wise, when older.

MISS P.   But their minds
    Are so unlike!—

CECIL.   And never can be matched

23

Until they learn to share each other's aims.
Souls are not mated when two forms of
    flesh
Join hands, or merely share each other's
    arms.

Miss P. And you would have them like each
    other?

Cecil.   Yes.
It seems important if they are to marry.
Like ought to go with like. And paths that
    push
Young men and maids together, whet their
    wits
And make their weddings wise ones.

[Miss P.   Always?

Cecil.   No;
But oftener, yes much oftener so, than else-
    wise.
Where true love is the treasure to be sought,
One glimpse of nature is a better guide
Than all the forms of calculating art
That ever powdered an instinctive flush,
Or rouged pale hate, in any masquerade
That men call good society.]

Miss P.   But few
Would think you had so much romance in
    you.

[Cecil. All have romance, if only they have
    soul.

They differ but in their expressions of it.
*Enter—Right Rear—*Jem *with a tray holding*
refreshments.

Miss P.   And most of them believe, with Deacon
Blaver,
It should not be expressed in school.
Cecil.   Why not?
Romance is but the day-time of the soul
Well sunned by love, beneath which, when we
dwell,
Each act of duty and each thought of truth
Is haloed with a light that seems like heaven's.
To spirits rightly moved, the whole of life,—
Home, school, religion—all lead through ro-
mance.
                (Jem *speaks aside to* Cecil.)
(Blaver *and* Miss P. *rise while* Cecil *gestures to-*
ward the chairs, Jem *and the refreshments.*)
Cecil.   Oh, pray be seated, and take more.
Miss P.   Thanks.
Blaver.   Thanks.
(Jem *removes from the table the empty glasses and*
plates, and substitutes full ones.)
Miss P.   And do you then approve, do you
admire
Lean, short-haired women, and lank, long-
haired men,
Exchanging shawls and coats, and stripping
life

Of character, to make it caricature?

*Exit—Right Rear—*JEM.

CECIL.   I do not much admire the straw in
  spring

That forms the spread of flower-beds; but
  beneath

Sleep summer's fairest offspring.   What you
  moot

May show two sides. A man may be run down

Amid the clash and clangor of a street,

Because one ear is deaf.   In any path,

The rush of life may run down all who hear

But on one side.]

*Enter—Right—*FREEMAN.

[MISS P.   But when one side is right.

CECIL.   The right is that to which the world
  moves on.

You cross its track to stop it; it moves on,

You fall.]

(CECIL *bows and turns toward* FREEMAN. BLAVER
  and MISS P. *bow, then continue conversing.*)

[MISS P.   And this he does not mean to do

For my cause or for yours. Trust me for
  that.

BLAVER.   His friends must see he does not get
  so high

That falling far will hurt him.]

          (BLAVER *and* MISS P. *sit down; and talk
            aside, till, after a little,* BLAVER *points*

vigorously toward the Right Front.
Then both rise, taking plates and
glasses with them, and exeunt at the
Right Front.)

*Enter—Left Rear—*MADAM CECIL, MA-
DAM LOWE *and* LOWE, *carrying his*
plans.

MADAM CECIL.   We shall find him.
(*to* CECIL.)
Oh, here you are! Come look at these—
(*pointing to* LOWE's *plans*.) these plans.
Are just the thing the city needs. We two
Were searching all the house for you.

(MADAM CECIL *and* MADAM LOWE *remain near*
the Left Rear.)

CECIL *motions to* FREEMAN *indicating*
that he look at the plans with him,
which FREEMAN *does.*

CECIL (*replying partly to* MADAM C. *and partly*
speaking to LOWE).   I see.

LOWE (*pointing to a part of the plan*). And see
the church here?

CECIL.   Oh! is that the church?
But I thought you a Friend?

LOWE.   The company
Are world's folk—will not build a meeting.
So
We would not quarrel with them. We build
this.

FREEMAN (*laughing good-naturedly*).
      You beat the Masonic order.   They but make
      A show of their religion when they lay
      A corner-stone.   You lay out for it now.
LOWE.   Ah yes!   With me religion is the chief
      Consideration.   Think how poor our life
      Would be without religion.
FREEMAN.   Be less rich,
      You think.
LOWE.   Just so; for there is nothing like
      A church to elevate the character——
FREEMAN.   Of real estate, I see—
LOWE (*half realizing that he is being made a butt.*)
                              And people too.
[FREEMAN.   No people live here yet?
LOWE.   Ah, but they will——
FREEMAN.   If you do what is right to draw them
            here.
      To build a church is right—not so?—and
            right
      Is your religion.
LOWE.   Yes; but one might think
      His motives were not rightly understood.
FREEMAN (*glancing toward* CECIL *significantly*).
      I think we understand them perfectly.
LOWE (*looking particularly toward* CECIL).
      And like the plans then?
FREEMAN.   Oh, he must—as plans.
      They plan so far ahead.

Lowe.   A man who sees
  A mountain in his path that must be climbed,
  Will make more effort.   Effort is our need.
  With such a plan as this, our friends will know
  We need more money, and will find us more.]
Cecil.   Quite true.
(Madam Cecil *comes to them.*   Freeman *turns*
        to speak to Madam Lowe.)
Lowe (*to* Cecil).
                  Am glad to meet your approbation.
Cecil.   Not that, quite that!   Men take too
      many chances
  In drawing facts from fancies.   I shall need
  To weigh——
*Exeunt—Right Rear—*Freeman *and* Madam
              Lowe.

Lowe (*half in earnest turning to* Madam Cecil).
          If friends thus judge us as our foes do,
  What good then does it do to have a friend?
Cecil (*earnestly and good-naturedly*).
  To prove to all the justice of our souls
  That wish for friends both generous and
      just.—
              (*taking the plans in his hands.*)
  One cannot fully take these in, at first.
          *Enter—Right Rear—*Jem.
Madam C. (*to* Lowe, *as if with a covert meaning*).
  You leave them here.   We must look over
      them.

(*She motions toward* JEM, *to whom* CECIL
*hands the plans, at the same time
motioning to him to take them to the
Left.* JEM *turns, and presently,*)
Exit—Left Rear—JEM.

(*When* CECIL *and* MADAM C. *turn toward* JEM,
LOWE *turns toward the Right, evidently dis-
satisfied.*)
Exit—Right Rear—LOWE.

MADAM C. (*to* CECIL, *and evidently annoyed to see*
LOWE *leaving them*).

  Kraft, Hycher, Lowe and Blaver,—all, to-
    night,
  All frown at things that you have said to them.
  Why will you always give these men offense?

CECIL.   Because I give them truth.

MADAM C.   Truth is for fools.

CECIL.   I give it to them.

MADAM C.   Humph! It comes from fools.

CECIL.   Yes, if they think men want it I do not.
  They merely need it.

MADAM C.   Need? What for?

CECIL.   Their good—
  Their own, and—say—humanity's.

MADAM C.   The good
  All seek from men like you, is leadership.
  But he who leads men up, himself must
    mount
  Where he appears above them.

CECIL. How and where
He mounts, depends on that in which he leads.
A leader in the truth would better kneel
Upon the footstool of a throne, than sit
Upon it, crowned by falsehood.

MADAM C. Would you were,
But what I thought you were when we were
wed!

[CECIL (*kindly*).
Come, come, your wishes, like wild steeds,
escape
The reining of your reason, and may wreck it.
Why wish a station higher than we have?

MADAM C. For you—your influence.

CECIL. Nay, in that you err.
True words alone are weapons of true thought.
If I be free to use these, I am free
To be truth's champion. If, to gain the place
You wish me, or to hold it, being gained,
I let my tongue be tied, I live a slave.]

MADAM C.
A woman wrecked at sea, would better lash
The anchor to her throat, than try to breast
The waves of life in such a world as this,
Wed to a man without ambition. She
Could not sink sooner.

CECIL (*gazing and gesturing at their surroundings*).
Do you sink, my wife,
With such surroundings?

MADAM C. Yes, for power and wealth
  Both loom before you. When I tell it you,
  And strive to urge you toward them, you,
    blind loot,
  Squat, blinking like an owl; or, if you stir,
  But flutter, blunder, miss your aim, and fall
  From off the very branch, the topmost branch,
  You ought to perch upon.

CECIL. Alas, my wife,
  I thought you loved me for the man I was.
  I never wrought or wished for wealth.

MADAM C. Oh, drone,
  That I could sting you, as do bees their
    drones
  That make no honey!

CECIL. You do sting at times.
  That pleases you?—But you have better
    moods.
  I never could have thought I loved you else.
  Why blame my soul, because it must be true
  To higher aims and higher influence?
  If, seeking these, this world's promotion come,
  Let come! I take it then by right divine.

MADAM C. Fanatic! Do you think in men's
    mad rush,
  Each toward his own life's goal, they wrest
    the power
  That makes another serve them, without
    work?—

Skill? shrewdness? tact? and forcing to the
    wall,
Or down the precipice, each weaker rival?

CECIL. I do, if power that crowns them come
    from God.

MADAM C. The power that crowns one with
    success on earth
  Is earthly. Keen men know this. Not, not
    God:
  The devil rules the world.

CECIL.   God overrules it.

MADAM C. In far results, but in the near ones
    never!

CECIL. Then look to far results. Transferring
    there
  These transient whims,—ah you will find them
    melt,
  Like summer mist, while, rock-bound under
    them,
  Each goal remains that your true nature
    craves.
  Why seek for riches, when we have enough?

MADAM C. Enough! Oh, sluggard! Have we
    that?

CECIL.   We have—
  Enough for comfort, not enough for care;
  Enough to make us grateful for the wage
  Rewarding earnest work; but not enough
  To bind long habit to their fate whose course

While serving earth has made them slaves to
    it.
The peace of life crowns competence, not
    wealth.
The wise man wants no more.

Madam C.   But woman does.
        Exit—Right Rear—Madam Cecil.

Cecil.   Then let no wise man marry. Cursèd
    fate!—
[This trudging on and on in paths of right,
And knowing every pace takes one more
    stride
Away from all one loves!—From all one
    loves?—
No, no;—from all that, once, one thought he
    loved.
Oh, cruel customs of a cruel world,
Which damn us for those dreams that seem to
    be
Our holiest inspirations! Cruel dreams,
That never prove delusions, till the world
Welds bonds for us that death alone can
    break!
And cruel bonds that make all happiness,
In one so bound, impossibility,
Unless he live a sneak's life—who is this?]
        Enter—Left Rear—Celia.
Why Celia!

Celia.   I have come to tell you, friend,

The man I fear is here. I saw his face,
And like a thunder-cloud foretelling storm——
CECIL. Come first where we shall not be over-
　　　heard.
　　　*Exeunt—Right Front—*CECIL *and* CELIA.
　　　*Enter—Right Rear—*FREEMAN *and* FAITH.
FREEMAN. You love me, Faith. Your manner
　　　tells me so.
FAITH. Your rival, Freeman, is no man, mere
　　　man.
FREEMAN. You are deceived. You vow through
　　　—to—a man.
　　And he will treat you—how?—His door is
　　　locked:
　　He holds the key. Your uncle, though a
　　　priest,
　　Has eyes upon your wealth. The thing is
　　　proved.
　　Your dying father feared this. Faith, I knew
　　His wish for you. Trust him, trust me, your
　　　friend,
　　Disrobed of mystery, save th' eternal one
　　Which thrills us now, whom heaven has made
　　　for mates.
[FAITH. I would not give you up so, save to wed
　　A holier spouse.
FREEMAN. 　　　　Yet one that is, at times,
　　A Moloch, clasping in his arms of fire
　　Desires he kindles, but can never quench.

FAITH. Oh, Freeman, when you speak, I
tremble so!
You fill my soul with fears for you; but, ah,
With fears that are so sweet, again I fear
That my own soul is what I most should
fear.
FREEMAN. The wise fright off their fears by
facing them.
Will you not be my bride? Be this and use
Your freedom as your father would have
wished.]

*Enter—Left Rear—*FATHER HYCHER.

FATHER H. (*to* FAITH).
What?—Have I warned you, Faith, so many
times?
And you still parley with this infidel?—
Obey me now!—Away! No more of this!
(*Faith moves toward the Left Front—*
FREEMAN *starts to follow her.* FATHER
HYCHER *calls to him.*)
You will not follow her?—

*Exit—Left Front—*FAITH.

FREEMAN.   No?—wherefore not?
FATHER H.   I am her uncle.
FREEMAN.   Not her father, though!
FATHER H.   Her spirit's—I direct her steps.
FREEMAN.   Step-father?—
In that rôle men like you are just ideal!
But I am, that which you are not—her friend.

FATHER H.   You are a young man with a young
    man's dreams.

FREEMAN.   You are an old man; and an old
    man schemes.

  And she has wealth, and you have use for it.

[FATHER H.   And you think you have none!
    Oho, young man,

  When you have read yourself, you may be
    heard

  When trying to read others.   But we waste

  Our time.   I am her guardian; and you

  Should act the gentleman.

FREEMAN.   Which when I act,

  I shall not take my lessons all from you.

FATHER H.   Take this at least.—A gentleman
    is one

  Who never does the unexpected.

FREEMAN.   Well,

  By that test you can pass.   I grant it you.

  All you have done has been in character.

  You call me infidel; but, Father Hycher,

  The infidel is one who does not trust

  The God that made and moves the soul
    within.

  If Faith did not desire another life

  Than you have planned, you might be wise
    and kind.

FATHER H.   Poor youth, when you know more
    about the world——

FREEMAN.   I shall know more about such men
    as you;
  Know how the dust of earth can make one
      blind,
  And din can make one deaf, till skies can
      blaze
  And heaven's voice thunder, yet no sight nor
      sound
  Reach——
FATHER H. (*sarcastically*).   What?—
FREEMAN.   What was a soul!   But there are
    souls
  Are stolen too when stoled.   The devil's hand
  Out-does the deacon's.   There is nothing left
  But vestment.   All the barterer's priceless
      birthright
  Goes for the mess of pottage that he feeds on.
  Not strange such like to limit others' joys,
  Turn nature inside out and upside down,
  Claim spirit rules where all are slaves of sense,
  And heaven their realm, though all is rimmed
      by hell.]
FATHER H.   Humph, humph, my friend, you yet
    shall writhe for this.

    *Exit—Left Front—*FATHER HYCHER.
    *Enter—Right Front—*CECIL *and* CELIA.
CECIL (*to* FREEMAN.)
  Why, friend, you seem excited.   What has
    roiled you?

FREEMAN. Oh nothing, nothing, nothing **but**
    a toad
  That squat upon a flower here in your garden!
CECIL. Here is another flower may take **its**
    place.
  I must attend the guests, and this, our
    friend,
  Needs your protection. She will tell you why.
  I leave her with you.
      *Enter—Right Rear—*MADAM CECIL.
      (CECIL *continues to* CELIA, *taking her hand.*)
          And remember, Celia,
  You must not fail to stay with us to-night.
(FREEMAN *and* CELIA *move toward the alcove at*
        the Right.)
MADAM CECIL (*to* CECIL).
  I thought so! I have spied this play before.
  Men seldom waive the wishes of their wives
  Except to welcome other women's wishes.—
  You have forgotten you have other guests.
  A storm is coming on. They wish to leave;
  And we should speed their parting. Shall we
    go?
FREEMAN (*to* CELIA, *motioning toward the alcove*).
  By staying here, we may keep out the way.
      *Exeunt—Left Rear—*CECIL *and* MADAM
        C. FREEMAN *and* CELIA *seat them-*
        selves in the alcove.
*Enter—Left Rear—*FATHER *and* WIDOW HYCHER.
24

FATHER H. (*to* WIDOW H).

 Let him have all her money that you live on?—
 Not I!

WIDOW H. (*to* FATHER H.). He shall not call on
  Faith again.

FATHER H. She may be out?

WIDOW H.   She may.—And you, you liked
 The altar cloth?

FATHER H. Embroidered wonderously!

 Your candlesticks too go so well now with——

FREEMAN (*to* CELIA).

      Ideals from dark ages?

WIDOW H. (*to* FATHER H.). When you pray—

FATHER H. (*to* WIDOW H.).

 Their lights appear like starlight sprinkling me
 With spray-drops of the heaven-light whence
  it came—
 I think of you.

WIDOW H. (*to* FATHER H.).

     Of me, and not of God?

FATHER H. (*to* WIDOW H.).

 Of you because of God.—Who could forget
 Your share in rendering His house attractive?

FREEMAN (*to* CELIA).

 Especially in the front pew with her bonnet,—
 Heaved at him like some second flower-
  crowned censer.

FATHER H. (*to* WIDOW H).

 I think that all men must have noticed this.

FREEMAN (*to* CELIA).
    The usual result:—heads crown'd with flowers
    Nod most for bees that buzz and sting about
        them.

WIDOW H. (*to* FATHER H.]
    And Cecil—will you aid him?

FATHER H. (*to* WIDOW H.).   Humph! a cause
    Once lost is not the one I follow.

*Exeunt—Left—*FATHER HYCHER *and* WIDOW
             HYCHER.

CELIA (*to* FREEMAN).   Cause?—
    Does he mean Cecil's?

FREEMAN.   Hope so! Happy Cecil!—
    High noon will come for him when he can
      see
    A form like that one shadowing him no more.

CELIA. I think it always may seem noon to
      those
    Who trample all their shadows underfoot
    As he does.

*Enter—Right Rear—*LOWE *and* MADAM LOWE.
    (*The air becomes gradually darker.*)

FREEMAN (*pointing toward the Right Rear*).
             Very true! But what of those
    Who deem it wise to keep themselves in shade,
    Held as a shield to ward away the light
    With every ray of color that might reach
      them,
    As if they thought it their worst enemy?

LOWE (*to* MADAM LOWE).

The air seems weighted with a coming storm.

FREEMAN (*to* CELIA).

Their airs appear so.   Yes.

MADAM L. (*to* LOWE).   Must hurry home.

(*Thunder in the distance.*)

How near! We should have been at meeting!

LOWE (*to* MADAM L.)   Yes,

But if we had been there, how could one then
Have shown those plans?

MADAM L. (*to* LOWE). Of course, we had to
come,

But this man Cecil seems not pious.

LOWE (*to* MADAM L.).   No;

You heard how they made light of that new
building,—

One, too, for their own sect!

MADAM L. (*to* LOWE).

Yes, I have heard

Enough for once.   That irreligious music!

LOWE (*to* MADAM L.).

And noise and dancing!   It was fortunate
The supper-room was opened early.

MADAM L. (*to* LOWE).   Yes.

(*Distant thunder.*)

LOWE (*to* MADAM L.).

And one good thing!—this thunder storm will
end it.

*Exeunt—Left Rear—*LOWE *and* MADAM LOWE.

FREEMAN (*to* CELIA).

   I wonder if they really grudge each draft
   Of those enjoying what is past their taste?
   I hate to think it, yet at times, one must,
   That some men deem mere conscious envy
       conscience;
   And seem most zealous when they are but
       jealous.

(*Thunder louder than before.* CELIA *and* FREE-
      MAN *both rise.*)

   But hear the storm. I think it best you stay
   Inside the study.

(FREEMAN *points toward the Left Rear.*)

CELIA (*pointing toward the Left Front*).

              We can pass through here.

FREEMAN. And I must go, and call these men
     I know,
   Detectives—good ones—they will shadow him.

*Exeunt—Left Front—*FREEMAN *and* CELIA.

     *Enter—Left Rear—*BLAVER, LOWE, MISS
        PRIMWOOD *and* MADAM LOWE, *and*
        others, all with hats and cloaks, evi-
        dently prepared to leave the house.

BLAVER (*to* LOWE).

   I used to have some confidence in Cecil.

LOWE (*to* BLAVER).

   But now he shows this lack of enterprise!

BLAVER. A man like him will never aid my plans,
   Nor yours.

> *Enter—Left Rear; and Exeunt Right Rear*
> *—*Father Hycher, Widow Hycher
> *and* Faith, *prepared to leave the house;*
> *also* Freeman.

*Enter—Left Rear—*Madam Cecil, *followed by*
Jem.

Lowe.   And wise men, when they fear a fight,
Will never lend one weapon to a foe.

Madam C. (*to* Miss Primwood).
You leave us in a storm.

Blaver (*to* Madam Cecil).   No storm as yet.
I thank you for a very pleasant evening
          (*shaking hands with* Madam C.).

Madam C. (*shaking hands with* Blaver).
Good evening.   (*to* Jem.)
          Here, Jem, show them to the gate.

> Madam C. *motions to* Jem *who Exits at*
> *the Right Rear—*Miss Primwood,
> *then* Lowe, *then* Madam Lowe, *also*
> *others, shake hands with* Madam C.

Miss P.   Good-night.

Madam C.   Good-night.

Lowe.   Good-night.

Madam L.   Good-night.

Madam C.   Good-night.

> *Exeunt—Right Rear—*Blaver *with* Miss
> Primwood, Lowe *with* Madam
> Lowe *and others.*
> *Enter—Right Front—*Kraft.

KRAFT.   Where went your husband?

MADAM C.   He?—With guests, perhaps.

KRAFT.   Or, say, with Celia.

MADAM C.   What?—Your scheme
   has failed?

KRAFT.   Not yet; my men are here.
          *Enter—Right Rear—*JEM.
(*Thunder and lightning—*KRAFT *points toward*
                    JEM.)   You send for him,
   And I will send for her.

MADAM C. (*to* JEM).   Jem, find your master.
   I wish to see him.   Say it is important.
          *Exit—Left Rear—*JEM.
               (*to* KRAFT.)

   [Now let him leave her but one little mo-
      ment,
   As leave he must, and we shall have her
      seized.
   And may a pall, as black as tops this night,
          (*Thunder and lightning.*)
   Come down, and hide her face from us for-
      ever.]
        KRAFT *beckons toward the Right Front.*
          *Enter—Right Front—*TWO MEN.
*Exeunt—Left Front—*KRAFT *and the* TWO MEN.
          *Enter—Left Rear—*CECIL.
             (*Thunder and lightning.*)
CECIL (*to* MADAM CECIL).   What is your
   wish?

MADAM C.   What care you, for my wish?
Oh, I was but a fool, to wed a fool!
Like goes with like.   I now acknowledge it.
        (*Thunder and lightning.*)
You might have been—ah me!—what might
    you not?
Position, wealth,—all waited on your nod.
You have dismissed them by your course
    to-night;
But one hope now remains, and that through
    Kraft.
    Enter—Left Rear—in trepidation, CELIA.
        (*Thunder and lightning.*)
CELIA.   Help! help!
CECIL (*to* CELIA).

                Come here.   What is it?
CELIA.   He—with men!
    They come to take me.
CECIL.   That they shall not do.
MADAM C.   Wait, wait! Her guardian claims
        her.   Who are you?
CECIL.   A man who shields a woman.
MADAM C.   If she lie?—
CECIL.   Then he can prove it.
MADAM C.   Dare you tell him that?—
    Him, Kraft,—the man on whom alone de-
        pends
    Your chance now for promotion?
            (*Thunder and lightning.*)

CELIA (*to* CECIL).   Do not harm
   Yourself.

CECIL (*to* CELIA).   One harms himself the most
     when letting
   One weaker than himself be harmed.—Hide
     here!

(*He points toward a window curtain at the*
                Rear.)

    *Exit—behind the curtain—*CELIA.

MADAM C. (*to* CECIL).
   You do not know.—They claim her as a slave.

CECIL (*to* MADAM C.).   I save her as a woman.

MADAM C.   But the law—
   The sentiment—the spirit of the State.—
   You dare not shield her.

       (*Thunder and lightning.*)

CECIL.   Wherefore dare I not?

MADAM C.   No man has ever yet with us been
     left
   Not ruined—left alive—who ventured this.
   Your influence, your position, property,
   Your life, my home, my hope for you,—all, all,
   Would all be forfeited.

       (*Thunder and lightning.*)

CECIL.   Well, let them go.
   When they have stripped me of all things
     besides,
   I shall have left a clean, clear conscience, death
   And heaven.

MADAM C.   You madman!

CECIL.   Not as mad as you:
I wait for proof.

MADAM C.   And if they prove their case?—

CECIL.   I wait then till they take her.   But
they come.
            (*Thunder and lightning.*)
      *Enter—Left Front—*KRAFT *with two men.*

KRAFT (*to* CECIL).
   Is Celia here?
      (*advancing toward the Left Rear Entrance.*)
                         I say, is Celia here?

CECIL (*standing in front of the Left Rear En-
      trance—and looking around*).
   I do not see her here.

KRAFT.   I too have eyes.
   I did not ask that.   She was in this house.

CECIL.   She was my guest; if she be still within
   She still then is my guest.

KRAFT.   I am her guardian.

CECIL.   And so am I, while I remain her host.
            (*Thunder and lightning.*)
      (CECIL *looks at the men behind* KRAFT.)
   You seem to wish to guard her well,—too
      well.

KRAFT.   I do and shall—for she belongs to me.

CECIL.   Well, prove your case.

KRAFT.   You ask for proof from me,—
   A gentleman?—

CECIL.   I ask for proof from you.

KRAFT.   You hint I am no gentleman?

CECIL.   I say
> You are not gentle in your present mood;
> And that child is—too gentle far for you.

KRAFT.   What?—You defy me?—I shall search
> for her.

>   (*Thunder and lightning*).

CECIL.   Not till you get by me!

(CECIL *pulls out a pistol.* MADAM C. *seizes it.*)

KRAFT.   And that we shall!

> (KRAFT *dashes at* CECIL, *followed by his
> men. A pistol-shot is heard.* CECIL
> *falls. Violent thunder and lightning.*)

*Enter—Right Rear—*FREEMAN *with two detectives.*

FREEMAN.   Here! seize them! Stop the villains,
> every one!

*Exeunt—Left Front—*KRAFT *and men, followed
> by detectives.*

> *Enter—from behind the curtain—*CELIA,
> *and bends over* CECIL, *excitedly ex-
> amining into his condition.*

FREEMAN (*snatching the pistol from* MADAM C.).
> Aha, you are the murderer? you? eh?—
> you?

MADAM C.   I did not fire it.

FREEMAN (*examining the pistol*).

>   One ball gone! Who did?—
> Confess it, or convict your lover, Kraft.

CELIA (*wringing her hands over* CECIL'S *prostrate body*).
   Oh, he is dead for me!—The only man
   I ever loved is dead for me, for me!
       (*Thunder and lightning.*)

CURTAIN.

ACT SECOND.

SCENE FIRST:—*A sick chamber. At the Left, just behind the Front Entrance, is an alcove. In this, visible to the audience, is a bed. In front of the bed is a chair and a small table, and on the latter are bottles and glasses. On the bed is an effigy of* CECIL *who is apparently lying there insensible. Forming the back curtain of the stage is a representation of the wall of an ordinary bedroom.*

> ENTRANCES: *by doors at the Right and Left; also, farther back at the Left, connecting with the space behind the bed in the alcove.*
>
> *The rising curtain reveals a* PHYSICIAN *sitting in the chair beside the bed, and* CELIA *just entering the room, or standing near him.*

CELIA (*to* PHYSICIAN).

How fortunate for Freeman and myself
That Kraft and Madam Cecil should have fled
And left with us the man they thought was
    murdered!
Now we can nurse him, as he should be
    nursed.—

How does he seem this morning?

PHYSICIAN.   Very low.

CELIA.   Too low, you think, to rally and recover?

PHYSICIAN (*rising from the chair and offering it to
          CELIA*).

No man could tell—no other case just like it.
One would not think a bullet lodged as this
          one
Enough to insulate the brain entirely,
Yet not a nerve will act.   He scarcely seems
To see, or hear, or even feel one touch him.

CELIA (*looking at* CECIL).

It seems like death.

PHYSICIAN.   Yes, very much like death.

CELIA.   He seems to think, though.

PHYSICIAN.   Yes; for he is living.

CELIA.   In states like this, what can a person
          think of?

PHYSICIAN.   Why, he may dream of what he
          did, and was,
And wished he was, before he reached them.

CELIA.   So?

PHYSICIAN.   There could be nothing else for
          him to think of.

CELIA. I sometimes hope he knows that I am by.

PHYSICIAN (*rising and preparing to leave*).

Perhaps he does.   At any sign of it,
A word might make him conscious of your
          presence,

And keep him so. They say that things more
    slight
Than flickering flames, attracting conscious-
    ness
At times, if they but set the nerves to thrilling,
Wake slumbering senses into life again.
CELIA. Why, that would be like calling back
    to earth
A spirit after it had flown.
PHYSICIAN.   It would.
CELIA. You think it could be done?—that
    human tones,
Though he might not conceive what thought
    was uttered;
That human touches, though he might not
    know
Just who it was that held him, hand in
    hand,—
That these might find him where the spirit
    dreams,
And comfort him, and draw him here once
    more?
PHYSICIAN. Who knows?—Why not?
CELIA.   I thank you for the thought.
  You come to-morrow?
PHYSICIAN.   Yes, good day.
CELIA.   Good day.
    *Exit—Right—*PHYSICIAN. CELIA *moves*
      toward the door with the PHYSICIAN.

> *Then she returns to the bed, sits in the chair beside it, and apparently takes* CECIL'S *hand in her own.*

SCENE SECOND:—*The stage is darkened, and the curtain forming the back of the room in Scene First rises, leaving everything on the stage in front of this curtain the same as in Scene First.* CELIA, *however, no longer sits by the bed in the alcove. At the rear of the stage, is an extensive sylvan landscape, trees, rocks, mosses, etc., backed by higher rocks and distant mountain scenery. The leaves are colored as in autumn, and the sky as at sunrise. Backing, near the center of the stage, slightly elevated and containing seats overlooking the stage, is an arbor. Some of the stone or moss-covered steps leading up to this can be used as seats. Around and behind the arbor are other steps leading upward. Entrances, used in this scene: Right and Left Rear; and at the Back, behind the arbor, and reached by passing upward either through it or around it.*

> *From the moment that the stage is darkened, and while it is gradually being illumined again, part of the following is chanted by a choir, either invisible to the audience, or, clothed in white, and half seen at the rear of the stage:*

Oh, who has known the whole of light,
　That knows it day by day,
Where suns that make the morning bright,
　At evening, pass away?
Before the day, beyond the day,
　Above the suns that roll,
There was a light, there waits a light
　That never leaves the soul.

Oh, who has weighed the worth of light,
　That gauged it by the gleam
That came within the range of sight
　And thought the rest a dream?
Before that sight, beyond that sight
　Unending and supreme
There was a light, there waits a light,
　Where things are all they seem.

　　　Once or twice toward the close of the sing-
　　　　　ing, CECIL *who is now in the bed sits*
　　　　　up, in a bewildered way, passing his
　　　　　hand over his forehead. As the singing
　　　　　ceases, he stands on the floor, leaving
　　　　　the effigy of himself lying on the bed
　　　　　behind him. He now appears clothed
　　　　　in white. As he begins to gaze wonder-
　　　　　ingly about him,
　　　　Enter—Left—an idealized form of CELIA,
　　　　　clothed also in white. CECIL *does*
　　　　　not see her till after she has spoken.
CECIL.　Ah, where am I?
25

CELIA. With me.

CECIL (*looking at her in astonishment, yet shrinking from her as if in awe*).

And who are you?

CELIA. Your friend.

CECIL (*drawing nearer her*).

My friend?

CELIA. Do I seem else?

CECIL (*with pleased bewilderment*). Nay, nay,
  You seem it all: you seem far more than
    this;
  Yet where—when—was it, that I knew you
    so?

CELIA. You knew me so?—You think you knew
    me, then?

CECIL. Yes, knew you; and I know you; yet
    seem not
  To know where, when or how I learned of you.
      (CECIL *gazes around, then, looking back
        at the bed that he has left, he suddenly
        starts upon seeing there the effigy of
        himself.*)
  What? what?—Is that my body?—Am I dead?

CELIA. You seem to be alive.

CECIL. If feeling be
  The test of life, I do live.—And yet that—
(*returning toward the bed and looking at the
    effigy.*)
  That is my body.

CELIA (*meeting him as he turns about, and point-
      ing to his own form*).
                    Nay, but look you here.—
What then is this?
CECIL (*placing his hand on his chest*).
                    This?—Oh, so light, so free,
It seems an essence framed of flutterings,
Ethereal as the trillings that a lark
Leaves up in heaven when it has left for
      earth.—
And you call this a body?
CELIA.   That one there,
          (*pointing toward the bed.*)
Holds not your thought?
CECIL.   Nay, it has flown to you.
CELIA.   And wherefore, think you, has it flown
      to me?
CECIL.   I do not know.   I half believe my soul
Has all my life been flying thus to you.
[Why, when you speak, your voice the echo
      seems
Of some familiar strain, with which all sounds
That ever I thought sweet were in accord.
And when my dimmed eyes dare to face your
      own,
Each seems a sky within which is inframed
A world that holds my lifetime; and the light
Beams like a sun there, scattering doubt and
      gloom.] (*looking around.*)

But what a world you live in!—Golden skies?—
Is it the sunset?

CELIA.   Nay; you see no sun.

CECIL.   Is it the Indian Summer?

CELIA.   Nay; you see
The air is far too clear.

CECIL.   Is there a breeze?—
I feel it fan me.

CELIA.   Yet the leaves move not.

CECIL.   Why, every leaf glows fairer than a
    flower!—
It must be autumn.

CELIA (*plucking a leaf, and handing it to him*).
              Nay; these leaves are fresh.

CECIL.   I think I dream:—all things appear so
    strange;
Yet doubt I dream:—they all appear so clear.

CELIA (*sitting on one of the lower steps, leading up
    to the arbor*).
Does nothing seem familiar?

CECIL (*sitting, in a half kneeling position, on a
    step beside* CELIA, *but lower than the one that
    she occupies, and gazing up reverentially
    toward her*).
                No—yet, yes.
[I dimly can recall what now appears
A troubled, stormy sea, yet not a sea;
And in the depth that which I call myself
Seemed held and heaved as in some diving bell.

But evermore in reveries and dreams,
But most in dreams when outward sense
    would sleep
My soul would be released, and rise and reach
Fresh air, in which was breathed what gave
    fresh life;
Then, sinking downward, wake and work
    again,
Till time for rest and fresh refreshment came.
But never could my powers at work below
Remember aught that blest them when above.

CELIA.   And now you dream that somehow they
    came here?

CECIL.   Oh, do not tell me that I now but
    dream!—
Nay, call it heaven?—Or is the rest of sleep
But absence from the body while we draw
New drafts of life from that which gave us
    life?

CELIA.   What do you think?

CECIL.   I do not think at all.
I only know I would that I were Adam,
And you were Eve, created while I slept.
Or is it true that all our souls create
The things that they aspire for?—And are
    you,—
You whom my very spirit seems to clasp
And thrill forever at each tingling touch,
Are you, indeed, the form of my ideal?

Oh love, you seem as if at one with God;
And yet I never thought a God could be
So dear. (*kneeling.*)
           There have been monks in ecstasy
Who saw—or thought they saw—the Virgin.
    I—
I could not credit them. But now, it
    seems——

CELIA.   You think that I——

CECIL.   I know not what you are.
I only know my soul had sought for you;
And now has found the search was not in vain.
Why, and how is it that I know so well—
How have you told me—what you are to
    me?

CELIA.   I have not told you this; and He alone
Who formed the spirit knows the how and
    why.

CECIL.   Who formed?—Why, that is God.   I
    thought me dead.
Yet here, I see not——
          (*gazing around and upward.*)

CELIA.   You had hoped, at death,
To pass to Paradise, and be at rest.
Move on: I have detained you.
    (*rising, and waving him off with a gesture.*)

CECIL (*rising anxiously*).   I move on?—
And you stay here?—I cannot.   There is not
The littlest finger of the littlest nerve

In all my frame here, that could summon
    power
To move where you moved not.
CELIA.   Ah, then your will
    Is mightier than you deemed it? You can rise
    But when you wish to rise? The haunts of
        heaven
    Need not have walls to keep you out of them?
(*seating herself on a step higher than she occupied
        before.*)
CECIL (*sitting beside, but below her*).
    Keep out of them?—Why, your sweet form
        alone
    Has brought me now a million, million times
    More than I ever dreamed that death could
        bring me.
CELIA.   But where is your religion?
CECIL.   All was love.—
CELIA.   And not the Christ—?
CECIL.   Why, yes—that which he was—
    For which he died,—the spirit in the man,—
    In me, in you.—Ah, now it seems as if
    Each face I loved on earth but imaged yours!—
    Why is it, dear one, that you seem to be
    So fully all things that they all could be?
    And what love is it?—what, the halo here
    That seems to orb you in the sphere of God?
CELIA.   Had you seen more of that, you might
    find out.

CECIL.   I would I could!

CELIA (*rising, as does also* CECIL).

>   And shall I help you to it?

CECIL.   I knew there was no wish within my soul
That would not find an echo in your own.
Where shall we go that we may find—?]

CELIA (*pointing toward the Right*).   You see
Those coming?—Let us watch, and listen to
them.

> (*They enter the arbor, where, in view of the
> audience, they overlook the stage.*
>
> *Enter—Right—*LOWE *and* MADAM LOWE
> *in gray Quaker costumes, resembling
> in most regards those of* CECIL *and*
> CELIA.
>
> (*Blue-gray light illumines the stage.*)

CECIL (*to* CELIA).

They look like Lowe, the Quaker, and his wife.

LOWE (*to* MADAM L.).

I feel so weary, yet we wanted rest.

MADAM L. (*to* LOWE).

Did I not walk with thee, I half might doubt
The leading of this path.

LOWE.   I doubt it not,
When leading thee.—Who ever saw thee
decked
In vain attire?

MADAM L.   Or thee not grave and gray?

LOWE.   Or heard thee romp?

MADAM L.   Or thee hilarious?

LOWE.   Or found thee once the toy of giddy
       fancy?

MADAM L.   Or thee, of disconcerted calcula-
       tion?

LOWE.   None ever!—Yet I fear this path.—I
       thought
   I heard—and oh, I dared then listen twice!—
   I thought I heard strange singing—

MADAM L.   Birds?—I thought
   I saw—and oh, I dared then look there twice!—
   I thought I saw a wicked, grinning ape.

LOWE.   Hush, hush! Think not of these things.
       Nay, but think
   Of things that God hath made.—I wonder if
            (*becoming shrewd.*)
   The holy city be completely built.

MADAM L.   They might give thee a contract.

LOWE.   Well, they might!
   [And if the saints be not all Friends——

MADAM L.   Sh—sh—
   Not that!—so loud!—I fear me, lest we doubt.

LOWE.   To doubt is charity, where to believe
   Is to condemn. Who knows but we could
       thrive
   Deprived of Friends—build churches.

MADAM L.   Say not that.
   We may be taken down yet, where they use
       them.

LOWE. I fear me some may use them here.
    For look!—
    (*Part of the stage is illuminated with red light.*)
    The colors on the leaves, the very sky,
    Seem sadly gay.
MADAM L.   Oh, do not look at them!
    They glow to tempt the lusting of the eye.]
LOWE. Sh!—what is that? Loud noise and
    music too!
(BLAVER *and* MISS PRIMWOOD *are heard singing.*)

    Oh, up and spout, and down and shout,
    And show the spirit off and out.

MADAM L. Oh, there may be a fiend here! Let
    us hide.
Exeunt—Right—LOWE *and* MADAM L. *hurriedly.*
    Enter—Left—BLAVER *and* MISS PRIM-
       WOOD *in blue clothes resembling those*
       of CECIL *and* CELIA. *The stage is*
       illumined with dark blue light.
CECIL (*to* CELIA).
    See!—Blaver and Miss Primwood, I should
    say.
BLAVER. We should have found the place ere
    this; or heard
    The blowing of the trumpets, or the shouts——
[MISS P. Of all the elders, yes.
BLAVER.   We soon shall reach

The place "where congregations ne'er break
    up."—
Oh, I could talk forever!

Miss P.   So could I!—
Yet,—do you know?—if I were not with you,
I half should tremble, lest my feet were near
The silence of the——

BLAVER (*in a frightened way*).
                 Do not speak of that!
Keep talking.—Oh too true!—There are no
    shouts.]
No one has got the power here.

Miss P.   It may be,
They all have got it.

BLAVER.   What if that were so?—
Suppose they had.—Suppose that no one here
Could ever find a spirit to reform—
Not one to preach to,—how could saints here
    know
About one's gifts?

[Miss P. (*agitated*).
           Yes, yes; but keep on talking.
To be with one who talks on, makes one
    sure
The silence is not near.

BLAVER.   Yes, let us talk.
Perhaps, at times, to change a tune or text,
The congregation pauses; and may hear,
And send the sexton for us.]

Enter—Right—stealthily, and dodging behind trees, LOWE *and* MADAM L.

MISS P. (*pointing toward the Right*).

Who are they,
So still, so backward, skulking through the shade?

BLAVER.   So backward and so still!—Are both bad signs.

[MISS P. Though this were Paradise, there might be here
Another serpent.

BLAVER.   Or those like him!—Would
Be backward too, and not stand up for aught.

MISS P.   Would slip away.

BLAVER.   Be still in doing it.]

MISS P. (*clinging to* BLAVER'S *arm*).

How wise that I did learn to be a woman,
And cling to man! Ah, were I here alone——

BLAVER. Those two seem slipping just like drunken sneaks
Evading prohibition laws.—I have it:
Heaven calls me to my mission. See them quail
When I exhort them! What is more religious
[Than ministering discomfort? Rile folks up,
Their dregs appear; they see their own foul depths.]
You watch them now.—Hoho! hoho! hoho!

(BLAVER *is gesturing toward the Right Entrance.*)
> *Enter—Right—*FATHER HYCHER, *in a
> long red cassock, and* WIDOW HYCHER,
> *in a red gown resembling a cassock.
> The stage is suddenly illumined with
> red light.*

FATHER H. (*to* BLAVER).

Hold, preaching fiend! How dare you block
   my path
And raise that impious and schismatic shout?
Down on your knees.

[(*then to* LOWE *and* MADAM LOWE, *who appear
     at the Left*).

                    Down on your knees.

MADAM LOWE.   Vain souls,

Trained on the earth to influence men through
   force,
In realms where spirits have not forms that
   force
Can harm, must find their occupation gone.]

*Exeunt—Left—*LOWE *and* MADAM LOWE.

CECIL (*to* CELIA, *as he looks at the* HYCHERS).

Father and Widow Hycher, or their doubles!—
[The Quaker dame has not forgot her training.

BLAVER (*to* MISS P., *looking toward* MADAM L.).

Expected to surprise her! — failed! — She
   knows
The devil is deformed, and so wears robes.

Miss P.   They both wear like robes!—Are for
        woman's rights?
    And think the woman's best is in her gown?
Widow H. (*to* Blaver, *pointing to* Father H.).
    He bade you kneel.
Blaver (*to* Widow H.).   Am I your suitor?—
            No;
    Nor his.   You neither suit me.
Widow H. (*pointing to* Father H.).   It is time
    You go to——
Blaver.   You go there yourself.   Ay, ay;
    Be missionaries for me.   I will not
    Be tempted that way then.
            (*to* Miss P.)   How strange that forms
    We meet in Paradise all seem to garb
    Our worst aversions!
Miss P. (*anxiously*).   Yes, but—oh—exhort
        them!]
Blaver (*to* Father *and* Widow H.).   Hoho,
        hoho!
    Who rails at preaching proves his need of it.
[Widow H.   I feel as if a storm were near, and
        yet
    Were blowing music for me.
Father H. (*to* Widow H.).   Heard in heaven,
    Storms blowing from the mouth of hell make
        music.
Blaver (*to* Miss P.).   Their colors! they—they
        flag the foe for me.

Are red as fire—are fire, perhaps; if so,
Need stirring up, and showing—blowing up
And out.   Hoho, hoho!]
   (*The* HYCHERS *disappear behind a rock.*)
                   Why, they seem gone?—
Skulked off?—We might have known they
   would.   Come follow.
You sing, and I will shout.
          (*moves toward the Right*).
MISS P.   Not that way, no!
     (*Both turn to the Left*).
BLAVER and MISS P. (*together*).

     Hoho! hoho! hoho! hoho!
     We've all things here you need to know.

*Exeunt—Left—*BLAVER *and* MISS PRIMWOOD.
(*Reappear at the Right,* FATHER HYCHER *and*
       WIDOW HYCHER.*)
WIDOW H.   If I were not with you, I half
   might fear
That we had wholly missed the narrow path,
But with my shepherd near me, all is well.
[FATHER H.   How strange that I have found not
   yet a flock,
Nor sheepfold, not a single hedge, forsooth,
In which to drive a single soul!
WIDOW H.   Like that—
Where all were kept so safe—no schism
   there!—

The walls were always echoing back the
    words
You spoke; and no one else was let to speak.

FATHER H.   All heard what they believed.

WIDOW H.   Could they do else
Than to believe what they were always
    hearing?—
Dear words, how we must thank them for our
    faith!

FATHER H.   Without our words men might be
    left with nature.

WIDOW H.   Just think of that!—And where
    would nature bear them?

FATHER H.   Off from the church, I fear.

WIDOW H.   Yes, yes, and off—
Off from the priest.

FATHER H.   From God, as well?

WIDOW H.   I fear—
For He is so unnatural.

FATHER H.   You mean
Is supernatural.

WIDOW H.   Mysterious!—
Creates our reason, yet condemns its use.
I never used my reason—did not dare.

FATHER H.   You were a modest, model woman,
    yes.

WIDOW H.   And you a model man—no monk
    with me;
Yet ever showed the world a pious face.

FATHER H.   I did.   They lied who said I did
       not care
   For truth.   How oft, for it, I held my tongue!
WIDOW H.   And so held on to truth—
FATHER H.   And kept it sacred.
WIDOW H.   And easy too for us, who need not
       find it.
   For my part, I would rather have no truth
   Than risk damnation, planning how to use it.
   How kind the priest to do our thinking for
       us,
   And make us, through not thinking, think
       just right!
FATHER H.   But you did thinking—when I
       thought—
WIDOW H.   Of course,
   When you thought for me.—Is that what you
       mean?
   And now, and here, too, you will think for
       me?
FATHER H.   Could I do else?]
WIDOW H.   And when we reach the gates,
   You promise not to leave me; for, you know,
   I never learned the language of the spirit;
   And might not know it, were not you beside
       me.
FATHER H.   I—yes—but if——
WIDOW H.   There was no *if* in what
   You used to say.
       26

*Exeunt—Left—*Father Hycher *and* Widow
Hycher.

> (*The red light changes to golden, and* Cecil
> *and* Celia *come out from the arbor,
> and, while speaking, gradually descend
> to the stage.*)

Cecil. They did not see us.

Celia. No,
For they did not look up.

Cecil. I know, but why?—
Where all things round them were so new and
strange?

Celia. The spirit is the slave of its desire.
They did not care to look above themselves.

[Cecil. Pray tell me who they were. They
seemed so near,
And yet so many million miles away.
They looked like people, too, whom once I
knew;
Yet moved like cuckoos jointed on a clock,
Accenting nothing they have thought them-
selves,
Or have the force to make another think.

Celia. They seemed as if lost souls.

Cecil (*startled*). Lost souls, you say?

Celia. Did you not note them—how they wan-
dered on;
Nor knew their destination?

Cecil. Heaven forbid!

CELIA. Why pray for this?—You think that
  force rules here,—
 That spirits are not free to wander where
 Their own ideals bear them?
CECIL.   Those they formed
 On earth, you mean?
CELIA.   Where else could they be formed?
CECIL. And whither, think you, will ideals bear
 Those whom we just have seen?
CELIA.   Where would you deem
 These could be realized—save on the earth?
CECIL. But some of them seemed looking for
  their Christ.
CELIA. I fear those looking but for their own
  Christ
 May sometimes fail to find the Christ of God.
CECIL. But will they never find Him?
CELIA.   Do you think
 That those in search for but a false ideal,
 Could recognize Him, even should they find
  Him?
CECIL. Is not the Christ of God in all the
  churches?
CELIA. Is He not preached through men?
CECIL.   And are not men
 Controlled?—inspired?
CELIA.   And, if so, from what source?
 Are there no spirits in the line between
 Divinity and man?—And what of man,—

This urn of earth in which the true seed
    falls?—
There was an Arab in Mohammed's time;
In Joan of Arc's there was a maid of France.
CECIL.   But would you grant their claim?
CELIA.   Some keen as you
  Believed it true.   And is it charity
  To deem them dupes?
CECIL.   But one must rate them thus,
  Or call upon their prophets.
CELIA.   Think you so?
  One hears of gypsies telling what comes
    true.
  Does this truth prove them seers of all the
    truth?
  Believe not every spirit; prove——
CECIL.   But how?
CELIA.   How but by what is told, and character
  Of him who tells it?   To the true soul, truth
  Appeals to taste, as beauty to the sense;
  Its test is quality.   The like comes from like.
  Their inspiration is the nearest God's
  Whose life and love seem nearest Him.
CECIL.   May those
  Not near Him be inspired too?
CELIA.   Why may not
  Some lower phase of spirit-power, earth- borne
  To live for matter only, still intent
  To live for matter, take abode in them,

And work its will upon their willing souls?
Why differs it, though they may rise on
    earth
Impelled through emulation to enforce
Their wills on others; or, through appetite
May fall, and yield control of reason's reins
To that which drives them on to lust and
    crime?—
A spirit that inspires through selfishness
To mean success or failure, equally
May vex as by a devil made incarnate
Oneself and all about him.

CECIL.   Poor weak man!

CELIA.   Weak ever—save when conscious of his
    need.]

*Enter—Left—*FREEMAN *and* FAITH *dressed like*
       CECIL *and* CELIA.

FREEMAN (*advancing, speaking to the two, and
    pointing toward the Back*).

  Does this path lead us upward?

CELIA.   Yes, it does.

FREEMAN (*looking at* CECIL, *and speaking to
    him*).

  Why, why, friend, is this you?

           (*to* CELIA.)   And Celia too?—

CELIA.   Your friends, at least, whoever we may
    be.

(CECIL *and* CELIA *shake hands with* FREEMAN
       and FAITH.)

CECIL (*to* FREEMAN).

And Freeman—you with Faith?—I join your
joy.

Why, it fulfills my dream for you.

FREEMAN.   And mine!

(*to* FAITH, *and gesturing toward their surroundings.*)

How much, with each new step, th' horizon
widens.

[FAITH.   How could one bide below!

FREEMAN (*thoughtfully, and pointing toward the
Left*).   Ask Father Hycher.

FAITH. And he—he was a good and learnèd man!

FREEMAN. Less good than learnèd, darling.
Your pure soul

Breathed such an atmosphere about itself,

Your very presence could impart an air

Of sacredness to all brought near to you.]

FAITH (*to* CELIA, *while* FREEMAN *turns to* CECIL).

So strange it is how much more wise and wide

His views are here than seem the views of
those

Who, on the earth, appear'd so much more
learnèd.

CELIA. Not strange!—Though spirit-life be
lived in thought,

Where thought pervades the atmosphere like
air,

What can its measure be, for any mind,

Save that mind's receptivity?   If so,
When freed from bounds conditioning human
        thought,
It is a mind not filled so much as open,
Where waits not bigotry but charity,
Although with little learning, that first thrills
To tides that flow from infinite resources.

FREEMAN (*who has turned to listen to the latter
        part of what she has been saying*).
    Is this a revelation?

CELIA.   Ay, to those
Who heed the truth behind the words I use;
And yet for those who heed this truth them-
        selves
I do not need to term it revelation.

FREEMAN. We soon, I hope, can test it for
        ourselves.
    Farewell, kind friends, until we meet above.
(FREEMAN *and* FAITH *shake hands with* CECIL
        and CELIA.)

CELIA. Farewell.

CECIL.   Farewell.

(FREEMAN *and* FAITH *pass upward through, or
        around the arbor, till, finally they disappear.*)
*Exeunt—at the Back—*FREEMAN *and* FAITH.

CECIL (*looking at them as they ascend*).
    Oh happy, blessèd pair!
            (*Part of the following is then chanted by the
            choir, either invisible, or visible at the*

> *rear of the stage.   During the singing,*
> CELIA *and* CECIL *gradually ascend*
> *to the arbor where both sit.*

Two springs of life,—in air and earth;
  Two tides,—in soul and sod;
Two natures,—wrought of breath and birth;
  Two aims,—in cloud and clod;—
Oh, where were worlds, or where were worth
  Without the two, and God?

Two movements in the heaving breast,
  Two, in the beating heart;
Two, in the swaying soldier's crest;
  Two, in the strokes of art;—
Oh where in aught of mortal quest,
  Are e'er the two apart?

Two times of day,—in gloom and glow;
  Two realms—of dream and deed;
Two seasons—bringing sod and snow;
  Two states—of fleshed and freed;—
Oh where is it that life would go,
  But through the two they lead?

Two frames that meet,—the strong, the fair,
  True love in both begun;
Two souls that form a single pair;
  Two courses both have run;—
Oh where is life in earth or air,
  And not with these at one?

CECIL (*pointing in the direction taken by* FREE-
  MAN *and* FAITH).
  And now they rest?

CELIA. Why not? What now remains
  Of an ideal to bear them back to earth?—
  Or what to learn from mortals?

CECIL. Learn from mortals?
  [Can mortals aid immortals?

CELIA. Life is one.
  Our daily deeds bring sweeter dreams at
    night;
  And sweeter dreams more strength for daily
    deeds.
  If thought may pass from sphere to sphere,
    why not
  The benefit of thought?

CECIL. Why, this were strange!

CELIA. If strangeness were a test of what is
    false,
  Most things that are believed would not be
    true.

CECIL. But high and heavenly spirits helped by
    human?]

CELIA. Why should not all in heaven or earth
    be helped
  By all with whom in spirit they are one?
  [Were you on earth, the while your soul aspired,
  Could mine not move up with you? What you
    learned,
  Could it not ever be a part of me?

CECIL. Why, this is that for which I so have
    longed!

And once with one I thought that I had found
　it.
Ah, can it be the halo crowning her,
Was your sweet face behind the face I saw?—
Yet—were it right to turn from her to you?

CELIA.　All ties are right that make true life
　　　more bright.
Think you that she had not her own ideal?
　　　(*gesturing toward the Right.*)
And were her soul but free to pass to it,
Do you imagine she would pass to you?]

CECIL (*looking toward the Right*).
My wife with Kraft?—How can it be?—and
　　　yet——

(*The stage is suddenly illumined with brown light.*)
　　　*Enter—Right—*KRAFT *and* MADAM CECIL,
　　　　*dressed in dark brown clothes, shaped
　　　　like those of* CECIL *and* CELIA.

MADAM CECIL (*to* KRAFT).　It matters not what
　　we have done.　Have faith.

KRAFT (*to* MADAM CECIL *with suppressed fear*).
But should I meet my wife whose will I broke,
Whose slaves were not set free——

MADAM　C.　　　　　Have faith, have faith!

KRAFT.　Or should we two meet Cecil——

[MADAM C. (*in abject fear*).　　　Oh, oh, oh,
Speak not of that! It all is paid.　Have faith.

KRAFT (*doubtingly*).
Yet some would talk of proving faith by works.

MADAM C. I joined the church when scarcely
    sweet sixteen,
And never danced, except away from home.
KRAFT. And I, when I was twenty; and I never
    Let people see me backslide.
MADAM C.   And I always
  Professed to take an interest in the meetings.
KRAFT. And how men praised me for my church-
    subscriptions,
  And for my faith that God would, someway,
    pay them!
MADAM C. Yes, we were both so careful to seem
    right!
KRAFT. But yet, should we meet Cecil——]
MADAM C. (*shuddering*). Oh, oh, oh,
  Not him! not him!
          (*recovering herself suddenly.*)
             He never can come here.
KRAFT (*eagerly*).
  You think so—eh?—Why not?
MADAM C. (*sententiously*). He lost his faith.
KRAFT (*with cringing hope*).
  Is that so?—Yes?—but how?
MADAM C.   Why, just because
  Our pastor said, one time, of slavery,
  The institution was divine, God's own,
  He never after set foot in that church.
[KRAFT (*with self-congratulatory delight*).
  Oh, is that so!

MADAM C.　　　Besides, he sometimes owned
　To other——

KRAFT.　　　Other what?

MADAM C.　　　　　Misgivings.

KRAFT (*with assumed horror*).　　　　Not
　Believe in things men preached?

MADAM C. (*sanctimoniously*).　He doubted
　them.

KRAFT (*decisively*).
　Then he did not have faith.

MADAM C.　　　　　No; he did not.

KRAFT.　I learned the catechism in my youth;
　And always said, when asked, that it was
　　true.

MADAM C.　Thank God for that!　He was not
　　trained as you were.

KRAFT. You know I would not let an ignorant
　man,
　A slave or poor white, meet me in my parlor.

MADAM C.　No; never!

KRAFT.　　　　When a man is ignorant
　About the doctrines—doubts them,—how can
　he
　Expect that God will welcome him?

MADAM C.　　　　　Just so!
　We never have a God we understand
　Until we learn to judge Him by ourselves.]

　　　(CELIA, *beckoning to* CECIL *who follows
　　　her, comes from the arbor, and moves*

> *toward* KRAFT *and* MADAM C., *who,*
> *being at the front of the stage facing*
> *the audience, do not see them.*)

KRAFT (*in self-congratulatory way*).

Your husband then had really lost his faith?
I wonder if my wife had not lost hers.

MADAM C. Did she not free her slaves?—Our
　　pastor said
The institution was divine.

KRAFT (*deliberatingly*).　　　Yes, yes.

MADAM C. She did not think it so.

KRAFT.　　　　　　　　But I did, I,—
I broke her will.

MADAM C.　　　And saved her.—

KRAFT.　　　　　　　What?—Oh, yes!—
Saved her from the results——

CELIA (*to* KRAFT *and* MADAM C., *as she points*
　　to CECIL).　　　　What sophistry
Is this?

MADAM C. (*falling on her knees before* CECIL, *in*
　　abject fear).
　　　　　Oh, Master, did I not have faith?

KRAFT (*also falling on his knees before* CECIL).

Did I not often say "Good Lord" in prayer?

[MADAM C.　Did I not bear my cross?—

KRAFT.　　　　　　　A diamond cross
I gave her?—

MADAM C.　　　I embroidered one. I showed
My faith by works.

KRAFT.   I, in my business,—

  Oh, how my slaves would work at those church
      fairs!]

CECIL (*to* CELIA).

  Are they insane?

CELIA.   In part.

CECIL.   Heard you the name

  They called us?

CELIA.   His who said that "Inasmuch

  As ye have done it to the least of these,

  My brethren, ye, have done it unto Me."

MADAM C. Oh, Master, wherefore are we here?

CECIL (*to* CELIA).   Where do

  They think themselves?

CELIA.   Where false and hellish moods

  Create a false and hellish world to live in.

CECIL (*to* KRAFT *and* MADAM C.).

  What seems the trouble? What is it you fear?

KRAFT. Oh, Master!

MADAM C.   Master!

[CECIL   Why do you say that?

MADAM C. You are so holy, and we are so base.

KRAFT. Oh, wherefore did I kill you?

MADAM C.   Wherefore, oh,

  Oh, wherefore did I load you with abuse?—

  I did not know you then.

CECIL.   Nor know me now.

  Am I your master?

KRAFT.   It was you we harmed.

CECIL. What would you that I do for you?

MADAM C. Oh let
Us pay it back.

KRAFT. Yes, let us pay it back.

CELIA. Pay what back? What?—You said,
"It all is paid.
Have faith." Your faith means faith that
God forgives.
If he forgive you, why not feel forgiven?

MADAM C. You mock us.

KRAFT. Mock us.]

CECIL (*to* CELIA). Tell me what to say.
And is there nothing one can do for them
To free them from their misery?

CELIA. They say
There is, and truly. Though the Lord for-
give,
In spirit how can spirits feel forgiven
Ere they undo the wrong their lives have
wrought?
Ere this had been undone, not even laws
Of Moses let the trespasser receive
The benefit of sacrifice; and how
Could heavenly joys crown even perfect love
Save as it served the soul it once had harmed?

CECIL (*to* MADAM C. *and* KRAFT).
What is it, then, that you would do for me?

KRAFT. What you had done, had we not stayed
your work.

CECIL (*to* CELIA).

 What?—Is it possible?—my plans, my hopes
 Can be fulfilled yet? and fulfilled through
   these?—

    (*to* KRAFT *and* MADAM C.)

 Well, it may be so. You may serve your time.

[MADAM C. Ah, now I know, indeed, that
   Heaven is true!

KRAFT. And now I know, indeed, the Lord
   forgives!]

CELIA. But prove your faith by your fidelity.

    (CELIA *points toward the Right Rear En-*
    trance. As she does so, Enter—Right
    Rear— JEM *and* MILLY. *Their dresses*
    are of a grayer shade, but otherwise they
    resemble those of CECIL *and* CELIA.
    As KRAFT *and* MADAM C. *turn*
    toward the Right, they see JEM *and*
    MILLY, *and draw back affrighted.*)

MADAM C. See those grim messengers of tor-
   ture coming!

CECIL (*to* CELIA).

 Why, those are Jem and Milly, our old slaves!
 She tried to thwart me, when I set them free.

CELIA. She thinks them fiends.

CECIL.   How blind! Their dusky hues
 To me seem fair-formed shadows cast before
 The light of coming angels.

    (CELIA *and* CECIL, *at her apparent bidding,*

*seat themselves again on some of the
steps leading up to the arbor, and from
there listen to the following.*)

MADAM C. (*to* JEM *and* MILLY, *kneeling before
them*). Spare my soul!

JEM. A little thing ter spare!—I 'spects I will.

MADAM C. You will not drive me off to tor-
ment then?

JEM. Come, come, ole missus, yer mixed up on dis.
De debil not so black as he am painted.
He's white,—a missus too! When yer gets
dah (*pointing down*),
Jes' take one look in dat ah lake. You'll see
'im.

MADAM C. Oh, oh, then you have seen him?

JEM. Wall, I's been
Dun gone down da below,—a slave, yer see.
But now, I's heah.

MADAM C. And I must be your slave?

JEM. No; we's not mean enough ter own no
slaves. (*gesturing toward* MILLY.)

MADAM C. You would not drive us to the
darkness?

JEM. No
We's come away from dah, or 'spected so
Till we met——(*he looks at her sharply.*)

MADAM C. Who? Oh, take me not——

JEM. Fur 'im?—
Law sakes alive! Yer kneelin'!

27

MADAM C.   I will serve
  For all my life——
JEM.   De debil?—better not!
(JEM *and* MILLY *turn to leave at the Right Rear
Entrance.*)
MADAM C.   I must pay back the service forced
        from you.
  You will not, cannot, must not cast me off.
JEM (*turning around toward her*).
  Dem folks dat's free perfers ter choose deir
        help.
*Exeunt—Right Rear—*JEM *and* MILLY, *hurriedly.*
MADAM C. (*to* KRAFT *who seems to desire to
        linger*).
  Oh, we must overtake them!
          (*She pulls* KRAFT *after her.*)
*Exeunt—Right Rear—*MADAM C. *and* KRAFT.
(*As they leave, the stage is illumined with golden
light.*)
CELIA (*looking after them*).   Who can tell
  What ages it may take to overtake
  The wrong one's own wrong lashes into
        flight!
CECIL.   Where are they going?
CELIA.   Earthward, so it seems.
CECIL.   And will she serve her slaves?
CELIA.   Why should she not?
  Why should not those who were the most
        oppressed

Have most that serve them where but souls
    are served?
All things inverted and turned inside out,
The last in station may become the first,
The lowly lordlike and the high the low,
The crown'd the chain'd, the crucified the
    crown'd.
[CECIL. But how and where can spirits right
    their wrong?
CELIA. Wherever spirits influence the spirit.
CECIL. Ah, then, through others' lives they
    work their work?
CELIA. Perchance they may; perchance they
    may do more.
CECIL. Do more?—What mean you?—live
    again on earth?—
Nay, if they shall, they have lived; yet who
    ever
Met mortal yet whose memory could recall
A former state?
CELIA.   He might recall the state
Without the circumstance. To know, be-
    speaks
Experience. To be born with intuitions
And insight, is to know. To sun new growth
Why should not all be given an equal chance
Unshadow'd by dark memories of the past?
CECIL. But if the past were bright?
CELIA.   If wholly so,

Would one need progress? or could he be
　　cursed
With deeper woe than thought that could
　　recall,
Enslaved in flesh, a former liberty?
Why lure to suicide, that, breaking through
The lines determining development,
May plunge the essence down to deeper depths
There planted till new growth take root anew?

CECIL.　Must all new growth be planted in the
　　earth?

CELIA.　Is any germ that grows not planted
　　there?

CECIL.　What trains it then?

CELIA.　　　　　　Some say that where it falls
In age, clime, country, family, fleshly form,
The mighty wheels of matter—earth and
　　moon,
And sun and planets, all the unseen stars
Of all the universe that round it roll—
With one unending whirl grind out its fate;
Yet only earthly fate.　Flung to and fro,
And torn by care and toil and pain and loss,
The spirit knows in spirit it is free;
And true to its high nature, may pass through
The terror of the ordeal with all
The finer flour of nature's grain preserved.

CECIL.　So though careers be fated, souls are
　　free?

CELIA. The consciousness of freedom comes
  from force
 Which is of heaven; the consciousness of fate
 From that which is of earth; and both are
  true;
 Or that which makes all feel them both is
  false.

CECIL. But if some spirits thus return to earth,
 Why not all spirits?

CELIA.   Who has traced for you
 The history of spirits? If they came
 From God, as matter came, why came they
  not
 With matter?

CECIL. What?—Through beasts and birds, you
  mean?

CELIA. Why not?—Why should not these have
  endless life?
 Why, if they have it, should their course be
  checked
 Ere they attain the highest?—and, if not,
 Why should their essence not move up through
  man?

CECIL. Is man the son of beasts?

CELIA.   In flesh why not?—
 But may be born of flesh and of the Spirit.
 Devoid of spirit, all the body's nerves
 Are lifeless as the wires, when rent apart,
 Which once were thrilling with electric force.

But ah! that force, though flown to air, comes
    back
To give new life wherever new forms fit it.
So, while the whole creation of the flesh,
In groans and travails of successive births,
Prepares each new formation for its need,
Why should not psychic force, the breath of
    Him
In whom all live and move and have their
    being,
With rhythm mightier than the pulse of lungs,
Or day and night, or autumn and the spring,
Pass up through all the lower ranks of life,
Through birth and on through death, from air
    to breath,
From breath to air, till, last, it reaches man;
And, taught the lesson there of human hands
Which master matter, and of each man make
A fellow-worker in creation's work,
And, taught the lesson of the human voice,
Which for each new conception frames a word
To phase and phrase it, and of each man
    makes
A fellow-thinker in creation's thought,—
Why should not this force, moulded by the
    hand
And head, attain in man its final end,
And dowered with will and reason, freed at
    death

From its material framework, hold its mould,
And reach the last result of all that is,
Where that which served the serpent is the
    son,—
A spirit in the image of the Father?

CECIL. These words recall an ancient eastern
    dream;
And, in one's waking hours, can it be true?

CELIA. Think you a true soul ever served a
    thought
Not souled in truth, whatever were its form?

CECIL. But what then of the Christ?

CELIA.   Did he not say
He lived in spirit ere he lived on earth?—

CECIL. He said he came for others.

CELIA.   Do you think
A spirit such as his would need to come
For his own good?

CECIL.   And yet that sacrifice?—

CELIA. He sacrificed the spirit-life for life
On earth, and life on earth for spirit-life.

CECIL. And but fulfilled a common rôle?

CELIA.   Not common,
Did he fulfill our spirit's best ideal;
For spirits live in thought. How can they
    know
Of any God beyond their thought of him?

CECIL. But if they know the Son?

CELIA.   They know, at best,

A "Son of Man," as well, too, as "of God,"—
In spirit one with Him, but not in frame.

CECIL.   And yet a "Saviour"—

CELIA.   What inspires, but spirit?—
Or saves, but inspiration? He—enough—
All must move upward would they find the
        Christ.   (*rising and pointing upward.*)

CECIL (*rising*).

But ought they not to work for others too?

CELIA.   In spirit those work most for truth, who
        most
Are true; for all are led, yet all are leaders.
Thus does the line of being bridge the gulf
Between the world of worm and fire,—the
        hell
As well as home of all not saved from matter—
And that eternal rest where souls, made free
From longer craving a material frame
Through which to signal their vain selfhood,
        lose
Their lower life to find a higher life,
Where now their spirits are at one with His
Whose life of love is theirs who love his
        life;
And, even as the Christ is in the Father,
So, too, become joint heirs with Him of all
        things.

(CELIA *and* CECIL *move upward, and finally
                disappear.*)]

*Exeunt—at the Back—*CELIA *and* CECIL.
   *In the meantime, part of the following
   is chanted by a choir, either invisible
   or visible at the rear of the stage.*

In the world of care and sorrow
   Cloud and darkness veil the way,
But in heaven there waits a morrow
   Where the night will turn to day,
Where the spirit-light in rising,
   Yet will gild the clouds of fear,
And the shadows, long disguising,
   Lift and leave the landscape clear.

When the soul, amid that glory,
   Finds its earthly garments fall,
Harm and anguish end their story,
   Health and beauty come to all;
No more fleshly chains can fetter
   Faith that longs to soar above;
None to duty seems a debtor,
   And the only law is love.

There is ended earthly scheming,
   Earthly struggle sinks to sleep;
Souls have passed from deed to dreaming,
   And they have no watch to keep;
For the world has wrought its mission,
   And the wheels of labor rest;
And the faithful find fruition,
   And the true become the blest.

(*The stage is darkened; and the curtain that
   formed the back of Scene First in this
   Act falls upon it.*)

SCENE THIRD:—*Same as Scene First of this Act.*
While the stage is still dark, unseen by the
audience,

> *Enter — Left — CECIL, in dressing-gown*
> *covering completely the dress worn*
> *by him in the last scene.   He reclines*
> *on the bed, where his effigy was in the*
> *First Scene of this Act.*
>
> (*The stage is made light.*)
>
> *Enter—Left—CELIA, dressed as in Scene*
> *First of this Act.   In addition, she*
> *brings a hat and shawl, which, as she*
> *becomes visible to audience, she is seen*
> *putting on.*
>
> *Enter—Right—JEM.*

CELIA (*to* JEM).

The time has come to take my morning walk.
I almost fear to leave him.   You will stay
While I am gone, and keep good watch?

JEM.   Yes, Missus.

Fo' Gawd, dey done dare hahm de ole Marse
now.

What dey would hahm would be de udder
pusson.

> *Exit—Left—CELIA.*

(*After waiting a moment, JEM opens the door at*
the Left, looks about, closes the door, then
crosses to the door at the Right, opens it,
looks out, and speaks.)

Now yer's all safe, suh. She 'ab gone away.
> *Enter—Right—*KRAFT, MADAM CECIL *and*
> *two* MEN, *all dressed in out-door*
> *costume. All of them except* KRAFT
> *cross the stage toward the couch.*
> KRAFT *remains behind, and, taking a*
> *bank-note from his pocket-book, holds*
> *it in front of* JEM'S *mouth.*

KRAFT (*to* JEM). Will this patch keep that
    mouth shut?

JEM (*taking the money and pocketing it.*)
                    Law now, Marse,
    And pocket, too, suh.

KRAFT.   You are wise, my man.
> (KRAFT *crosses to the alcove where* MADAM
> C. *and the two* MEN *have been looking*
> *at* CECIL. *He looks at* CECIL, *and*
> *speaks to them.*)

No doubt! — You see the man is living
    still.
    You both can swear to that?

FIRST MAN.   Oh, yes.

SECOND MAN.   Yes, yes.

KRAFT (*to* JEM).
    What says the doctor, Jem?   Will he recover?

JEM. I 'spec' he 'spec's it.

KRAFT (*to* MADAM CECIL).   We are safe, at
    least.
    Has lived now long enough—for that.

MADAM C. Yet I
Could almost pray to know that he was dead!
CECIL (*in bewilderment, starting suddenly, and
sitting up in the bed*).
And did you think I wanted to be living?

CURTAIN.

ACT THIRD.

An interval of two year is supposed to elapse between the occurrences in Acts Second and Third.

SCENE FIRST:—*A room in the house of* FREEMAN, *who has married* CELIA, *and is living with her in a Northern "Border" State. Near the center of the room, set with dishes for a meal, is a table. Bread and a pitcher of milk have already been placed on it. Three or four chairs are near the table. At the Left is a closet, and about the room other articles of furniture. Backing, a wall containing a window or door; also a mirror near the Left Rear. Entrances by doors at the Right and Left near the Front.*

The rising curtain reveals JEM *with overcoat and hat on, standing in front of the table, also* MILLY.

JEM (*to* MILLY).

De station am a mile off. Whar's de dahky
Dat wouldn't get hungry 'foah he got dat fah?
(*taking bread from the table and putting it into his pocket.*)

Dey all don't want to see 'im stahve; not dey!
An' dry up, no!

(*taking up the milk-pitcher, and looking at it.*)
           Why, 'sakes alive! dah's marse—
And what's he call me calf faw?

(*pouring out, evidently against* MILLY'S *protests,
    a tumbler-ful of milk, drinking it, then
    hiding the tumbler in the closet.*)
                           Dat am good.
Dis dahky's glad dat ole Marse Cecil's comin'.
But ole Marse Cecil,—wondeh how he'll take
To seein' his Miss Celia Missus Freeman.
It 'peahed as how he liked dat ah young gal,
An' when ole Missus Cecil she got out
An' married dat Marse Kraft, why, you an'
    me,
We 'spected how Marse Cecil 'd like to get
As fuh de oder way wid his Miss Celia.—
But now Marse Freeman's got her, got her
    tight.

*Exit—Left—*MILLY *who has evidently heard
        someone coming.*

    *Enter—Left—*FREEMAN *and* CELIA.

FREEMAN (*to* JEM).
  It's time to go, Jem.

JEM.   Go?—I's goin',—gone!

        *Exit—Right—*JEM.

CELIA (*arranging the dishes on the table, and
    suspiciously examining the bread-plate and*

*milk-pitcher, while shaking her head at the
departing* JEM).

[Did Faith look well?]

FREEMAN (*seating himself in one of the chairs, and
taking a newspaper from his pocket and
unfolding it*). [Much as she did of old.

But paler—that is, till she chanced on me.

CELIA.   And then?

FREEMAN.   She flushed.

CELIA.   It needed but a spark
To kindle the old fire.

FREEMAN.   In her?—or me?—
I saw no light.   I only thought of ashes.

CELIA.   I know her nun's veil seemed a shroud
to you.

FREEMAN.   Your white one, Celia, when I married you,

Seemed like an angel's.   Now that you have
dropped it,   *

I know it was.

CELIA.   I thank you.   Yet, at times,
I fear mere pity led you to propose.

FREEMAN.   Was it your pity led you to accept?

CELIA.   You know you thought that I had closed
the door

To every other suitor by my act

In closing it on all except us two

When we were nursing Cecil.

FREEMAN.   And you know

You thought that I had closed the door on
 Faith,
Because of that which Father Hycher said.
But—nonsense!—what if pity were a motive?
CELIA. Pity is but a sadder kind of love—
FREEMAN. No love at all. But as a motive to
 it—
A door to open,—why complain of it,
If only opening where we wish to go?
(CELIA, *having ended arranging the things on the*
 table, stands back looking at it).]
And all is ready—is it?—for our guest?
CELIA. To think that Cecil should be here, and
 well!
FREEMAN. And such a note as his too! Why, a
 boy,
A boy in love, could not more gracefully
Let tumble forth from his embarrassed lips
The whole sweet burden of his blushing
 cheeks,
Than he did, pelting, helter-skelter, out
Those metaphors at us, to vent his joy
In welcoming our own!
CELIA.   How strange he felt so!
FREEMAN. Strange?—I am worthy of you; you
 of me;
And both of us of Cecil's interest.
He knows how we two nursed him. Now, at
 last,

His voyage at an end, his health restored,
It ought to give him joy, and pride as well,
To learn how we, through love for him, at
    first,
Have come to love each other. Every soul
Is proudest of the good itself has fathered.
CELIA. I know; and Cecil has a heart so kind!
But I must go, and get the breakfast ready.
FREEMAN (*rising and taking* CELIA'S *hand*).
But, first, my Celia, let me break my fast.
                    (*kisses her.*)
One kiss of yours could make the thrilling
    lips
Go fluttering all day long like Cupid's wings
To bear sweet words of love to all they meet.
            *Exit—Left—*CELIA.
[(FREEMAN *apparently addressing the reflection of
    himself in the mirror.*)
I told no lie. She lights my life with joy.
But, oh, had she been Faith, joy had been
    bliss!—
Poor Celia, she shall never learn the truth.
She thinks my nature water. I did once:
As each new face looked love upon its
    depths,
I thought they might be filled with that; but
    ah,
My heart is like a photographer's glass
Whereon the image once impressed remains;
28

And Celia's face is always framed in Faith's.
I fear I love the picture for the frame.—]
Why, Cecil here already?—must be he—

*Enter—Left—*Milly, *crossing the room and
opening the door at the Right.*

> *Enter—Right—*Cecil *followed by* Jem.
> *Both wear out-door costumes,* Cecil
> *an overcoat. He also carries a cane
> and limps. As he enters, he shakes
> hands with* Milly *and with* Freeman.

A hearty welcome, friend! I saw you coming.
How well you look! You are well too, not
    so?

Cecil (*removing his hat, which* Jem *takes*).
    Oh, yes.

Freeman (*noticing that* Cecil *limps*).
            Lame yet?—

Cecil.   Shall always be.   One foot
Was caught inside the grave.   I pulled away;
But drag the foot-stone.

Freeman (*helping* Cecil *take off his overcoat*).
                Not the head-stone though!

Cecil.   I hope not.

Freeman (*handing* Cecil's *overcoat to* Jem, *who
    takes it in addition to the hat*).
            Here, Jem, take these out with you.
    (Freeman *turns to get a chair for* Cecil.)

Jem (*aside to* Milly).
    I'd like to see what ole Marse Cecil'll do

When he fine out Miss Celia's Missus Freeman.

I know, from what he say, dat he don't 'spec
so.

*Exit—Right—*Jem.

*Exit—Left—*Milly.

Freeman (*placing a chair behind* Cecil).

Sit here. (*also handing* Cecil *the newspaper*).

Cecil (*sitting in the chair and looking around the
room*).

I thank you.—What a pleasant home!

And have you heard, of late, about my wife?

Freeman. You knew she married Kraft?
How mean in her!

Cecil. Oh, no; not that!

Freeman (*sitting*). But getting her divorce—
Accusing you!

Cecil. Kraft managed it, of course.

I had deserted her.

Freeman. You could not help it.

Cecil. No; thanks to her—and heaven! But
let that rest.

When one has well nigh slept the sleep of
death—

You know I thought me dead—it seems not
sad,

On waking, to begin one's life anew.

Freeman. And we too thought you dead.

Cecil. I acted so?

FREEMAN. You acted not at all. You did not
stir.

CECIL. No wonder! Had you seen what I saw
then,

Your senses would have been as hushed as
mine.

FREEMAN. What was it?

CECIL.   One might say a vision—dream—
Perhaps a trance.—Wait, till I tell you it.

FREEMAN. If dreams came true, a man might
prize them more.

CECIL. At times, they do come true. Mine will.
The power

That handles Kraft can make that devil spin

Like potter's clay to work out his designs.

It all was prophesied.

FREEMAN.   Was prophesied?

CECIL. Yes,—in my vision,—all about—your
marriage.

FREEMAN. My marriage?

CECIL.   Yes, and then such joy for me!—
And sure to come too!

FREEMAN.   Sure?—I envy you.

CECIL. I thought me dead. I woke and all
was life.

Above, I saw the stars; far east, the dawn.

If earth rolls on, it yet will bring full day.

FREEMAN. And bright may heaven, too, make
it!

CECIL. That it will.
Earth is a field where hidden treasure lies.
All search for it. Their searching wakes their
thoughts,
And draws out their desires, and aims their
acts.
At last, they look and live for that alone
Which lures beneath appearances. Few find
it.
The few that do, find that which makes the
world
Worth living in, and worth yon circling dome,
The crown God made it, jeweled with the
stars.
FREEMAN. And you have found it?
CECIL. Freeman, yes, I have;
And know why sometimes earth seems holy
ground,
And those that tread it Godlike. Then
Heaven's face
Back there behind the veil shines dimly
through it.
But wait. I yet will tell you. In our souls,
Far down within, are depths like sunken seas
All dark!—yet only when concealed from light
And from the face of love they else might
image.
And my soul—you should know its depths to
know

My coming joy; yet need not. You will
    guess it.

FREEMAN. Your mood alone can make one
    guess enough

To offer his congratulations now.

(FREEMAN *rises. So does* CECIL, *and they shake
hands.*)

And some one else here will be glad to do it.
        *Exit—Left—*FREEMAN.

*Enter—Left—*MILLY *carrying a dish which she
places on the table.*

CECIL (*reseating himself and talking at first to*
MILLY *and, later, to himself*).

How kind his welcome! It is worth some loss

To know we own some friends.—And Faith,
    too, Faith,—

She too, he says, will be so glad to see me.

I always liked her; and I always knew

The two were lovers, and they knew I knew it.

This must have been the reason why his note

Made such a mere brief mention of his mar-
    riage;

As if, forsooth, I knew the news already.

I thought I must have missed one letter from
    him.

But no; what need of sending me her name!—

Who could she be but Faith!—This very room

Seems like her too. No setting so becomes

A jewel of a woman as a home,—

A loving home like this. Thank God, some
    souls
Need not to die before they find their mates.
        *Exit—Left—*MILLY.
        *Enter—Right—*CELIA.
What?—Celia here? And I was never told
    it?—(*He rises to greet her.*)
Why, Freeman said that I should find a friend.
I have—the friend to whom I owe my life.

CELIA (*shaking hands with* CECIL).
Had it been lost, it would have been for me.

CECIL. And now when saved, let it be saved for
    you.

CELIA. For me and all who love you.

CECIL (*to* CELIA.)   Ah, who love!
I would that I could stay forever with you.

CELIA. You would not go away?

CECIL.   What, would you wish me
To make my home with you?

CELIA.   Why, yes.—Why not?

CECIL. But I must work.

CELIA.   Yet people sue—not so?—
In any place?

CECIL (*taking her hand*). Shall I begin it here?

CELIA. Begin and keep on too.

CECIL.   I think I will.

CELIA. It would so please us all!

CECIL.   And could you think
That I could feel at home away from you?

CELIA.   How kind in you to say that!—You will
       live
   Right here with me and Freeman?
CECIL.   You and Freeman?
CELIA.   Why, certainly!—He wants it, too.
CECIL.   I see.—
   You two together saved my life, of course.
CELIA.   Of course we saved it, if it could be
       saved.
CECIL.   And so you live with him?
CELIA.   Because of that—
   It was our mutual interest in you.

           *Enter—Left—*FREEMAN.

       (*Just as he enters*, CELIA, *bowing to* CECIL
            *and gesturing toward the table, indi-
            cates that she must prepare for the
            meal, and moves toward the Left.*)

           *Exit—Left—*CELIA.

       (CECIL *seats himself again.* FREEMAN *re-
            turns to the closet near the Left, and,
            while carrying on the following con-
            versation, finds there a small bottle,
            which, when presently he leaves the
            room, he takes with him.*)

CECIL.   She tells me I must live with you and
       her.
FREEMAN.   Yes, we had hoped so.
CECIL (*looking at* CELIA's *retreating form.*)
                         Freeman, this is bliss!

FREEMAN. Yes, we are very happy.

CECIL. That we are!—
Men do not often wed their own ideals.

FREEMAN. I know it. I have thought it
through; and yet,
Without that, life can have some brightness
left.

CECIL. Without that?—You mistake my mean-
ing, Freeman.
I need not live without that. No, indeed!
She loves me, Freeman; not a doubt of it.

FREEMAN. Who?

CECIL. Celia.

FREEMAN. Celia?

CECIL. Celia, yes.—Why not?

FREEMAN. You mean?—

CECIL. Oh yes, you think she is too young!
But, Freeman, love is of eternity, and knows
No youth, nor age;—is like the air of heaven
That tosses in its play the dangling fringe
Athrill with grace about our outward guise,
And runs its unseen fingers through our
hair,
And brushes to a glow our flushing cheeks,
But has more serious lasting moods than
these.
It is the substance of the breath we breathe
That keeps the blood fresh, and the heart in
motion;

And; e'en when these give out, it still is there
To buoy us up and bear on high the spirit.

FREEMAN.　　Oh, yes!—but Celia?—

CECIL.　　　　　　Wait, and let me tell you.
That evening when that pistol shot was fired
That almost freed my spirit, Celia thought
I sank unconscious.　So I did but not
Before heaven let me hear her cry—of me!—
"The only man I ever loved is dead!"
Then came my more than dream.　I saw her
　　spirit,—
A spirit one with mine; and that is why
I run no risk.　I know that she loves me,
And I love her; and we can both thank God
For cloud and storm and flash that struck me
　　down,
And heaven in life that followed death in
　　life.—
I see you doubt me.　Is it past belief?

FREEMAN.　Why—but—excuse me—I—

CECIL.　　　　　　You know not what
Is in a woman's heart!

(CECIL *looks down at his paper as if reading.*)
　　　　　*Enter—Left—*CELIA.

CELIA (*to* CECIL, *as she places upon the table a
　　dish that she brings, and arranges other
　　dishes on it*).　Now I am coming
To stay with you awhile.

CECIL (*to* CELIA).　To be with those

Who really love one, is a new delight.
You said you loved me, Celia.

CELIA.   Why, of course—
Just as I always have, and always must.

*Exit—Left—*FREEMAN, *lifting his hands in a
               bewildered way.*

CECIL (*noticing that* FREEMAN *had left*). Of
     course!
Look—Freeman's vanished, Celia.—Have a
     care.
To love too much may make him envious;
And chewing on the cud of jealousy
Is not a pleasant practice for one's friends.
For though you give them naught to work
     upon,
So much the more the grinders work away
And grind themselves the sharper,—ay, and
     grind
The words that pass them too—made sharp
     as arrows
To pierce the soul they hit.

CELIA.   No fear of him!—
We both love you.

CECIL.   Ah, I shall punish him!
When he comes in,—shall send him after Faith.

CELIA. No; you must not do that.

CECIL.   Oh, yes, I shall.

CELIA (*taking a seat*).
You would not dare.—

CECIL.   Not dare?—Ha, ha, ha, ha!

CELIA.   No, no; I beg you not to——

CECIL.   Not to, Celia?

CELIA.   You must not.

CECIL.   Must not? — And you really mean
   it?—

   Well, if you be in earnest, I will not.

   But, bless me, if I see the reason why.

CELIA.   He loves Faith.

CECIL.   Yes; and where would be my joke,
   Unless he loved her?

CELIA.   There was deep, deep love,
   I sometimes think it saddens him to-day.

CECIL.   What? what?—not happy in his married
   life?

CELIA.   Oh, one could not say that—so kind,
   you know.

CECIL.   Yes, yes?—and she?—is she not kind
   to him?

CELIA.   Who?—Faith?

CECIL.   Yes, Faith.

CELIA.   He never hears from her.

CECIL.   What?—Are they separated?

CELIA.   Separated!

   She went—you had not heard it?—to a
   convent.

CECIL.   She did?—Poor Freeman!—When was
   that?

CELIA.   Last year.

CECIL (*in a perplexed way*).
  But when was Freeman married?
CELIA.   Why, last March.—
  He wrote you all about it.
CECIL (*startled*).   No; not all,—
  Not half a page.
CELIA (*surprised*). Why, twenty pages, friend!—
  We both wrote twenty; and you never got
      them?
CECIL. Why, no; you see I had not heard of
      Faith—(*hesitatingly*).
  And you now — you are living with him
      here?
CELIA. Yes, living!—Did you think that we
      were boarding?
CECIL (*slowly, and struggling to conceal emotion*)
  You know—it seems—why, strange—when—
      he loved Faith.
CELIA. What?—That he married me?—He
      told me all;
  But Faith seems dead.
CECIL (*controlling himself*).
                    And he is kind, eh, Celia?
CELIA. Yes, very kind.
CECIL.   Forgive me, will you, Celia?
  You see that I have always loved you, Celia,—
  Just as a father loves a child, you know;
  And if my love be anxious for you, Celia,
          *Enter—Left—*FREEMAN.

(*He is not observed by* CECIL *or* CELIA.
*He replaces in the closet the little
bottle taken from it, when in the room
the previous time. While doing so,
he evidently hears the following conversation.*)

You will not think it strange?

CELIA.   Nay, not a throb
In all my heart, but you could rightly know it.

CECIL.   Your heart's wish is fulfilled?

CELIA.   Yes, yes, my love
Is deep and true. No wife could love one
   more.

               *Exit—Left—*FREEMAN.
               *Enter—Right—*JEM.

CECIL.   Then you have two friends,—him and
   me. You stand
Between us.

CELIA (*rising*).   I must go now.

CECIL (*rising*).   Yes, my daughter!

               *Exit—Left—*CELIA.

(CECIL *looks toward* JEM *whose sympathetic
   attitude shows that he understands* CECIL'S
   sacrifice.)

So close the clouds of heaven upon my
   dream!—
Do not repeat my talk to you this morning.—
I sometimes think the devil rules this world,
And wise men rule it with him.—But no, no!—

Oh, what a universe of agencies
Are centered in one life that may be both
The God and devil of the soul it loves!
[Yet wits were given one to outwit the world.
If Celia be what I have dreamed she is,
The world must work its work upon her will
Without one touch of mine, or hint, or sigh,
To make her life more tempted or less true.—
Oh, cursèd world, in which forswearing love
Is our best proof that we would foster it!
But wait!—What moves me?— Am I but a fool
Controlled by dreams?—No, no; I had a
    dream;
But this, at least, is none,—that each who
    aids
An angel upward for himself prepares
Angelic friendship; and if there be spheres
Where spirit can reveal itself to spirit,
And sympathy be sovereign, there must be
One soul supremely loved. I dreamed no
    dream.
High, knightly chivalry whose love protects,
Thy knightly honor *is* the sacred thing
Of which thy pride is conscious. But—oh
    God!—
To be just on the threshold of all bliss:
And fail.—Fail?—No. Let Freeman have
    her now
A few brief years.—I dream with her forever—]

But, Jem, you seem to have some message for
　　me.

JEM.　Some white folks heah as wants ter speak
　　wid yer.

CECIL (*in surprise*). With me?—I have no
　　friends here.—Bid them enter.

　　　　Enter—Right—as JEM *holds open the
　　　　　　door,* THREE GENTLEMEN. *They
　　　　　　wear overcoats and hold their hats in
　　　　　　their hands.* CECIL *exchanges bows
　　　　　　with them, and motions toward the
　　　　　　chairs.*

And will you sit?

FIRST GENTLEMAN.　No, thanks. We have no
　　time.

Our party's first convention meets to-morrow.
The news is ominous. We may have war.
We came as a committee to request
To hear from you.

CECIL.　　　　　To hear from me?—and why?

FIRST GENT.　You suffer from the wrongs of
　　slavery

That we oppose.

CECIL.　　　　　But here I am a stranger.

FIRST GENT.　Good reputation is to good men
　　what

Fine perfume is to flowers. A charm it has
Which lures the sense that heeds it to a search
That will not cease till finding its fair source.

CECIL. You do me too much honor.

FIRST GENT. Honor us;
And let our people hear you.

CECIL. If my words——

FIRST GENT. The words of men whose deeds
     have proved them true
Are also true.

CECIL. Thanks. If you think them so,
They may at least command your interest.
And he whose words can wake the earth to
     thought
Has heaven's own warrant that he should be
     heard.
Yes; I will come.

FIRST GENT. Thanks.

SECOND GENT AND THIRD. Thanks.

          (*All move toward the Right Entrance.*
          JEM *who is nearest it opens the door
          there.* CECIL *and the* GENTLEMEN
          exchange bows.)

CECIL. We meet to-morrow.

Exeunt—Right—the THREE GENTLEMEN *and*
          JEM.

————

SCENE SECOND:—*An open field or village green.
Backing in the distance, village houses, and
beyond them hill scenery. Extending diagonally
across the Right Rear corner is a cottage fronted*

29

by a porch, the latter being a platform elevated about a foot above the rest of the stage. At the Left of the stage are trees and a tent, apparently one of a soldiers' encampment beyond it.

ENTRANCES: *Right, between trees; Right Rear from a door opening from the cottage on to the porch; Back Center from behind the cottage; Left, Front and Rear, from behind trees, or the tent.*

As the curtain rises, MILITIA *and* POPULACE *are seen grouped at the Left.*
(They sing as follows:)

The trumpets call to action
 Through all the threatened land
No more is heard of faction.
 The time has come to band.
  What soul can see
The state in fear and fail to be
Beneath the flag, enrolled with all
 That heed the trumpet's call?
  No patriot is he who can see
  The state in fear and fail to be
  Beneath the flag, enrolled with all
  That heed the trumpet's call.

The best of men are brothers.
 The worst can be a foe;
And not for self but others,
 True men to battle go.
  No longer meek,
Where wrong is cruel, right is weak,

Or aught has brought the base to band,—
 They throng to lend a hand.
  No true man is he who can see
  The state in fear, and fail to be
  Beneath the flag, enrolled with all
   That heed the trumpet's call.

Who, think you, live in story
 That live for self alone?
Who care to swell his glory
 That cares not for their own?
  In every strife
That stirs the pulse to nobler life,
The man that has the thrilling heart,
 He plays the thrilling part.
  No hero is he who can see
  The state in fear, and fail to be
  Beneath the flag, enrolled with all
   That heed the trumpet's call.

 *Exeunt—Left—*Militia *and* Populace.
*Enter—Back Center—*Cecil, *and a* Gentlemen.
 *Enter—Right—*Faith, *dressed as a nun.*
Cecil (*to* Gentleman).

 These clouds of war break like a thunder-clap
 Amid clear skies of summer; but will bring
 Our plant of freedom to a finer fruitage.
   *Exit—Left—*Gentleman.
   (*suddenly noticing* Faith.)

 Faith Hycher?
Faith (*to* Cecil). Yes—on business.
Cecil.   With me?

FAITH. Old friends of ours are here—have interest
In land near by us. Being of the South
They came to deed it so as not to lose it;
And stand arrested. People deem them spies.

CECIL. Who are they?

FAITH. Why, my mother, Father Hycher,
Lowe, Blaver, Kraft——

CECIL. His wife too?

FAITH. Yes.

CECIL. Humph, humph!

FAITH. Their holdings were not small. The time was brief.
All came here who might need to sign their papers.

CECIL. And what can I do?

FAITH. Say you know them—you
And Freeman.

CECIL. You have seen him—Freeman?

FAITH (*hesitating*). No—

CECIL (*kindly*). I understand you.

FAITH. It was not his fault:
I was deceived.

CECIL. By whom?

FAITH. By Father Hycher.

CECIL. Yet now you wish to help the Father?

FAITH. Yes.

CECIL. As I should help the Krafts?—You think I should?—

[Faith, you and I have loved supremely,—yet
Our love has loved another.—Could this be
Of that form which we walk with in our
    dreams?

FAITH. Why——

CECIL. Did you ever think that all our dreams
  Are in ourselves; and this form too may be
    there?
  They say that human brains, ay, all our
    frames
  Are doubled.—If so, why?—For use?—then
    whose?—
Who is it twins existence with us here?—
What if it be our living, better self
Which under consciousness we vaguely feel
Dreams while we wake and wakes the while
    we dream,
Recalls what we forget, incites, and is
Less form than spirit, but, because a spirit,
Heaven's representative, our guardian, guide,
And all that tells of God?   You know all praise
The men dependent only on themselves.
Yet why?—Is it so noble to be free
From love, or wish for love? Or own these
    men
A subtle consciousness of nobler love
Which, in the spirit-life, is all in all?
Know they that earthly forms which seem
    divine

But image that within which is divine?—
Though you have wed the church, Faith, I
  have not;
And yet the bonds that bind us may not
  differ.—]
If so, Faith—yes—your friends shall have my
  help.

FAITH.   How kind!

CECIL.   For you, for me, for all whose paths
Of honor and of sympathy divide,
One choice alone remains—to dwell content
With loneliness, and one's ideal, and God.

(*Both bow.*)

*Exit—Left—*FAITH.

*Enter—Right Rear—coming suddenly from the
  cottage on to the porch,* CELIA.

CELIA (*to* CECIL).   Save, save my husband!

CECIL.   Save from what?

CELIA.   From death,
From certain death.

CECIL.   To march to war is not
To march to certain death.

CELIA.   My throbbing heart
Would spend its blood in blushes for my shame
Till it forgot to give my being life,
If, by a single sigh, I durst keep back
One soldier from the ranks of this just war.

CECIL.   What mean you then?

CELIA.   That he has volunteered

To be a spy, and in the very town
Where he has lived, is known, and hated too.
He can but be detected.

CECIL. You are right.

I see him coming.

(*pointing to the Left.—*CELIA *looks at him,
inquiringly.*)

You would better leave us.

*Exit—Right Rear—*CELIA.

*Enter—Left—*FREEMAN, *dressed as an officer.*
(*to* FREEMAN).

Your wife says you have volunteered to be
A spy, where you are sure to meet with
death.

FREEMAN. I may succeed.

CECIL. You scarce can hope to do so.

FREEMAN (*with assumed indifference*).

And what if not?

CECIL. Then you are not the man
To trust on such a mission.

FREEMAN. Not?—How so?

CECIL. No man, if wise, will waive from what he
plans
The prospect of success. If you attempt it,
Trust me to thwart you.

FREEMAN. Humph! You seem officious.

CECIL. One needs to be at times; and now
your life
And Celia's happiness are both at stake.

FREEMAN. Not Celia's happiness.

CECIL. What do you mean?

FREEMAN. I mean, since men have talked so
  much against
Our owning blacks, the time is coming fast
For some to talk against our owning whites.

CECIL. And what suggested this?

[FREEMAN. You know—We both
Have seen both men and women treat their
  peers—
In wedlock, yes, but also out of it—
As if they owned them; and society
Approved, enforced their course. Mere selfish-
  ness
Has been enthroned so long in men's affairs,
That naught seems worthy of respect to
  some
Of which it only is not king and guide.

CECIL. And pray, too, what of that?]

FREEMAN. If Celia find
More joy in your society than mine,
Then let her find it. Did I marry her
To limit her delights?

CECIL. Why, Freeman, friend,
Look here at me—You are an upright
  man,
  (*placing his hand on* FREEMAN'S *shoulder.*)
And so am I. But, ere I knew you married,
Was it—with all that she and I had been—

So strange that I should have—those—whims
  of mine?

FREEMAN. She told you that she loved you.

CECIL.   Yes, she did:
 But as a daughter.
    (FREEMAN *looks incredulous.*)
         I am not the man
 You should distrust.

[FREEMAN.   Who knows what men can be,
 Till pierced where tenderest! It was the fleet
 Achilles could be wounded in the heel;
 And some have heads, and some have hearts
  to hurt.

CECIL. I say she said she loved me as a daughter.
 I quote her right.]

FREEMAN.   She said no more than that?

CECIL. When speaking of her love, she said no
  more.
 She gave no slightest hint that meant not
  that.

FREEMAN. Yet you love her?

CECIL.   In the degree I do,
 Her honor I would guard, as, too, mine
  own;
 And guard her love too. She has told me all.
 She loves you as a true and faithful wife.
 So let me save you for her. Be no spy,
 But captain, colonel, general,—who knows
 What fortune may await the tide of war!

FREEMAN. And you?

CECIL.　　　　　Am I, think you, a man to play
A second fiddle to your tune of love—
With instrument all broke beyond repair,
Make discord of the music of your life?
I promise you to leave here.

FREEMAN.　　　　　Leave your home?—
You have no other.

CECIL.　　　　Some will open for me.
　　　(pointing toward the tent.)
There were one here, did my infirmities
Not keep me from the army.
　　　(Shouts are heard at the Left.)
　　　Enter—Left—A guard of MILITIA *headed
　　　　by an* OFFICER, *and conducting* BLA-
　　　　VER *and* MISS PRIMWOOD—*now
　　　　the wife of* BLAVER — LOWE *and*
　　　　MADAM LOWE, KRAFT *and* MAD-
　　　　AM CECIL — *now* MADAM KRAFT
　　　　—FATHER HYCHER *and* WIDOW
　　　　HYCHER, *attended by* FAITH. POPU-
　　　　LACE *follow.*

FREEMAN *(in evident astonishment).*

　　　　　　　Who are they?

CECIL. I think you know them.

FREEMAN *(noticing* FATHER HYCHER).

　　　　　　Father—?—Now will I
Get even with him.

CECIL.　　　　There is no such thing

As getting even with a low-lived soul,
Without one's lowering his own self.
     (*to the* OFFICER.) And who
Are these?

OFFICER. All spies.

OTHER PEOPLE. To shoot.

ANOTHER.   And all have land
 To confiscate.

OFFICER (*to* CECIL). They tell us that you
 know them.

CECIL. Why, yes; and Freeman too.—Ah,
 Madam Blaver!
  (CECIL *and* FREEMAN *shake hands with*
   MISS PRIMWOOD—*now* MADAM
   BLAVER—*with* MADAM LOWE, WID-
   OW HYCHER, LOWE *and* BLAVER,
   but not with the others. CECIL *con-*
   tinues to the OFFICER, *gesturing*
   toward the ladies, including MADAM
   CECIL—*now* MADAM KRAFT.)

Our war is not with ladies, I believe?
 (*The* OFFICER *apparently agrees with him.*)

FATHER HYCHER. I am a clergyman.

CECIL   Quite true; and we?—
 (*looking for assent to* FREEMAN.)

FREEMAN. Of course, we have no strife here
 with religion.

LOWE. I am a Friend.

CECIL.   He is.

LOWE. With me the chief
　Consideration is religion.

BLAVER. And I
　A prohibitionist. Our pleas were all
　Based on religious grounds.

OFFICER. And what of that?

FREEMAN (*laughing*). You fail to catch its
　　　bearing?—When they take
　Their oath of loyalty, why, they will keep it.
　(*The prisoners make startled signs of dissent.*)

CECIL. And this, too, may be said,—that as a rule
　The Friends are on our side; and are not
　　　fighters.
　So too with prohibitionists.

FREEMAN (*to* CECIL, *in a laughing way*).
　　　　　　　　　For once,
　Religion seems to help them in their practice.

OFFICER (*taking* KRAFT *roughly by the shoulder*).
　But here the case is clearly different.
　We know him, and his party.

MADAM CECIL-KRAFT (*to* CECIL). Could I talk
　A moment with you?

CECIL. Oh, yes, if it please you.

(CECIL *and* MADAM CECIL-KRAFT, *walk to one
　　　　side.*)

MADAM C. You know my father died.

CECIL (*nodding toward* KRAFT). Before you
　　　married? (MADAM C. *nods in assent.*)
　A happy man!

MADAM C.   He left some property.
It now is in this land.

CECIL.   In Kraft's name?

MADAM C.   Yes.
(*hesitatingly, after pausing a moment.*)
There was an informality——

CECIL.   In what?

MADAM C.   My marriage—

CECIL.   I should think so!—

MADAM C.   Not in that,
But in the mode of transfer. I would deed
You half—

CECIL.   No, thank you — neither half nor
all,

MADAM C.   And you would have me lose my
property?

KRAFT (*coming forward, followed by* FREEMAN).
No; surely you will help us?

CECIL.   Surely?—why?

KRAFT.   You know I am no spy.

CECIL.   How do I know it?

KRAFT.   My character——

CECIL.   What character?

KRAFT.   And you
Would have me shot?

CECIL (*to* FREEMAN).
                Shot at, perhaps?—Not so?—
By proxy, eh?—And in a better cause
Than his past deeds deserve?

FREEMAN.   I see.
          (*to the* SOLDIERS.)   Say, friends,
We all would save the lands of loyal men.
All loyal men about us are enlisting.
If Kraft be loyal, he will do the same.
(*The* SOLDIERS *make signs of approval.*)
                    (*to* KRAFT.)
What say you?
KRAFT (*hesitatingly*).
                    Had I—a—commission——
FREEMAN.   That
Would prove unwise the one who gave it you.
CECIL (*to* KRAFT, *putting his hand on* FREEMAN'S
          shoulder).
Places of trust are only for the trusted;
And high commissions but for men with
          missions.
FREEMAN (*to* KRAFT).   What say you—prison or
          private?—Make your choice.
KRAFT (*abjectly*).
Why, if I must——
FREEMAN.   It looks as if you must.
     Enter—Left—hurriedly, TWO GENTLEMEN.
(*Commotion among the* POPULACE *near them and
                    following them.*)
POPULACE.   Hurrah!
          *Enter—Right Rear—evidently attracted by
               the commotion,* CELIA, *followed by* JEM
               and MILLY, *and stand on the porch.*

FIRST GENTLEMAN (*to* CECIL). They nominated you.

CECIL.   For what?

FIRST GENT.   For representative at Washington.

SECOND GENT. (*shaking hands with* CECIL).
And I congratulate the district too

CECIL.   But I?—a stranger?

FIRST GENT.   No, no; one well known.

SECOND GENT.   The only home you have now
must be here;
For here they brought and nursed you, when
so ill.

FIRST GENT.   And when the factions could not
else agree,
They all could join on you.

PEOPLE.   Hurrah! hurrah!

SECOND GENT.   And nomination here is sure
election.

PEOPLE.   Hurrah! hurrah! hurrah! A speech!
a speech!

CECIL (*ascending the porch, where he stands with*
CELIA *at his Right*).
This is no time for words.   The world needs
work;
But one whose forced infirmities prevent
His bearing arms and marching to the front,
May choose the course that you commend to
him.

(Cheers from the crowd. CECIL *gestures toward
        the* SOLDIERS.)

But do not think you only move to war;
Or deem that I stay here to dwell in peace.
To men whose purposes, like ours, push on
To work out high designs, all life on earth
Is girt with warfare, where the light of heaven
That brings us each new day's enlightenment,
Contends with darkness, and there is no
        peace.
Our very bodies are but phantoms formed
Of that same darkness that we must oppose,
And we must fight, if nothing else, ourselves.
Ay, whether we may march our frames to
        greet
The cannon's mouth, or duty's commoner call,
Go where death threatens, or long seems to
        tarry,
One destiny, at last, awaits us all:
Upon life's little stage the play will close,
The curtain drop, and leave the actor dead.
Yet, soldiers, what care you, or what care I?—
The souls that fight for truth, beyond scenes
        here,
Find life that does not end in tragedy;
For all our world is but a theater
Outside whose walls, where shine the stars of
        heaven,
The actors with their rôles and robes laid by

May all meet smiling in the open air.
And now—to play our several parts—farewell.

(*bowing to those before him, then turning to* CELIA
and taking her hand.)

(*Blast of bugles, as the* SOLDIERS *fall into line,
with* KRAFT *well guarded.*)

CURTAIN.

END.

30

THE AZTEC GOD, AND OTHER DRAMAS

By GEORGE L. RAYMOND

16MO, CLOTH EXTRA, $1.25

"It is not with the usual feeling of disappointment that one lays down this little book. One reads 'The Aztec God' with pleasure. . . . 'Cecil the Seer' is a drama of the occult. In it the author attempts to describe the conditions in the spiritual world exactly as they exist according to coinciding testimony of Swedenborg, of the modern Spiritualist, and of all supposed to have explored them in trance states. Indirectly, perhaps, the whole is a much needed satire upon the social, political, and religious conditions of our present materialistic life. . . . In 'Columbus' one finds a work which it is difficult to avoid injuring with fulsome praise. The character of the great discoverer is portrayed grandly and greatly. . . . It is difficult to conceive how anyone who cares for that which is best in literature . . . could fail to be strengthened and uplifted by this heroic treatment of one of the great stories of the world."—*N. Y. Press.*

"One must unreservedly commend the clear, vigorous statement, the rhythmic facility, the copious vocabulary, and the unvarying elevated tone of the three dramas. . . . The poetic quality reveals itself in breadth of vision and picturesque imagery. One is, indeed, not seldom in peril of forgetting plot and character-action in these dramas, because of the glowing imagination."—*Home Journal.*

"The time and place make the play an historic study of interest, aside from its undoubted high poetic quality and elevation of thought. . . . The metre of the dramas is Shakespearian, and that master's influence is constantly apparent. It is needless to say to those who know the author's remarkable abilities that the plays are substantial and reflect perfectly the author's mind."—*Portland Transcript.*

Modern Fishres of Men. 12mo, cloth, gilt top . $1.00

"This delightful novel is written with charming insight. The rare gift of character delineation the author can claim in full. . . . Shrewd comments upon life and character add spice to the pages."—*Nashville Tennessean.*

"Deals with love and religion in a small country town, and under the facile pen and keen humor of the author, the various situations . . . are made the most of . . . true to the life."—*Boston Globe.*

"Such a spicy, racy, more-truth-than-fiction work has not been placed in our hands for a long time."—*Chicago Evening Journal.*

"Essentially humorous, with an undercurrent of satire . . . also subtle character delineation, which will appeal strongly to those who have the perceptive faculties highly developed."—*San Francisco Bulletin.*

A LIFE IN SONG

By GEORGE L. RAYMOND

16MO, CLOTH EXTRA, $1.25

"An age-worn poet, dying amid strangers in a humble village home, leaves the record of his life in a pile of manuscript poems. These are claimed by a friend and comrade of the poet, but, at the request of the cottagers, he reads them over before taking them away. The poet's life is divided into seven books or 'notes,' because seven notes seem to make up the gamut of life. . . . This is the simple but unique plan, . . . which . . . forms but the mere outline of a remarkably fine study of the hopes, aspirations, and disappointments of life, . . . an American modern life. . . . The author sees poetry, and living poetry, where the most of men see prose. . . . The objection, so often brought against our young poets, that form outweighs the thought, cannot be urged in this instance, for the poems of Prof. Raymond are full of keen and searching comments upon life. Neither can the objection be urged of the lack of the human element. 'A Life in Song' is not only dramatic in tendency, but is singularly realistic and acute. . . . The volume will appeal to a large class of readers by reason of its clear, musical, flexible verse, its fine thought, and its intense human interest."— *Boston Transcript.*

"Professor Raymond is no dabbler in the problem of the human spirit, and no tyro in the art of word painting, as those who know his prose works can testify. These pages contain a mine of rich and disciplined reflection, and abound in beautiful passages."—*Hartford Theological Seminary Record.*

"Here are lines which, if printed in letters of gold upon the front of every pulpit, and practised by every one behind one, would transform the face of the theological world. . . . In short, if you are in search of ideas that are unconventional and up-to-date, get 'A Life in Song,' and read it."—*Unity.*

"Some day Dr. Raymond will be universally recognized as one of the leaders in the new thought-movement. . . . He is a poet in the truest sense. His ideals are ever of the highest, and his interpretation is of the clearest and sweetest. He has richness of genius, intensity of human feeling, and the refinement of culture. His lines are alive with action, luminous with thought and passion, and melodious with music."— *Cleveland World.*

"The main impulse and incident of the life are furnished by the enlistment of the hero in the anti-slavery cause. The story of his love is also a leading factor, and is beautifully told. The poem displays a mastery of poetic rhythm and construction, and, as a whole, is pervaded by the imaginative quality which lifts 'a life' into the region of poetry,—the peculiar quality which marks Wordsworth."—*Christian Intelligencer.*

"It is a great work, and shows that America has a great poet. . . . A century from now this poem will be known and quoted wherever fine thought is appreciated, or brave deeds sung."—*Western Rural.*

BALLADS AND OTHER POEMS

By GEORGE L. RAYMOND

16MO, CLOTH EXTRA, $1.25

" In the construction of the ballad, he has given some notable examples of what may be wrought of native material by one who has a tasteful ear and practised hand. If he does not come up to the standard of the ancient ballad, which is the model, he has done as well as any of the younger American authors who have attempted this kind of work, and there is true enjoyment in all that he has written. Of his other poems, the dramatic poem, ' Haydn,' is finished in form, and has literary value, as well as literary power."—*Boston Globe.*

" The author has achieved a very unusual success, a success to which genuine poetic power has not more contributed than wide reading and extensive preparation. The ballads overflow, not only with the general, but the very particular, truths of history."—*Cincinnati Times.*

" It may well find readers in abundance . . . for the sake of the many fine passages which it contains. . . . 'Ideals made Real' has one point of very high excellence . . . we have in the conception of the character of Edith the work of a genuinely dramatic poet. . . . In Edith we have a thoroughly masculine intellect in a thoroughly feminine soul, not merely by the author's assertion, but by actual exhibition. Every word that Edith speaks, every act that she does, is in accord with this conception. . . . It is sufficient, without doubt, to give life to a less worthy performance, and it proves beyond doubt that Mr. Raymond is the possessor of a poetic faculty which is worthy of the most careful and conscientious cultivation."—*N. Y. Evening Post.*

" A very thoughtful study of character . . . great knowledge of . . . aims and motives. . . . Such as read this poem will derive from it a benefit more lasting than the mere pleasure of the moment."— *London Spectator.*

" Mr. Raymond is a poet emphatically, and not a scribbler in rhyme.' *London Literary Churchman.*

" His is no mere utterance of dreams and fancies. His poetry takes hold on life ; it enters the arena where its grandest and purest motives are discussed, and by the vigor and beauty of the language it holds itself on a level with the highest themes. . . . Every thoughtful reader . . . will wish that the poems had been longer or that there had been more of them. It would be possible to quote passage after passage of rare beauty."—*Utica Herald.*

" . . . Rhythmical in its flow and deliciously choice in language . . . indicating a deep acquaintance with human nature, while there is throughout a tone that speaks plainly of a high realization of the divine purpose in life . . . Not the least charming characteristic is its richness in pen-and-ink pictures marked by rare beauty and presenting irresistibly that which the poet saw in his mind's eye. . . . We confidently promise that any one taking it up will enjoy the reading throughout, that is, if there is any poetry in him."—*Boston Evening Journal.*

BOOKS BY PROFESSOR RAYMOND

Dante and Collected Verse. 16mo, cloth, gilt top . $1.25

"Epigram, philosophy, history—these are the predominant elements . . . which masterly construction, pure diction, and lofty sentiment unite in making a glowing piece of blank verse."—*Chicago Herald.*

"The poems will be read with keenest enjoyment by all who appreciate literary genius, refined sentiment, and genuine culture. The publication is a gem throughout."—*New Haven Leader.*

"The poet and the reformer contend in Professor Raymond. When the latter has the mastery, we respond to the justice, the high ideals, the truth of all he says—and says with point and vigor—but when the poet conquers, the imagination soars. . . . The mountain poems are the work of one with equally high ideals of life and of song."—*Glasgow* (Scotland) *Herald.*

"Brother Jonathan can not claim many great poets, but we think he has 'struck oil,' in Professor Raymond."—*Western* (England) *Morning News.*

"This brilliant composition . . gathers up and concentrates for the reader more of the reality of the great Italian than is readily gleaned from the author of the *Inferno* himself."—*Oakland Enquirer.*

Pictures in Verse. With 20 illustrations by Maud Stumm. Square 8vo, in ornamental cloth covers . . $ .75

"Little love poems of a light and airy character, describing pretty rustic scenes, or domestic interiors. . . . As charming for its illustrations as for its reading matter."—*Detroit Free Press.*

"Simple songs of human every-day experience . . . with a twinkle of homely humor and a wholesome reflection of domestic cheer. We like his optimistic sentiments, and unspoiled spirit of boyishness when he strikes the chord of love. It is all very true and good."—*The Independent.*

The Mountains about Williamstown. With an introduction by M. M. Miller, and 35 full-page illustrations from original photographs; oblong shape, cloth, gilt edges. Net, postpaid $2.00

"The beauty of these photographs from so many points of vantage would of itself suffice to show the fidelity and affection with which Professor Raymond pursued the theme of his admirably constructed poems. The introduction by his pupil, friend, and associate is an exhaustive study. No better or more thorough review could be written of the book, or more clearly point out the directness and power of Professor Raymond's work. . . . Among his many books none justifies more brilliantly the correctness and charm of his rhetorical instruction, or his facility in exemplifying what he commends."—*Hartford* (Conn.) *Courant.*

Rhythm and Harmony in Poetry and Music. 8° . $1.75

"The reader must be, indeed, a person either of supernatural stupidity or of marvellous erudition, who does not discover much information in Prof. Raymond's exhaustive and instructive treatise. From page to page it is full of suggestion."—*The Academy* (London).

PROFESSOR RAYMOND'S ART-BOOKS

Art in Theory. 8vo, cloth extra. . . . $1.75

"A well grounded, thoroughly supported, and entirely artistic conception of art as a whole, that will lead observers to apply its principles . . . and to distrust the charlatanism that imposes an idle and superficial mannerism upon the public in place of true beauty and honest workmanship."—*The New York Times.*

"His style is good, and his logic sound, and . . . of the greatest possible service to the student of artistic theories."—*Art Journal* (London).

The Representative Significance of Form.
8vo, cloth extra. $2.00

"Evidently the ripe fruit of years of patient and exhaustive study on the part of a man singularly fitted for his task. It is profound in insight, searching in analysis, broad in spirit, and thoroughly modern in method and sympathy."—*The Universalist Leader.*

"An original thinker and writer, the charm of his style and clearness of expression make Mr. Raymond's book possible to the general reader, though worthy of the study of the student and scholar."—*Hartford Courant.*

Painting, Sculpture, and Architecture, as Representative Arts. With 225 illustrations, 8vo. . $2.50

"Expression by means of extension or size . . . shape . . . regularity in outlines . . . the human body . . . posture, gesture, and movement . . . are all considered. . . . A specially interesting chapter is the one on color."—*Current Literature.*

"The whole book is the work of a man of exceptional thoughtfulness, who says what he has to say in a remarkably lucid and direct manner."—*The Philadelphia Press.*

The Genesis of Art-Form. Fully illustrated. 8vo. $2.25

"In a spirit at once scientific and that of the true artist, he pierces through the manifestations of art to their sources, and shows the relations, intimate and essential, between painting, sculpture, poetry, music, and architecture. A book that possesses not only singular value, but singular charm."—*N. Y. Times.*

"A help and a delight. Every aspirant for culture in any of the liberal arts, including music and poetry, will find something in this book to aid him."—*Boston Times.*

Proportion and Harmony of Line and Color in Painting, Sculpture, and Architecture.
Fully illustrated. 8vo. $2.50

"No critical person can afford to ignore so valuable a contribution to the art-thought of the day."—*The Art-Interchange* (N. Y.).

"One does not need to be a scholar to follow this scholar as he teaches while seeming to entertain ; for he does both."—*Burlington Hawk-Eye.*

"The artist who wishes to penetrate the mysteries of color, the sculptor who desires to cultivate his sense of proportion, or the architect whose ambition is to reach to a high standard will find the work helpful and inspiring."—*Boston Transcript.*

BOOKS BY PROFESSOR RAYMOND

Poetry as a Representative Art.   8°   . $1.75

This book is an attempt, in accordance with modern methods, aided by the results of modern investigation, to determine scientifically the laws of poetic composition and criticism, by deriving and distinguishing the methods and meanings of the various factors of poetic form and thought from those of the elocution and rhetoric of ordinary speech, of which poetry is an artistic development.   The principles unfolded are illustrated by quotations from the first English poets.

"I have read it with pleasure, and a sense of instruction on many points."—*Francis Turner Palgrave, Professor of Poetry, Oxford University.*

"Dieses ganz vortreffiche Werk."—*Englische Studien, Universität Breslau.*

"An acute, interesting, and brilliant piece of work.   .   .   .   As a whole the essay deserves unqualified praise."—*N. Y. Independent.*

The Essentials of Æsthetics.   Fully illustrated.   8° $2.50

A compendium of all the art-volumes, designed as a Text-Book.

"So lucid in expression and rich in illustraton that every page contains matter of deep interest even to the general reader."—*Boston Herald.*

"It can hardly fail to make talent more rational, genius more conscious of the principles of art, and the critic and connoisseur better equipped for impression, judgment, and appraisement."—*New York Times.*

The Orator's Manual.   12mo   .   .   . $1.50

A Practical and Philosophic Treatise on Vocal Culture, Emphasis, and Gesture, together with Hints for the Composition of Orations and Selections for Declamation and Reading, designed as a Text-book for Schools and Colleges, and for Public Speakers and Readers who are obliged to Study without an Instructor, fully revised with important Additions after the Fifteenth Edition.

"It is undoubtedly the most complete and thorough treatise on oratory for the practical student ever published."—*The Educational Weekly*, Chicago.

"I consider it the best American book upon technical elocution. It has also leanings toward a philosophy of expression that no other book written by an American has presented."—*Moses True Brown,* Head of the Boston School of Oratory.

The Writer (with POST WHEELER, Litt. D.)   12mo $1.00

A Concise, Complete, and Practical Text-book of Rhetoric, designed to aid in the Appreciation, as well as Production of All Forms of Literature, Explaining, for the first time, the Principles of Written Discourse by correlating them to those of Oral Discourse.

"A book of unusual merit . . . prepared by practical teachers, and the end in view is evidently to teach rather than to give information."—*The Pacific Educational Journal.*

"The pupil will forget he is studying rhetoric, and will come to express himself for the pure pleasure he has in this most beautiful art."—*Indiana School Journal.*

Books by Professor Raymond

Ethics and Natural Law. 8vo . Net, $2.25.

A Reconstructive Review of Moral Philosophy, Applied to the Rational Art of Living,—a Book that is in effect a Continuation and Completion of the Author's well-known Æsthetic Works, showing the Relationship of the Principles underlying Art to the Culture of Character.

"The student of ethics will considerably fortify his knowledge of the history of ethical thought by reading the book, especially the first twelve chapters. In these Mr. Raymond embodies, with copious references, his extensive knowledge of what has been written and thought by moral philosophers. On pp. 63–67, for instance, will be found in footnotes a kind of classified anthology of all the definitions given of conscience by modern writers. The various ethical theories holding the field do not, he thinks, recognize as indispensable the coöperation, in every slightest detail of thought and feeling, of the two necessary factors of every desire; and he claims that his own doctrine keeps to the purpose he avows in his opening chapter,—to draw no inference, and to advance no theory, not warranted by known facts as ascertainable in connection with the operations of natural law. . . . Chapters XIII to XXIII deal acutely and comprehensively with the various sides of American life."—*London* (England) *Times.*

In an article entitled *A Desirable Acquaintance, Prof. A. S. Hobart, D.D. of Crozer Theological Seminary,* after mentioning his twenty years' experience in teaching Ethics, says, "I find this book the only one that has come within the range of my reading which has, for the basis of its system, what I have found to be satisfactory. The writer assumes that there is in the nature of things a law of ethical conduct as continuous and self-evincing as is the law of physical health. . . . The study of psychology has opened the mind to inspection as we open the back of a watch-case and see the wheels go round; and this study lays its crown of victorious explorations at the feet of ethics. . . . His view is that conscience is the sense of conflict between bodily and mental desires. . . . therefore not a guide; it is only a sense of lostness in the woods, that wants a guide. Good sense and good religion are the guides to be consulted. By many illustrations and very clear reasoning he verifies his view. Then, . . . he takes up the task unusual in such books—of showing how the leading moral qualities can and ought to be cultivated. In view of my own careful reading of the book I venture to call attention to it as a most fertile source of instruction and suggestion for ethical teaching.—*The Baptist.*

"The book is clear and comprehensive. His theory in regard to conflict is reasonable, and the principles deduced from it have philosophic foundation."—*Boston Transcript.*

"Professor Raymond extracts a fundamental principle that largely reconciles existing ethical theories . . . makes distinctions that have vitality, and will repay the necessary study and application."—*Scientific American.*

Books by Professor Raymond

A Poet's Cabinet and An Art Philosopher's Cabinet.

Two books containing quotations, the one from the poems, and the other from the æsthetic works of George Lansing Raymond, selected by Marion Mills Miller, Litt.D., editor of *The Classics, Greek, and Latin.* Each book 8vo. cloth-bound, gilt top. $2.00

"Dr. Raymond is one of the most just and pregnant critics, as well as one of the most genuine poets, that America has produced. . . . His verse generally, and his prose frequently, is a solid pack of epigrams; and hundreds of the epigrams are vigorous, fresh, telling, worth collecting and cataloguing. . . . Probably from no other American but Emerson could a collection at all comparable be made. Many of the phrases are profound paradox. . . . Others are as hard-headed as La Rochefoucauld. . . . Some are plain common sense, set in an audacious figure, or a vigorous turn of phrase. . . . But few or none of them are trivial. . . . As an æsthetic critic, Professor Raymond is, by training and temperament, remarkably versatile and catholic. He is almost or quite equally interested in architecture, painting, sculpture, music, poetry. . . . Each is as definitely placed in his system as the several instruments in a great orchestra. . . . If Dr. Raymond had been born in France, England, or Germany, he would, no doubt, have enjoyed a wider vogue. But it is just as well that he was none of these; for the, as yet, æsthetically immature New World has sore need of him."—*Revue Internationale,* Paris.

"We risk little in foretelling a day when all considerable libraries, private as well as public, will be deemed quite incomplete if lacking these twin volumes. Years after the thinker has paid the debt to nature due, his thoughts will rouse action and emotion in the hearts and minds of generations now unborn."—*Worcester* (Mass.) *Gazette.*

"This Poet's Cabinet is the best thing of its class—that confined to the works of one author—upon which our eyes have fallen, either by chance or purpose. We can't help wishing that we had a whole book-shelf of such volumes in our own private library."—*Columbus,* (O.) *Journal.*

"The number and variety of the subjects are almost overwhelming, and the searcher for advanced or new thought as expressed by this particular philosopher has no difficulty in coming almost immediately upon something that may strike his fancy or aid him in his perplexities. To the student of poetry and the higher forms of literature . . . the volume will be of distinct aid."—*Utica* (N. Y.) *Observer.*

"Dr. Miller's task in selecting representative extracts from Professor Raymond's works has not been a light one, for there has been no chaff among the wheat, and there was an ever present temptation to add bulk to the book through freedom in compilation. He thought best, however, to eliminate all but the features which revealed the rare rich soul and personality of the poet, and each quotation is a gem."—*Albany* (N. Y.) *Times-Union.*

"To study the works of any one man so that we are completely familiar with his ideas upon all important subjects—if the man have within him any element of greatness—is a task which is likely to repay the student's work. . . . This fact makes the unique quality of the present volume . . . quotations which deal with practically every subject to be found in more general anthologies." *Boston* (Mass.) *Advertiser.*

Books by Professor Raymond

The Psychology of Inspiration. 8vo, cloth. (New Revised Edition). Net, $2.00; by mail, $2.14

The book founds its conclusions on a study of the action of the human mind when obtaining and expressing truth, as this action has been revealed through the most recent investigations of physiological, psychological, and psychic research; and the freshness and originality of the presentation is acknowledged and commended by such authorities as Dr. J. Mark Baldwin, Professor of Psychology in Johns Hopkins University, who says that its psychological position is "new and valuable"; Dr. W. T. Harris, late United States Commissioner of Education and the foremost metaphysician in the country, who says it is sure "to prove helpful to many who find themselves on the border line between the Christian and the non-Christian beliefs"; and Dr. Edward Everett Hale, who says that "no one has approached the subject from this point of view."

The first and, perhaps, the most important achievement of the book is to show that the *fact* of *inspiration* can be *demonstrated scientifically;* in other words, that the inner subconscious mind *can* be influenced irrespective of influences exerted through the eyes and the ears, *i. e.*, by what one sees or hears. In connection with this fact it is also shown that, when the mind is thus inwardly or inspirationally influenced, as, for example, in hypnotism, the influence is *suggestive* and *not dictatorial.* Not only so, but such faith as it is natural and right that a rational being should exercise can be stimulated and developed in only the degree in which the text of a sacred book is characterized by the very vagueness and variety of meaning and statement which the higher criticism of the Bible has brought to light. The book traces these to the operation and requirements of the human mind through which inspiration is received and to which it is imparted. Whatever inspires must appear to be, in some way, beyond the grasp of him who communicates it, and can make him who hears it *think* and *train him to think*, in the degree only in which it is not comprehensive or complete; but merely, like everything else in nature, illustrative of that portion of truth which the mind needs to be made to find out for itself.

The sane, fair, kindly attitude taken gives of itself a profitable lesson. The author proves conclusively that his mind—and if his, why not another's?—can be at one and the same time sound, sanitary, scientific, and essentially religious."—*The Examiner*, Chicago.

"The author writes with logic and a 'sweet reasonableness' that will doubtless convince many halting minds. It is an inspiring book."—*Philadelphia Inquirer.*

"It is, we think, difficult to overestimate the value of this volume at the present critical pass in the history of Christianity."—*The Arena*, Boston.

"The author has taken up a task calling for heroic effort, and has given us a volume worthy of careful study. . . . The conclusion is certainly very reasonable."—*Christian Intelligencer*, New York.

"Interesting, suggestive, helpful."—*Boston Congregationalist.*

Books by Professor Raymond

Fundamentals in Education, Art, and Civics: Essays and Addresses. 8vo, cloth. Net, $1.40; by mail, $1.53

"Of fascinating interest to cultured readers, to the student, the teacher, the poet, the artist, the musician, in a word to all lovers of sweetness and light. The author has a lucid and vigorous style, and is often strikingly original. What impresses one is the personality of a profound thinker and a consummate teacher behind every paragraph."—*Dundee Courier*, Scotland.

"The articles cover a wide field and manifest a uniformly high culture in every field covered. It is striking how this great educator seems to have anticipated the educational tendencies of our times some decades before they imprest the rest of us. He has been a pathfinder for many younger men, and still points the way to higher heigbts. The book is thoroughly up-to-date."—*Service*, Philadelphia.

"Clear, informing, and delightfully readable. Whether the subject is art and morals, technique in expression, or character in a republic, each page will be found interesting and the treatment scholarly, but simple, sane, and satisfactory . . . the story of the Chicago fire is impressingly vivid."—*Chicago Standard*.

"He is a philosopher, whose encouraging idealism is well grounded in scientific study, and who illuminates points of psychology and ethics as well as of art when they come up in the course of the discussion."—*The Scotsman*, Edinburgh, Scotland.

"Agreeably popularizes much that is fundamental in theories of life and thought, The American people owe much of their progress, their optimism, and we may say their happiness to the absorption of just such ideals as Professor Raymond stands for."—*Minneapolis Book Review Digest*.

Suggestions for the Spiritual Life—College Chapel Talks. 8vo, cloth . . Net, $1.50; by mail, $1.63

"Sermons of more than usual worth, full of thought of the right kind, fresh, strong, direct, manly. . . . Not one seems to strain to get a young man's attention by mere popular allusions to a student environment. They are spiritual, scriptural, of straight ethical import, meeting difficulties, confirming cravings, amplifying tangled processes of reasoning, and not forgetting the emotions."—*Hartford Theological Seminary Record* (Congregationalist).

"The clergyman who desires to reach young men especially, and the teacher of men's Bible Classes may use this collection of addresses to great advantage. . . . The subjects are those of every man's experience in character building . . . such a widespread handling of God's word would have splendid results in the production of men."—*The Living Church* (Episcopalian).

"Great themes, adequately considered. . . . Surely the young men who listened to these sermons must have been stirred and helped by them as we have been stirred and helped as we read them."—*Northfield* (Mass.) *Record of Christian Work* (Evangelical).

"They cover a wide range. They are thoughtful, original, literary, concise, condensed, pithy. They deal with subjects in which the young will be interested."—*Western Christian Advocate* (Methodist).